Fair Dinkum
Teaching
and Learning

Fair dinkum
is an Australian term
meaning
genuine, true, real.

Fair Dinkum Teaching and Learning

Reflections on Literacy and Power

Garth Boomer

Director, Curriculum Development Centre
Canberra, Australia

BOYNTON/COOK PUBLISHERS, INC.
UPPER MONTCLAIR, NEW JERSEY 07043

Library of Congress Cataloging in Publication Data

Boomer, Garth
   Fair Dinkum teaching and learning.

   1. Language arts—Australia.   2. Literacy—Australia.
3. Language arts—Australia—Data processing.   I. Title
LB1576.B524   372.6'0994   84-21670
ISBN 0-86709-139-8

For information address Boynton/Cook Publishers, Inc., 52 Upper
Montclair Plaza, P.O. Box 860, Upper Montclair, NJ 07043.

Printed in the United States of America
85 86 87 88 10 9 8 7 6 5 4 3 2 1

Acknowledgments and Notes
on All the Chapters

Piggy Nick: That's a Good Word first appeared in *The Spitting Image,* Garth Boomer and Dale Spender, Rigby, Adelaide 1976. *Where Has the Eye Gone in Schools* is the previously unpublished edited transcript of an address dictated for a conference on language in education in 1976. *Tell Me a Story* has previously appeared in *Words and Windmills* Vol. 12, No. 1, 1980. It was written in 1977. *Becoming the Reader over One's Own Shoulder* was presented to the annual conference of the Australian Reading Association in Perth, 1979. It was subsequently published in *How to Teach Reading and The Year of the Child,* ed. T. Bessell-Browne, R. Latham, N. Reeves, A.R.A., Perth, 1980. *Writing Fair Dinkum in Primary Schools,* previously unpublished, was prepared as follow-up to a conference of elementary teachers in 1979. *Some Thoughts on Programming for the Language Arts,* also previously unpublished, was prepared as pre-conference reading for a conference of elementary teachers in 1980.

Oracy in Australian Schools is the text of a keynote address to a national conference on oral communication held in Armidale in 1979. It was published in *Developing Oral Communication Competence* ed. W. J. Crocker, University of New England, 1980. *A Parent's Guide to Literacy* has not been published previously. It was distributed as a draft paper by The Language and Learning Unit in South Australia for discussion amongst teachers in 1980. I am grateful to Christine Davis who contributed to the writing and helped me edit the guide. *Literacy: Where Should Australia Be Heading?* was my contribution to a panel debate at the opening of the national reading conference of the Australian Reading Association in Perth, 1979. It subsequently appeared in *The Australian Journal of Reading* (Vol. 3, No. 1, March, 1980). *Addressing the Problem of Elsewhereness* was written as a position paper for a national seminar on Action Research held at Deakin University in 1981. It has not previously been published.

Towards a Model of the Composing Process in Writing was prepared for a seminar on the composing process conducted as part of the ANZAAS Conference held in Adelaide in 1980. It has not previously been published although it has been widely used as a conference discussion paper. *The Literacy Machine* is the text of an address to the South Pacific Reading Conference, Auckland, 1982. It has not previously been published. *Zen and the Art of Computing* is the text of an address to the annual summer school on computers and education, conducted by the Education Department of South Australia in 1983. It appeared in the newsletter of Angle Park Computing Centre in March, 1983. *The Wisdom of the Antipodes* is the full text of an address to the National Convention of the International Reading Association in Chicago, 1982. It appeared in edited form in the *Journal of Reading* (Vol. 26, No. 7, April, 1983).

I have not substantially reworked any of these pieces, but I have edited and changed sections to remove local references and to avoid undue overlap between chapters.

Introduction

I am a part of all that I have met;
Yet all experience is an arch where thro'
Gleams that untravelled world whose margin fades
For ever and for ever when I move.

(TENNYSON)

Each of these pieces is an arch through which I have moved progressively over the past decade. To each new arch I bring my previous capacities to see, and as I pass through my seeing changes.

I think that I now see issues of literacy and power more clearly than I did in 1975. I certainly see them with more complexity. From wonder at the personal achievement of my young son in *Piggy Nick: That's a Good Word*, I have come to understand more deeply the significance of social interaction and social shaping as shown in *Becoming the Reader Over One's Own Shoulder*. From a certain impatience with schools and teachers which simmers in *Where Has the Eye Gone in Schools?* I have progressed towards some understanding of the way in which all of us are coerced by structures built into society and its institutions. Thus, in *The Literacy Machine: Towards a Universal Program for Literacy* I try to explain the "cosmic egg" which continually threatens to contain us. From despairing about how little teachers achieve, I have come to admire the way they keep on struggling.

You will see me as a "change agent" and teacher educator vacillating from piece to piece between suggesting specific teaching strategies (*Some Thoughts on Programming for the Language Arts*) and the formulating of generative principles and theories which might free us from the tyranny of habit (*The Wisdom of the Antipodes*). I run between my own theorizing (inspired by good practice and favorite storytellers such as Britton, Rosen, and Moffett) and the complex and contested sites of schooling where teachers have to make things work.

I have chosen to leave you with some recent arches through which I am attempting to see issues "universally" and to lay out maps of very large territories indeed. The last three chapters are, in effect, summations and consolidations of my journeyings since 1975.

Conscious of my tendency to let unfettered imagination distort my seeing, I asked some outstanding Australian teachers to respond as friendly critics to my visions by describing some of their own practices which relate to what I have said. I am grateful to them for offering their voices to interrupt, enhance, and alleviate my texts.

*   *   *

The book is addressed particularly to teachers who, like me, are addicted to learning more about the art and science of English teaching. My goal is more knowledge for better action. The method is action and reflection upon action.

While my career path has given me extra privileges in terms of time for "action research," I believe that my progress over a decade might act as some kind of incentive to teachers at any level who wish to take up a more deliberately reflective stance towards their own teaching actions. For this reason, I have written short autobiographical notes before each chapter that set down aspects of the context, the challenge, the intent, and the method. The third person "pilgrim's progress" pose (and style) is an attempt to both personalize and depersonalize the notes—to give me a chance to look at what happened to me the last dozen years or so while also suggesting that the "he" of the experiences could be any teacher with similar urges to know more about what he or she is doing. If the pose seems a little arch at times, I hope you'll recognize that using the first person might have been worse.

Thus, while the abiding theme of the book is literacy, there is a subtheme of action research or theorizing about practice that may suggest to other teachers strategies and areas for further field work in teaching English.

Looking back through the arches, I now see that this is a book about

- the power of intention
- the importance of practical theories
- the value of personal investigations
- the shaping power of contexts and structures
- the struggle between habit and creation
- the importance of action and reflection

Contents

I

In which the English teacher, as postgraduate student, in 1972 begins his career as a deliberate reflector.

Harold Rosen of the University of London Institute of Education had been introducing his course by playing recordings of natural language in context, particularly to explode the myth that working class language is "deficient." Members of his master's course were challenged to present a seminar on a small piece of field work involving the recording of language at work.

The myth of deficiency is often applied to the very young who tend to be seen as incomplete adults rather than as applied linguistic scientists in their own right. It seemed an interesting test to find out what a three-year-old said to himself at bedtime.

Perhaps the beginning researcher was lucky to strike such a gold deposit in his first essay into the field. Certainly all English teachers are not blessed with such an obliging source of data as the voluble Simon, hero of this chapter. Nevertheless, English teachers are surrounded by other potential gold fields—the group talk on poetry, the writing habits of six-year-olds, the reminiscences of ex-students, indeed their own running commentary in the classroom.

But, watch the ethics when you eavesdrop!

Fortunately, Simon, now fifteen, is not strongly resentful that he was exploited. When asked what he now thinks about his three-year-old tour de force he admits to slight embarrassment and feels that "royalties should have been paid." "At least," he says, "you were pretty sure to get the truth. If you'd told me what you were going to do, or asked me to demonstrate, I'd have shut up."

He puts his finger on a real problem for the ethnographer. As soon as you introduce the tape recorder into the context you change the context. In this case, we are privileged to witness a full-blown, unexpurgated text.

Piggy Nick—
That's a Good Word

Simon and Catherine and Jean and I were living in a one-bedroom garret in a block of three-story flats in London. We'd been in England only a couple of weeks and I noticed that Simon's pre-sleep monologues had grown to proportions that would have done credit to Cecil B. de Mille. He'd been in the habit of talking to himself back in Australia, but the transplant to London seemed to have given his bedtime spiel a new impetus.

Unethically, but in the interest of science, I decided to do a Watergate on him. I planted a tape recorder behind the bedhead. The nighttime ritual was to put Catherine and Simon down in the double bed while Jean and I read or watched television in the "lounge." When it was our bedtime we had to transfer the children to makeshift beds in the lounge.

Catherine, who was then five years old, always dropped off to sleep very quickly, leaving Simon, then 38 months, alone with himself. On the night of the second of October 1972 his only property was his teddy bear. Catherine was asleep alongside him.

What follows is my transcript of what he said. The tape, which I still keep as a precious document, is available as confirmation that I have not doctored what was said other than to give an orthographic approximation for some of the sounds.

(simulated sleep noises)
    Pssh . . . Pssh . . .
(10 second silence)
    Scratch . . .
(assorted sounds)
(2 minute silence)
    Prr
    Daddy's the boss, daddy's the boss, daddy the daddy is the
    boss   *(chanted)*

(indistinct sentence)
(20 second silence)
> The water bag
> The hot water bag   (Catherine has taken a hot water bag to bed)
(laughing)
> Hallo, Hallo, Halloo, Halloo, Halloo
> Yup the up the poo
> Jiggety, jiggety jog
> The mouse ran up the clock
> The mouse ran down
> Jiggety, Jickety—(pause) jock
(mumbling, then 1½ minute silence)
> Is that Greg or Nanna or Grumpy or Alison   (his cousin, back in Australia)
> I haven't got any honey
> Do with it to do with it
(indistinct sounds)
> That won't hurt   (Earlier that day, Simon had fallen off the
> Look at that   makeshift swing at the back of the flats.
> P'yoopy, yoopy, yoopy, yoop   A couple of young English children from
(indistinct whispering)   the flat downstairs comforted him.)
> Sit down, sit down (dramatized) (Here, after only a few weeks in London,
> Why you crying   he does a creditable imitation of the Eng-
> Oh, hosh, hosh   lish accent—"hosh" equals "hush.")
> We don't mean to cry do we
> No
> That's right
> O yes you do
> I'm happy now
(indistinct sounds)
> We have a swing
> O pee doodle
> Fell off the swing   (true of Humpty Dumpty)
> . . . clumsy
> Why you crying, don't cry, hosh don't prosh will
> you don't cry
> Going to have a little drop.
> Dumpy, dumpy dip   (continues humming in this vein)
> Look . . . my handle
> Now got lot . . . two handles
> Wash it
> He has enough
> had enough
(indistinct sounds)
> Night time   (simulated sleep sounds and humming)
> Shopping bag, shopping bag, shopping bag   (chanted)

Up the dee, up the dee, up the dee

Woo b doo   (to the tune of "London Bridge is falling down")

(1 minute silence, then extended humming)

Go to sleep now   (simulated snoring)

Night time

(laughing)

Hallo, hallo

(laughing)

Der, der, der, der

The fire'n, the fire'n, the fire fire

The feer, feer, feer   (to the tune of "The Farmer in the Dell")

The fire, fire, fire   (On our first day in London we took up

The fire, fire, fire, fire, fire   lodgings in a poky room in a hotel in Gower

. . . engine   Street. The traffic was loud. The kids rushed

The fire engine   to the window in amazement when a fire

It boom boom   engine went past at full blast. Simon was

Fire engine   really impressed by the "different" sound.)

It boom boom

Fire engine

I broom, broom, broom

The fire's out *(glissando)*

The fire's out, the fire's out *(sharp repetition)*

The fire's out *(repeated more softly)*

The fire's out *(still more softly)*

The fire's out *(louder)*

The fire's out, the fire's out *(sharp repetition)*

Fire's out *(glissando)*

The fire's out, the fire's out

Fire's out *(glissando)*

The fire's out *(echo effect)*

Fire . . . is *(pauses)*

Engine, engine

(indistinct sounds; grunting)

It's night time

It's night time *(chanted)*

The fire's out, the fire's out, the fire's out, the fire's out

The fire's in, the fire's out *(repeated)*

The fire's out, the fire's in

The fire's in

Der, der, der, der, der *(simulated siren)*

Din, din, din, din

The children go to the bicycles

. . . bikes

See the scratch there

Bang, bang

Bzz, Bzz, Bzzzzz
Tr . . . rouble makers *(swatting sounds)*
Stupid
Two kisses
Two kisses
One kiss, another little kiss
(hums a tune from "Gilligan's Island"—a television program—occasional words recognizable)
He's got two . . . *(simulated snoring)*
Teddy bear
Stop crying
Stop crying
Bassandra
Bassandra Boomer, Bassandra Boomer, Bassandra
Bassandra Boomer *(chanting)*
Bassandra Jean
We don't know what to do
We don't know what to do
Burp durp du durp du ("Pop Goes the Weasel")

(Cassandra is the name of the daughter of a Malay couple living in the same block of flats.)

(nonsense sounds to the same tune—the sound mmm predominates; finishes with . . .)
. . . cover you up
Uppy uppy yp yp
I'm dead
Ition box
What's on the ition box old boy
(indistinct sounds)
A soldier
Am I dead
It's hot
Hallo Caffy, Caffy
Caffrine, Caffrine *(to sleeping sister)*
(Yawn)
Night Caffrine
(ten second pause)
I told you . . .
A piggy nick
A piggy nick
A piggy back on me
Right under there *(chanting)*
Right under here on my head
I don't know what to do
I don't know what to do
I can't put her head

I don't know what to do
Pat her
(indistinct sounds)
Oh, no you can't
Oh, yes I can
(repeated three times)
Oh, yes I can
Oh, no I'm not
(repeated three times)
That's the slip
It is the slip to go in the water   (Friends back in Australia had a swim-
That's the water down there   ming pool with a slippery dip.)
and you jump
jumpy, jumpy, jumpy (chant)
We had a piggy
A piggy nick
(sound like R, rrr . . .)
A piggy nick
A piggy nick?
Oh, that's another good word
Squash in
(indistinct sounds)
I don't know what to do
A dear, dear, dear
A dear, dear, dear (repeated chanting)
A dear, a dear a do ya, you do, you do
you do ya
(1½ minute silence, then simulated sleep sounds)
Uncle Grant had a . . .   (Uncle Grant, back in Australia,
Car, car   had various nicknames for Simon,
(simulated sleep sounds—yawns)   including, "Car, car.")
Why did you turn it back there?
Catherine, I love you
(fifteen second silence)
Ready to go
Fireman, Fireman The Fireman
Bzz Bzz Bzz
Wee wee wee wee wee its
Is it a plane, is it a bird   (Obviously from the old favorite Is it a
It's a teddy bear   bird? Is it a plane? No it's Superman!)
It's an upside teddy bear
Goldilocks, goldilocks *(practiced to become something like*
"bawdy looks")
Leven, twelve, thirty, forty, fifty, sixty, seventy
eighty, ninety, seventy, eighty, ninety

Make a big moo
Muckety, muckety, muckety, muck, mucky, mucky, mucky, muck
The mouse went down, up and down . . . *(pause)*
Jiggety, jiggety, jock
Catherine where's your Humphrey   (her bear)
The mouse went down *(to a tune)*
Jiggety, jiggety, jock
. . . ran up the clock
The mouse went down *(increased tempo for this line)*
Jiggety, jiggety, jock *(slower)*
(This sequence repeated three times)
. . . Gosh you ran down
The mouse ran up the clock
The mouse went down
Jiggety, jiggety, jock
The mouse went up again *(no time)*
The mouse ran up the clock
The mouse ran down
Jiggety, jiggety, jock
I got an . . .
The mouse ran up the clock
(eight second silence; humming, one minute silence)
And we couldn't see the light out of that door
did we?   (The kids always liked to be
Didn't like it shut   able to see a light on at night.)
Then we didn't see the light in the light bulk did we? No we didn't
I can't get under my step
And I . . .
I'n Johnny
Big ladies and boys
Look at me I'n Johnny
Mnm Mnm Mnm . . . *(continued)*
Robert doody, Roberty doody   ("Doody" was the name for his penis.
Mnm   His daddy's first name is Robert.)
Cutthroat Jake
We just about ready
Cutthroat Jake
We just about ready   (from Captain Pugwash)
Cutthroat Jake
Just about ready to fight
Hush throw sh . . . ready to go
In the post office
The post office, the post office, the post
office *(rising intonation)*   (Mummy had taken them to
Ready to go   the post office that day.)

Now I don't know what to do
Oh no, no no no
I don't know what to do ee dee dot   (all this to "Pop Goes the Weasel")
Pip pit de dit dare
Mee-oo me-oo me-ooo me-ooo
And the airplane goes d dad   (Simon was intrigued and a little over-
I'n locked in   whelmed by the Jumbo Jet which brought
Mnm   us to London. He asked how you could
I'n yucking to him   get back down to earth if you wanted to.)
Big yucky I've been
I can't reach
How could we get down?
(indistinct sentence)
Off to the wood or the blocks or the   (Close to our flat there was
wood or the blocks or the wood or the   a pleasant wooded reserve.)
blocks or the blocks or the blocks. Box
order box order box forty dorty dorter
dox *(rhythmical)*
(hums "Pop Goes the Weasel")
(two minute silence; indistinct muttering)
Catherine put your head up
I like it better up
(eight second silence)
I don't know what to do ooo oo oo   ("Pop Goes the Weasel")
(2½ minute silence; whispering; 2½ minute silence)
(yawn)
(1½ minute silence)
I don't know what to do
(indistinct noises, 'mnm' predominant)
Wrap him up, wrap in up, wrapn up
Rapnuptum, rapnuptum, rapnuptum, mnm, mnm
(one minute silence)
I see wacko, wackee, wacko, wackee
wackee, wackee, wackee, co eee coo eee coo eee
And we have a runda bock
We have a lovely box
We have a lovely run a run
. . . a runny fun
. . . Over the cowshed   (breaking into the song "K-K-K Katie,"
I'll be . . . *(indistinct)*   a song he had taken a fancy to back
Waiting at the g, g, g, g, train   in Australia. I think Grumpy used to
Over the cowshed   sing it to him.)
I'll be waiting at the
g, g, g, g, g, kitchen door
Skippy, Skippy   (His favorite Australian television program
Skippy the nice kangaroo   had been "Skippy, The Bush Kangaroo.")

D, d, d, doo
Der, de der de der   (tune of "Skippy" which flows into
Sh   another television signature tune)
(mumbling)
Nice comfortable isn't it
(indistinct sounds)
Wakin you up
That's clever
I can knee up
Oh time to get up
No it's time to go to sleep
When I go . . .
Ring ding ling
Time to get up
Tired
(mumbling)
They're pushing me down aren't they   (I can't resist drawing attention
(two minute silence; yawn; indistinct sounds)   to the symbolism.)
Sing . . . yella
the ella sumporine *(sings)*
We all live in the ella sumporine   (to the tune of "We All Live
ella sumporine the ella sumporine   in a Yellow Submarine")
We all live in the ella sum . . .
(and the rest is silence)

*   *   *

Simon, taking on patterns of experience and soothing words like ballast, finally dives into the subconscious of sleep. We all live in a yellow submarine. We need to lay the ghosts and demons of each day before sleep washes over us. What can I say about Simon's amazing method of rocking his own cradle?

Years ago, inspired by the late Ruth Weir's study of the monologues of her son, Anthony, I mined my transcript with a scholar's zeal, doing word counts and analyses of the metalinguistic practices of vowels and consonants. I noted the way in which he built up phrases progressively; how he punned and rhymed and played and associated and dramatized; how he tenaciously worked to reconcile Australia and England.

In seminars at the Institute of Education I used Simon to illustrate the theories of Chomsky and Britton (Simon, in the spectator role) and Jean Piaget and Lev Vygotsky. I used him to "prove" that we all have a natural urge to tell stories and write poems and compose songs. Now I can't bring myself to repeat the linguistic dissections. I just want to show.

Look on his work you teachers and despair. Despair because you cannot teach him more than the merest fraction of what he teaches himself about language and life. Relax and enjoy your children and enjoy yourselves.

Response

A TEACHER DOES MATTER

YVONNE PAULL

Exposition

Am I to be haunted by an Ozymandian irony to despair; to despair for my inability to teach what children can teach themselves, for my inability to orchestrate the insides of their heads?

Unlike Shelley's traveler from an antique land, I do not see desolation, a desert stretching in all directions. I refuse to despair. I do not feel guilty. I will not be goaded (or seduced) away from my belief that teachers matter by the clouding of the relationship between teacher and learner.

Theme

A teacher does matter . . . and so does the child's broader social context; parents, media, peers—"Piggy nick" clearly demonstrates that. In addition, Simon's monologue also serves to focus our attention on the effectiveness of the information processing capacity of the mind. My response to "Piggy Nick"? Succinctly:

- I believe in the power of an individual's learning.
- I agree that neo-Ozymandian pride is an inappropriate teacher attitude.
- I assert that A TEACHER DOES MATTER . . . and it is on this OMEGA that I will focus.

Why do teachers matter? Let me "for instance" imagine. For me to *force* a child to imagine is beset with difficulties, but a child may readily *choose* to imagine. As a teacher *I* am in a position to *influence* those imaginings by the kinds of interventions I make in the child's learning environment, by the *quality* of the nutrient in the petri dish of the child's learning environment under my control.

The next question to ask, then, is what kinds of interventions are indicated by "Piggy nick"? What does Simon's transcript suggest about practice?

I have identified eight "pointers to practice":

- encouraging the use of the imagination
- respecting a child's social context
- accepting the individuality of persons and responses
- providing structures and plans
- encouraging experimentation with words and language
- emphasizing reading for enjoyment (reading for oneself and by others)
- "investigating" the media
- engaging in musical activities

and I have written them as teacher interventions, since teachers matter!

Variations on a Theme

Perhaps you can think of more interventions? Perhaps my list surprises you. "How did she identify that?" By the same mechanisms Simon employed in his monologue. By processing information. I identified these eight interventions by entering into a discourse with the *writer* of the text. I drew inferences and predicted from "Piggy nick" using my own unique memory store of information. But then again, perhaps not so unique. Was your list similar to mine, demonstrating underlying shared societal/professional experiences?

Development

Now, although I have said that Simon and I were both processing this information, I had a printed text to prompt the response. Simon's monologue occurred just prior to sleep. Where was his text?

His texts were several; nursery rhymes, songs, T.V. scripts and fairy tales entwined with the richness of social discourse. These texts and conversations had been memorized. By retrieval from long term memory, they were "available" for processing. These memories resulted in the "discourse with texts" transcribed for us, a discourse transcribed as text and revealing creative acts of imagination.

Of text and discourse, their nature and relationship, however, I will say little more lest I begin to wax learned and change my writing style. Suffice to say that I am very aware of you, my readers of *this* printed text. I try to conjure you in my imagination. I can infer and predict. Yet as I write and imagine I do not, will not, cannot know the effect of this writing as discourse on you. You will process my text (and "Piggy nick") as discourse, bringing yourselves to it. You as individuals will accept or reject style, content, interpretation, and *that* says something about classroom practice!

But, to return, RONDO-like, to my eight earlier-identified "pointers to practice," I have chosen to focus on only two; *providing structures and plans* and *engaging in musical activities,* although they are both inextricably interwoven with the other six.

Firstly, then, *providing structures and plans.* By structures and plans I mean, loosely, frameworks for the mind and imagination which can be retrieved easily from memory and utilized by individuals when required. I believe that an important teacher-intervention occurs in the provision of a multiplicity of frameworks, foundations, trellises, matrices, maps, patterns, templates, coathangers, call them what you will. Simon's monologue is full of them; e.g. songs, rhymes, stories. AND they have not manacled him, chained him, repressed him, imprisoned him, stifled his imagination. Rather, they have provided a springboard for creation and the imagination.

Secondly, I wish to highlight *engaging in musical activities.* Why? Well, certainly Simon drew on music-related language and language structures and sang snatches of tunes, but music happens to be one of my personal biases. As a person I have gained a great deal from engaging in musical activities. As a teacher I enjoy providing a variety of musical (or music-related) experiences for children (who also show every indication of enjoyment). These experiences encompass being spectators, performers and creators.

I once heard a definition of music which appealed to me. It said: "Music is a language using organized sound within time." I believe that music (and movement) can be as powerful as verbal language. Moreover, they provide two more dimensions for communication, and the very nature of music—its beats, rhythms, harmonies (and discords), textures, dynamics, forms (STRUCTURES!)—can only enhance an individual's understanding of spoken discourse and its nuances.

Recapitulation

So, you see. I *already* enjoy my children. I *already* enjoy myself. BUT, I maintain, nevertheless, that teachers matter. It doesn't matter that children can teach themselves. I, PERSON, matter as I, TEACHER, interact with the children. I defy any computer program to replicate ME! I, teacher, matter even though children hold the key to their own powerful learning, for I, teacher, can be powerful too, influencing both the social and psychological milieu of the learner through the uniqueness of teacher-learner interactions and significant interventions.

Coda

I, teacher, in turn, however, can be most powerfully influenced . . . by peers, parents, bureaucracies, public servants, the economy, social malaise, the media and children . . .

CHILDREN?   CHILDREN?

Oh no! I *certainly* WILL NOT DESPAIR!

II

In which the English teacher is now a parent of two children in elementary school (1976). He, himself, has been made a senior adviser in English teaching charged with supporting teachers and providing opportunities for professional development in a centralized system employing about 17,000 teachers.

In moments of crisis, they say, it often happens that one's whole life, or at least significant aspects of it, flow into consciousness. On this occasion, a major conference had been planned to bring together influential but fragmented elements in language education in South Australia, including teachers of English as a second language, reading specialists, tertiary educators, "remedial" teachers, primary teachers and teachers of secondary literature courses.

Politically, it is the beginning of the "back to basics" scare before, many think, there had ever been more than a slightly festive frontlash. Our English teacher-cum-action researcher has geared himself to make a significant impact on this gathering in the cause of uniting against a palpable enemy (the media and the monopolies). He has, however, left his preparation to the last minute.

Fate intervenes, and, smitten by a squash ball in the eye, he is confined to hospital on the eve of the conference, sedated and forced to remain perfectly still on the flat of his back with a complete blackout effected by double eye pads. But intention overcomes valium, temporary blindness, and immobility. He calls for a tape recorder, and significant aspects of his personal and professional life burst into consciousness. Little pieces of documentation from the time of Simon's monologue (1972) through to the present crystallize around a theme.

He comes to an unpremeditated synthesizing point in his professional growth. Is it not, however, recollection in tranquility. Indeed it is closer to looking back in anger.

Where Has
the Eye Gone in Schools?

This is Garth Boomer speaking to you on the flat of his back in the Royal Adelaide Hospital. It's somewhat ironical that I'm going to talk to you about illiteracy. At this very moment I am illiterate myself, because I am blind. I've got double eye-pads on, so you are only going to be able to judge my "oracy."

First you might ask why you haven't got my written paper. Well, I've always put off till tomorrow what I should do today, and I had intended to write this up on Monday. I had planned what I was going to say, and I think it's still in my head. What you won't get is all the corroborative details which might help to prove my point, and so, it will sound somewhat blunt, controversial, and dogmatic, but then that's probably what I usually am.

I'm going to make the theme of my talk, *Where has the eye gone in schools?* and secondly, I'm going to pinch a phrase from Jimmy Britton which goes like this, *"The intention unlocks tacit powers."* But I'm possibly going to disappoint you by not talking much about our present illiteracy scare. I'm going to leave that hanging in the air, and say, *Well, we've got a lot of people who don't write very well,* but there is possibly something much more deep-seated wrong with our schools. I'm not so afraid of the illiteracy scare, but I'm most afraid of the "de-personalization scare," the fact that for many people school is a gradual progression of denial of self. If there is a progressive denial of self in schools, you're probably going to get the progressive denial of making meaning (that is, saying what I think or what I mean), and so a progressive threat to literacy. Perhaps many of you here don't need to be convinced that by the time you got to the end of your English studies at school you were past masters or mistresses at saying what the teacher thought you ought to think. Many of you, if you went on to do University English, probably have an honors degree in hypocrisy; that is, how to quote the critics and make out it is your own. But let us go back to where it all starts. The transcripts of my son Simon's talking at thirty-eight months old might begin to

14

convince you that between the ages of nought to five, there's an enormous amount of language going on. (See Chapter 1.) And there's no better way of finding out what language is going on inside a kid's head than to listen to a child monologuing. That's as close as you will ever come to getting a pure eavesdrop on the mind.

Well! what sort of things did Simon do in his bedtime spiel? He rehearsed all sorts of things that had happened during the day, such as falling off a swing. He rehearsed flying over to England in an airplane and recreated a fire scene based on the sound of an English fire siren. But he also did all sorts of meta-linguistic things. He played games with language itself. He hummed with it, making up words like "piggy nick"; he practiced his consonants by making sound like "m-n, m-n, m-n, m-n, m-n," and "k–k–k–k–k," and he sang songs. He practiced the rhythms of the language, and it was terribly egocentric in content. He was reflecting on and rehearsing his own world. He was going back over friends in Australia, and television tunes that he heard in Australia. The way I explain it is that in effect he was rocking his own cradle. He was making sense of the day, before he could go off to sleep.

But the linguists would also tell us, and I believe that this is true from looking at transcripts, that he was also practicing his own grammar, building up sentences, breaking down sentences, composing new combinations. In Chomsky's terms he was generating infinite numbers of meanings from the rules that he had written for himself. By doing a Watergate, we found that his pre-sleep babbling made sense. He was making meanings that obviously satisfied him, and which meant things to us because we shared much of his world.

The next little text I am going to offer you is an essay or, not an essay, a story that Catherine, my daughter, wrote when she was six years old. She came home and got on the typewriter and typed a little story, one finger. Meanwhile at school she was writing inane sentences about, *What I Did Yesterday.* At home she wrote this little story:

A Typed Story *(one finger)*

I am a brown football. My oner is kenney. I began life on a cow. You see I am a lether football allso some other footballs startlife on pigs. One day kenney my oner was haveing a game of football with me and he kickied me over the fence. part 21t was was a big kick actuley it was a gint kick, it kicek me right into a rocket witch was gust about to take of with me in it. I was so scerd I jumped into a small space sute and had a very uncomfortable rid. When we were at their moon i jumped out of the space ship ascdently one of the spacement knocked me of the side of the moon and i dide.

the end

Catherine

Because I get so many teachers (particularly elementary school principals for some reason or other) saying to me that it is nonsense that children know most of their grammar by the age of 5, I decided to do a grammatical analysis of this particular piece of writing. It is not a brilliant piece of writing, but I thought I'd find out what she knew. I made a list and found that she knew adjectives, subject-verb-predicate combinations, complements, and continuous past tenses. She knew resultant clauses. She knew the notion of an appositional phrase, and so on. I inferred all sorts of grammatical knowledge from this piece. Of course, there were lots of spelling errors in it because she used words like "accidentally."

At school, however, in the next year when she was seven, she went through the stage of losing half marks for errors. Then a surprising change came over her writing. She didn't use words she couldn't spell, and because she was also being taught at the same time about the conventions of putting full stops and commas in the right places, her writing became very self-conscious. She began to spit out sentences like peas. But more importantly or more disastrously, she began to distort her own meanings in order to produce the impressive artifact, and so she actually told lies in her essays because she had to use words she could spell.

Now I'm painting a rather bleak picture of this, and don't get me wrong. Catherine is happy at school, and she will do very well, thank you. She gets very high marks for compositions because she can play that game. I simply want to sow in your mind the seed that in fact we begin at a very early age, even in our better primary schools I suggest, to get kids playing the game of "Let's impress teacher. Let's find out what's in teacher's head."

Let me share with you a letter which Catherine wrote only last week. It's a letter she wrote at home to her Grandmother in Brisbane.

Monday April 19

To dear Nana Naught

Thank you for the money.
I have put it in the money box that Uncle Fred gave me. I hung the string holder on the veranda but I am not useing the flanels becaus they are to good to be faded. For Easter I got a train with six eggs in it an Easter bunny and half an egg. The next day we went to Nanas and I got more eggs from her. On Sunday I went to church with Nana because I slept over night. After church we drove home with Aunti Elm. Then I went to a cemetary with David to put some flowers on a few graves. David and I walked around while Nana and Aunti Elm put the flowers on the graves.
After that we went back to Nanas for lunch. We had a rost and Dad said it was great. While we had been at church Daddy had washed the car and it is mush cleaner now. After lunch we went over to Auntie Hellens and I gave David and Alison their money from you and our present which was two Easter bunnies that were just like mine. Then they gave us our presents which was an Easter egg.
I asked Alison if she would like a game of cards and she lost by four points. I had fifty three and she had forty nine. Then we had afternoon tea but I only had a drink. Alison asked if we would like to play schools

and I said that I would be glad to. So we went out on the veranda. Alison had the table and I had the high chair because there was nothing else there. Then the boys came through with things to make a tent. I told Alison not to take any notice but she went out and got into trouble. Then it was time to go home and I colected all my eggs and got into the car. As soon as I got home I went to bed because I was very tired.

The End

Love from
Catherine

It was syntactically near perfect and in many ways one could say it was most competent. What interested me, however, was that this wasn't Catherine writing to her Nanna. To her parents it sounds bogus. It is Catherine, not writing a letter to Nanna, but Catherine producing an artifact, which is what she thinks a child should write to her Grandmother. And so it is studied. You can see her self-consciously using things that she had been taught like "while" and "after." However, a couple of little pollutants get in. She uses "then" and "went."

Now there's a story behind this. Last week, would you believe, she came home from school and I said, *"How did you do at school today?"* and she said, *"Well, it's a sad thing Daddy, 'then' has got a broken arm, and 'went' has got appendicitis, and we're not allowed to use them, they're really sick!"* Now, as someone interested in language and making meanings I was horrified that an eight-year-old girl should be deprived of two of the most useful words in the English Language, especially when you are at the narrative stage and wanting to tell stories. So I didn't know quite what to do about this as a parent, but I thought I'd be funny and make a joke. I said, *"Oh! what about 'get'?"* Well, you wouldn't believe it, but next night she came home very happy. She said, *"Oh! we had a beaut time at school today, Daddy; we had a funeral for 'get'; we're burying him, we're not allowed to use him any more."*

So there we have an eight-year-old girl (and you might say, "Oh! this isn't a typical primary school," but think again), here we have a girl deprived of "then," "get" and "went." I challenge any of you, at any time, to make good meanings in the English Language without using those words. Just think of all the tricks you're going to have to get up to in order to avoid using them.

(If you're wondering what the background noise is, it's bath time at the Royal Adelaide Hospital and various people are getting a back-rub. I'll probably have to wait until I finish this to get mine.)

So that was the third little extract to show what seems to be happening to Catherine's language. You see, there was a time when she separated school language from home language. She wrote these beautiful stories at home and played a different game at school. But now even her natural home writing, her letter writing, is being, as I see it, polluted by school, where the emphasis is not on making meanings, but rather on making language which is superficially correct.

Then I could take you on to a little experiment I did in Sydney two weeks ago. (The nurse is having a good time in the background. You just forget her noises and concentrate on me!) In Sydney the other week I got six Year 12 essays [17-year-olds] written at a local high school on the question, Is Polonius a Talkative Old Man, or Is There More to Him?" and I seeded into these six essays a seventh which I wrote myself. I gave these essays to senior English teachers and I said, *"I want you to grade them on an 'A–E basis'."*

What did I find when the results came out? That for every essay they usually covered the full range from A to E. But mine got an almost universal "E." In other words, I failed final year English in their eyes. Now, why did this fail?

Polonius

Polonius is not merely any of these things. He is not even a portrait. He is a character, written into a play of Shakespeare, who lives only when some actor in the latest production of Hamlet takes to the stage and interprets the lines into tones and mannerisms and foibles. According to the negotiation between the director and the actor, Polonius may be actively evil or simply a bag of wind. He may be old and pitiful or old and detestable. He may be self-satisfied or ditheringly insecure. But what the actor makes Polonius is not the end of it. Polonius is also defined by the other actors and the action itself.

I get sick of all this talking about characters in plays as if they actually exist. I mean, you can spend hours sitting around wondering whether Hamlet really wanted to get into his mother's bed, but why bother? Shakespeare has to be the greatest con-man who ever lived. People, particularly school teachers, really seem to believe his illusions. Come to think of it, he's not all that brilliant. The writers of No. 96 [a well-known soap opera of the time] con at least half of Australia, half of the time.

I wonder what the truth is about Polonius? Shakespeare, running short of a few bob, thinks up the idea of a play about this guy who can't make up his mind. He's really a brilliant prince who thinks deeply and who is largely misunderstood. Now if you want to convince the yokels in the front stalls that this bloke is profound you need an idiot to contrast with him. Enter Polonius who changes his mind with his underwear or has no mind at all, an old dribbler who never thinks precisely on the event. Added twist for the cultured royals in the balcony—profound Hamlet and twittering old guy both fly around in ever decreasing circles and do nothing.

And so, the old show-biz office boy comes up with the right combination again, especially if you throw in murder, incest, unrequited love and bones in a graveyard. Sure to bring huge offers for film rights and a winner as a ten part serial on BBC in glorious color. (Bit of a problem about dubbing. Maybe you'd have to use subtitles.)

Polonius? He's about as bogus as the snobs who try to convince us that Shakespeare is deputy-god.

Well, I'll admit that I didn't answer in an orthodox way. I first of all sent the question up a little bit by saying that Polonius isn't anything; he is simply a character in a play. I wrote a very sophisticated first paragraph. In fact, I'm sure I would have had ticks all over it, but then I began to break all the taboos. I used some linguistic table manners that didn't suit. My next paragraph started with the words, "I get sick of all these teachers . . ." Now I'm putting it to you that there are many, many English teachers throughout South Australia who, as soon as they see words like "get sick of" in an essay almost immediately start to get into their minds the set, "Here is a student who is going to fail."

But I didn't stop there. I went on to insult Shakespeare. Now what I showed in that essay, I think, was the whole range of linguistic abilities. I showed that I could use the sophisticated language of examinations, that I could also play with the language, and make light of various serious things. But you see what I didn't do. I refused to play the examination game, and it so threw these markers that they had nothing else to do but fail me. So they failed someone who had linguistic sophistication, but didn't show conventionally that he had read the play. For example, I didn't go on at tedious length to say what Polonius did in the play, and I didn't quote. Of course, I showed in all sorts of other implicit ways that I had read it, but they couldn't see my meanings for the words.

I give you that little run-down, brief and eclectic as it is, to hint to you that there may be something in my hypothesis that from about Grade 3 onwards we go about bludgeoning "I" out of kids' essays, and "I" out of kids' meaning making. And we reward them the closer and closer they come to being like us, and saying the sorts of things we value. Now, if this is true, it's no wonder that we do have a certain amount of illiteracy, because we know ourselves that if we haven't got any clear meanings to make, we tend to get all garbled up and to write nonsense.

Now you might wonder why, if you have detected it, there's a certain bitterness under my statements. Well, the bitterness comes because I had a personal experience which was rather traumatic last year. One of the handouts for your conference is a piece of mine called "Whose Afraid of the Illiteracy Scare?" This article was commissioned by the editor of *Education News*, and I sent if off to him only to get a letter back saying he would like it to be written in the third person, in a slightly more formal style. You can imagine my response to this because my medium was my message. I deliberately wrote the article in a personal colloquial style because I wanted to engage with my reader. I wanted to say what I was thinking. I didn't want to get into the deception of sounding like some sort of impersonal God who said, "There is evidence to suggest that . . ." and all these other language games that the learned play. And I wanted to show that if there is illiteracy in our schools, it is possibly because we outlaw this word "I." So I wrote back the usual "get stuffed" letter to the editor of *Education News*, and then we had a rather absurd "Kafkaesque" kind of exchange of correspondence in which he continued to ignore what I was trying to say.

So eventually I withdrew the article and now it's been printed in this shorter form. But the point I want to make about this is that I saw clearly, probably for the first time, just how a kid in school must feel when he's written something he really wants to say, and back comes a message from the teacher, not about what he said, but about the way that he said it.

This upstart of an editor, and I call him that advisedly, because his letters to me were pompous and arrogant, was saying to me, in effect, *"I can't allow you to appear in public like this; you are grossly untidy and your hair is long and you look too shaggy; allow me to dress you up and then I am sure what you say can be made to sound acceptable."* So I'm bitter about what seems to me a conspiracy against "I" and a conspiracy about saying what you think.

I'm really on about this connection between so-called literacy and being able to say what you think. And I've got a sneaking suspicion that our schools reward those people who best learn to say what they think they should think. I know it's true with me. I'm only just learning to say what I think.

Well, let's tie it up with a little bit of theory while my brain is still running. What have we got to support this? Some of the things that I am saying about the value of "I" and making your own meanings, I would have thought are self-explanatory. Susanne Langer says primitive humans learned language in the first place, not to communicate with, but out of the dance. They got an overload of emotions in their brains and something had to come out so they started to make sounds associated with emotions. So language had a rhythmic, affective, emotional beginning (and it is largely that same kind of function that Simon was using it for).

Then we go to the sociolinguists who tell us quite clearly that we don't use language largely to communicate with. We use language to make sense of ourselves certainly, to help in understanding the world. We also use language to bludgeon people with, to keep people at bay with, to regulate people with. In fact, if you take two-thirds of the language that goes on in schools, you're likely to find that it's regulative language, teachers regulating kids in various ways. But we don't use language all that often to communicate straight facts from one to the other, and that isn't precise communication anyway, because there's always a gap between what the speaker means and what the hearer understands.

If you accept what I've just said about language, we have this irony, that in schools most of our time is spent in trying to emulate a kind of transactional writing devoted to conveying information to someone who already has the information (the teacher). Now, some of you who teach at the early levels may be sitting there feeling that this does not happen in your school. Not true, I say! Let me have a look at any writing lesson taught in South Australian elementary schools and I'll bet you, except in a few cases, they're all engaged in the game of "impress teacher" rather than expressing what they really think. And I don't care if some of you are wanting to object at this moment. I would want you to prove it to me before I would recant. Even so-called "Creative Writing" is still another game of transacting with the teacher to get reward, rather than saying what we really think.

To get back to the theory of it again. Let's look at some of the research on this. The London Research that I've quoted in that article shows a tragic picture of what happens in England. Most of the writing done in schools, apart from English, is of the transactional kind, and it's written to the teacher as examiner. Now if we are on about illiteracy, and if literacy is the ability to make your own meaning so that someone else can understand, I would suggest that writing something to an examiner who already knows is about the worst strategy you could use in order to cultivate literacy.

And yet the evidence is unequivocal. I'm not going to quote you the figures because I can't remember them in my head. But it also happens in Australia. John Annells did a similar experiment in Tasmania last year and found that at Grade 8 Level the average kid writes about one and a half pages a day, and, of that, one-point-two pages of this writing are simply exercise work. Now, of course, you are all enlightened and you may not believe that this could possibly be so. The facts in Tasmania speak for themselves, and I would bet that we would find similar things in South Australia.

So I suggest we've got this situation where kids are all the time concentrating on finding out what's in someone else's head. And I keep coming back to that. I think it's a crucial point. It's a crucial point if you consider the language practices that have been current in so many of our schools for so long.

Take Aboriginal Education for example. How much of the teaching of Aborigines has been a teaching which says, "Why can't they be like us? Why can't they use our language patterns?" How much of the teaching in infant schools has been in trying to pump language into kids on the assumption that they haven't got any when they come? How much of the teaching of language in elementary schools has been a mindless rigamarole of doing exercises, filling in blank spaces, "Active English!" "Let's make English Live!"? God help us all! How much of the language in secondary schools has been writing about writing, instead of writing? Writing about someone else's novel instead of writing your own stories?

In fact, when you think of language and writing in schools in particular, you find that what happens is largely absurd. It bears no resemblance to what goes on in the real world. Out there we write to people who write back. In here we write to a "dead letter" office, or to someone who puts a grade on our work. No wonder we produce some language cripples by the end of secondary school.

But what do we know from theory about the teaching of formal grammar and exercise work? I get sick of saying this. 50 years of research shows that teaching formal grammar is of no use whatsoever in improving writing. You might as well play chess or scrabble. And yet we still get many, many people in their troglodyte caves all around the countryside believing in the old tales and myths and rituals about grammar. Why can't we settle this bogey once and for all? By grammar, I mean the teaching of verbs, adjectives and nouns, and what makes up a sentence. And I also include mindless exercise work, like filling in the blanks, or putting commas and semicolons in a trial paragraph. We also find a continuing stream of tests which will show that kids can't do things. Have we ever looked to see what kids can do?

This is where I want to get on to the point that I began with, that the intention unlocks tacit powers. Look at kids reading! We can give reading age tests to some kids of eleven to find they have got a reading age of nine. Could it be that they simply didn't want to read the reading test; that they had no intention of reading the reading test? How would they score on a piece that they really intended to read? And if a kid really wants to write something, what tacit powers are hidden, powers he's got that he hasn't ever called upon before?

And so I'm putting it to you (and discussion can follow on this) that the major thing we have to do in our schools is to get kids intending to make meanings, and intending to get meanings. We must get rid of a lot of this meaningless claptrap, this language exercise stuff which bears no resemblance to the way language is used in the real world. Even in some of the language brains represented here today, I'll bet some people think that there's a hierarchical set of skills that can be taught one by one in language. Well, language just isn't like that! Language is making meanings, and it's a very subtle, complex thing. If I may make a rather crude pun, language is as delicate as an eyeball, and too many people in our schools are poking around with it, instead of letting it actively see.

(I'm getting rather rhetorical at this stage because my time's running out and the valium is starting to take effect.) The points I want to make are these: let's bring meaning back into the teaching of language, or the learning of language, whether it's in Aboriginal Education, whether it's in secondary school reading or elementary school reading, or whether it's in language across the curriculum. Let's get kids using language to make sense.

And also if I can end this short talk on a positive note, let's remember that we learn language by using language in situations where we intend either to make meaning or get meaning for good reason.

Response

LETTER FROM THE CLASSROOM

JUDY PETERS

Dear Garth,

I couldn't have read this article at a more appropriate time. You see, only three days before, "then" had had an accident in my Year 6 classroom. Not a fatal one but I had devoted what I call a "writers' workshop" to brainstorming possible alternatives to the poor word and discussed instances where it might be eliminated altogether. That part of your argument made me pause guiltily and carefully think through my justification for that strategy. I'll respond to that challenge a little later.

Your basic tenet of schools as depersonalizing agents and the resultant loss of power this engenders in individuals has been one of my concerns for the past few years. I believe this problem is largely based in the relationship which normally exists between teacher and pupils; that traditional one of teacher directing and students acquiescing. With such uneven distribution of power, naturally the language of the students will be restricted to what they think the teacher wants.

With my own classes I have been trying to break down some of these barriers by redistributing more evenly the responsibility for setting up and maintaining the physical environment, personal behavior, what is learned and how this is evaluated. This has also involved revealing myself more as an individual by sharing my thoughts and feelings. Above all I've tried to make development of each individual's feeling of self-worth the main outcome.

I've found this whole process exhausting, personally traumatic, and fraught with friction involving parents, other staff, and the administration, whose natural conservatism is continually fueled by the whole media "illiteracy/ back to basics" hysteria you mentioned. But it is possible within a year to have kids unlearn some of the caution they've assumed and begin to say what they think and even challenge what they see as unfair or meaningless.

To have this take effect in what they write involves a further step of unlearning certain habits. From early on they seem to adopt a generalized "we" for writing about personal experience. I'm sure everyone has read examples of the "Last Sunday we went on a picnic" variety. This style of writing is symptomatic of the depersonalization you refer to. It automatically precludes kids from reflecting on their own experiences.

One way I've tried to put them back in touch with this experience is by having five-minute jotting sessions in which we quickly scribble down our reactions to some experience (such as waking up on the first morning of term) and then share them aloud. I stress that the aim is to reflect on their feelings and thoughts at the time and articulate them so vividly that they let others inside their heads. Even children who don't normally like to write scribble frantically during this time and are eager to read their piece. I think this is because reading aloud is a great equalizer and removes the threat of incorrectness which showing writing has for some people. That is, provided an atmosphere of mutual trust has been established in the classroom.

Early on, even in this situation, many children use "we" in their writing, but I take this up as a discussion point and they are able to see for themselves it is less effective than "I." We go all around the room with each person rephrasing one of their sentences, using the first person and also making it as involving as possible for the listeners.

This brings me to a point where I may differ a little from the view you've presented that the primary function of language is to "make sense of ourselves and to help in understanding the world." I agree with that completely, but I think that the way we clarify this view of our own position in the world is by trying to communicate it to others. Therefore I'm concerned with working with my class on ways they can make what they write more dynamic and engaging for the reader, as I believe this helps them elaborate their personal view.

This is the function of the writers' workshops I mentioned in my opening paragraph, including the one on that unfortunate word. We usually start
from some writing we've done or are about to do and discuss a particular aspect which will affect reader involvement. In the case of "then" the kids were
working on "This Is My Life" scripts for a roll-through TV show. In a sequen-
tial narration such as that, "then" can occur so many times that it is boring
for the audience, so we brainstormed alternatives. The kids had enormous
energy for this and wanted to keep it up long after I was tired of writing them
on the board. On another occasion we went on a similar search through poetry
books, and similes have appeared in writing ever since. In a way the kids are
partly trying to make me happy, but I think the child who wrote, "I woke as
if coming out of hibernation," has deepened his own perception of that moment
as well as created an "impressive artifact." Of course, I agree that this is all a
"non-event" if the only reader is me. Writing done is usually read aloud, made
into books, or displayed in some way, and I don't leave reading and response
to chance but organize the times for it to occur.

My own response to this writing presents me with the common problem
of all writing teachers: that what I say or write should actively encourage clarification of personal meaning, while at the same time assist the development of
necessary skills. I try to do this by discussing the content of a piece while it is
in the rough draft stage and, when this is to the author's satisfaction, collecting
the drafts for a final read before rewriting. At this stage I "mark" the pieces by
making comments in two columns headed, "Things done well" and "Things to
check for." I keep an ongoing record of these and so does each kid. They add
things and change things from one column to the other as the year goes on. I
feel this fits in with your idea of "looking to see what kids can do," and they
are very positive about these lists. Parents also respond well, as this satisfies
their desire for a record of progress.

I guess the most disheartening thing for anyone who tries to put kids back
in touch with themselves is knowing that the next year will probably see them
back jumping through hoops for someone else. In a recent interview with two
of my kids from last year now in Year 8, one explained:

> "Now the emphasis is on actual, real English, you know the apostrophes,
> all the rules, the troublesome words and everything. We're leaving stories
> a lot. This is the first story I've done in my English exercise book and
> normally we just don't write stories. We do oral comprehensions to test
> our listening skills—she reads out a small story and asks some questions
> on it and gives us a sheet and then she grades it."

Although this is depressing, what is encouraging is that throughout the
interview the kids showed that they are fully aware that they are playing a
game for the teacher which has nothing to do with the real use of language. So
at least they're no longer mindless victims of these depersonalization tactics
and can preserve a detachment that must give them more protection than those
who are.

III

Taken from the classroom into the comparatively impotent realms of consult-
ancy, the English teacher strives to find "objective correlatives" for his theory-
inspired ideas. He seizes on any opportunity to talk with young children, the
most accessible of which are his own son, now seven, and daughter, nine.

His study in 1972–73 started many itches which he continues to scratch
away at. For instance, the reflexive social psychology of G. H. Mead burrows
away in his mind, and a metaphor of adult-child relationships as a kind of
"dance of language" takes hold. We learn by internalizing action, reflecting,
and then externalizing the newly created inner world to which people respond,
which leads us in turn to new internalizations and so on.

At a pleasant think-and-talk retreat organized for a network of English
teachers and their families, he takes the opportunity to play with a teaching
idea that has Mead at the back of it somewhere.

He kicks himself afterwards for not putting a tape recorder on the floor
while he and four young children made up stories which he "scribed." If only,
he thinks afterwards, teachers could have access to the kind of formulation,
reformulation, and language interaction these children displayed as they composed aloud.

Still, the instinct of the researcher leads him to take away the texts. With
the permission of his co-authors, he celebrates the achievement publicly and
makes some observations about implications for teaching.

Tell Me a Story
An Experiment in Language Development

Introduction

I had been reading Dennis Lillee as told to Tom Pryor [Lillee is a famous Australian cricketer] and I wondered whether this sort of ghost-writing had possibilities for language development in schools. I know that schemes such as "Breakthrough to Literacy" build in opportunities for teachers to write up children's stories and messages, and I have blithely advocated for many years that we should teach beginning readers to read by allowing them to cheat ("to swim with one foot on the bottom") by giving them their own written-up stories as readers. In this way they would begin to internalize appropriate patterns of their own thoughts in written form.

What I had previously taken from Vygotsky, and just lately from Joan Tough, suggested to me that children gradually "fine tune" and develop their thinking strategies by internalizing patterns of thinking which they see enacted in the world (by observing dialogue, operations, etc.).

Chomsky tells me that a person's competence always exceeds the performance and that we will often undervalue a child's language ability, and intelligence, if we take performance as our guide. Furthermore, it is a linguistic fact that a child's vocabulary and meaning taking ability far exceed the productive, meaning making ability.

Musing on the matters above, I began to have some hunches:

1. Maybe the greatest challenge facing language teachers is to get children confidently pushing their receptive language competence into productivity without fear of penalty; that is, to get them hypothesizing in talk and writing while providing warm, positive, constructive feedback.

2. If children internalize the language patterns they observe around them, especially when it serves their own thinking and meaning making, then teachers may be able to accelerate language development by providing

26

more sophisticated language patterns when children are in the process of making meaning.

3. Perhaps the *linear* and *physical* aspects of writing make children appear to be worse writers than they are. Perhaps in their heads they write pretty fluently before further processing and externalizing cripples it. Perhaps, then, children will dictate like a book (i.e. in written form) if they know that that is the game.

4. Perhaps it would be a good idea to sit down with some children and get them to tell me stories where I was not simply a scribe but also a Tom Pryor with respect to Dennis Lillee, a clarifier, extender, stylizer, questioner, and mediator to the public.

So that's what I did.

What I Did

A group of people interested in language went with their families to Eudunda for a weekend and, with the Principal's permission, camped in the Area School, using the Year 1 and Year 2 "Smile Set" room as a dormitory. According to our interests and needs we spent our time making things, or reading or discussing.

I went off with Simon (7) and Catherine (9), my own children and Thea (11) and Leslie Mohr (9) for a storytelling session. When I explained that I wanted each to tell me a story which I would write down, they were at first a bit reticent. So we sat around on the floor for a while and talked about the kinds of stories we enjoyed. I can't remember how it happened now, but somehow the conversation got around to horror stories.

Eventually, with a bit of coaxing from me, Simon, the youngest and the most extrovert, started telling a story about the "Three Vampire Bats." The others mucked around but listened first with one ear and then with growing interest as the story unfolded. Then, with little further prompting, each of the others also told a tale.

As scribe, I operated as follows:

- I took down what was dictated and, whenever it seemed appropriate, read sections back to the storyteller (to allow the teller to add further information, to correct miscues, and to remind him of the plot so far).
- When the information being supplied seemed rather bare, I asked the sort of questions that I thought an interested audience might ask (e.g. "What was this cave?" "Why did people fear these bats?").
- Then when the storyteller answered these questions, we would negotiate about how to include the extra detail.
- This is where I would offer various options for saying it, leaving the final choice to the ear and aesthetics of the storyteller (e.g. "We could say the bats were *gourmets.* This means great food lovers. Or we could say they enjoyed eating or we could say they just loved food. What do you want?"). This was my way of leading. I led but I did not insist on the more sophisticated pattern.

- If I saw gross illogicalities I'd point this out indirectly (e.g. "You said a while back that the bats were from Italy and now you're saying 'Australia.' Which do you want?").

And so I hoped to preserve their *meanings* and their *spirit* while opening up for them new options, new ways of saying, and new insights into my thought processes as I acted both as writer and potential reader. In this way they might learn more about what it is to be a competent adult writer and more about the questions readers ask and the expectations they bring to their reading.

I leave the reader to judge the method by the product.

THE FOUR VAMPIRE BATS

by Simon Boomer
(as told to Garth Boomer)

Once upon a time in a deep, dark smoggy cave in Italy there lived four bloodsucking Vampire Bats. Everyone feared these frightful Bats because they could fly down chimneys and bite people's necks when they were asleep.

When they were thirsty they loved blood; when they were hungry they loved insects or dead flesh.

One gloomy night, they went out into the deep, dark, smoggy forest to find something to eat because in the forest there lived all sorts of animals.

And, in the heart of the forest, they found a dead deer covered with humming blowflies. But they were greedy bats and the blowflies were too small, and so the first Bat said, "We shall go to the other side of the island and see if there are any houseflies there."

And so they flew off into the night and soon they came upon a swarm of houseflies, the Vampires' favorite dinner, because, as you know, these Bats were gourmets.

They licked them all up and they were scrumptious.

After that they decided to find their best friends, the Bush Babies.

The Bush Babies lived in South Africa, but the Vampires had jet powered wings and so they soon found the Bush Babies playing happily in a big oak tree.

But then, all of a sudden, out of nowhere, three men came into the clearance with chain saws and cut down the big oak.

Luckily the Vampire Bats picked the Bush Babies up with their back feet just in time and they flew to another clearance in the area and put the Bush Babies down.

After resting for a while, they flew back to their deep, dark, smoggy cave in Italy with the Bush Babies who were still in a state of shock.

They carefully put the Bush Babies down on their beds and gave them each an ice cube because it was very hot.

And so the Bush Babies and the Vampire Bats are friends to this very day.

The End

N.B. A Bush Baby is a kind of koala bear, only smaller.

Comment

Simon did talk like a book. He's had a good deal of bedtime storying at home and he has obviously internalized many of the conventions and cosmetic niceties of the children's story and the fairy tale, even to such details as the quaint "in the forest there lived . . . ," a form not found in normal speaking.

He needed little coaxing to add more and more embroidery to his sentences. He expanded almost automatically. Even the three Vampire Bats became *four* to the naturally excessive composer.

Without getting at all ingenious, it is easy to see how well he has the style—the repetition of "deep, dark, smoggy cave," the formality of "We *shall* go to the other side . . . ," the trick of engagement with audience, " as you know."

As I say, it was easy to prompt his expansion and he handled most of the syntactical joining and subordination himself. Occasionally, I tried several constructions and let him choose. Anyway, each sentence had his blessing. It was interesting just to hear and watch him building up his composition out loud, just as a somewhat hesitant company director might do when dictating a difficult letter.

The story is somewhat incremental and rambling, but I was impressed by his ability to take account of each new element built in. I thought his feel for the dramatic moment was good and his closure was commendable and nicely familiar.

In the content there is a delightful mixture of conventional horror and the gentle romance of Disney. Simon's own memories of childhood are obviously present, especially in the "ice cube because it was very hot" episode.

The range of his vocabulary, his handling of complex syntactical structures, and his skill in developing plot left me wondering where and how he had learned it all.

THE THREE INDIAN CHIEFS

by Leslie Mohr

(as told to Garth Boomer)

There was once a tribe of young Indians and they had three gentlemen in the tribe, one smart, one greedy, and one careless.

One day it came time to vote on who would be the next chief.

When they had finished the votes, it came to be that those three Indians had equal votes. So they were set, by the old chief, a task.

The first task was to climb over the narrow bridge that stretched above Death Valley. Two Indians made it but the careless one slipped and fell and had his head chopped off by a sharp rock.

Next day the old man took the children into the forest. The children thought he was going to chop down trees because he had brought along his axes, but in fact, he was going to chop their heads off. He made them bend over and place their necks on a log and was just about to chop their head off, when Abba came along and they started singing *Waterloo* so loud that they deafened the old man, who ran off into the forest screaming in agony.

But luckily, the children were very great Abba fans and their favorite song was *Waterloo.* They started to dance and Abba could see that these were their greatest fans. And so at the end of their song Abba adopted them and took them to live with them on their hideaway island.

So now you know why Abba have two children and if you look closely when Abba are singing you will see, somewhere in the background, two children dancing with little axes on their necks to remind them of that almost fateful day so many years ago.

The End

Comment

I was at first disappointed with Catherine as she dictated what appeared to be a dead steal from Hansel and Gretel. But then she rang the changes in a most novel and topical manner. I still don't know whether this was intended at the beginning, but I do know that she made a point that the story was to be set in Sweden right at the start.

She mingles her early childhood fantasy with her later childhood obsessions with Abba and obviously identifies with the two lucky children who are adopted. Like the others, she has storying conventions at her finger tips (or rather at the tip of her tongue). The beginning, middle, and end ritual is handled most competently.

As a general comment on each of the stories, I was fascinated to see how each story grew, how each new fact was gradually wound into the plot and how it gradually developed through tension and climax to the satisfying closure. Gestalt? The poetic vision? Or more good luck than good management?

All in Together

This individual storying so intrigued me that I wanted to do some myself, and so, to finish the day I suggested that we make a group story where each of them could be a key character and decide their own parts in the plot.

It was great fun. We laughed and exploded with ideas about the "Hunchback of Eudunda Area School." They shouted ideas, rolled on the floor, made appropriate noises and I tried to conduct, stimulate, put in ideas of my own, and write down, before it all escaped.

The end product was the story which follows. They all thought it was great stuff so we left a copy for the children at Eudunda Area School as a memento.

Simon the Super Skunk, Atom Ant, Laughing Gas Leslie and Speedy Gonzales went home happy, and so did the scribe.

THE FANTASTIC FOUR AND
THE HUNCHBACK OF EUDUNDA AREA SCHOOL
As told to Garth Boomer by
Thea Mohr, Leslie Mohr,
Catherine Boomer and Simon Boomer
at Eudunda Area School,
Saturday, 13th November, 1976

Somewhere north from Adelaide you will find Eudunda Area School, a peaceful, happy place where the birds sing and trees sway softly in the summer breeze. You will find desks and toys and books and neat rooms where children work and learn.

But it was not always this way. There was a time when there was no peace at Eudunda, a time of terror and panic and destruction. This was Eudunda's darkest hour—the time of the *Hunchback of Eudunda Area School.*

It all started on a windy day in November, on Friday 13th to be exact. There was something eerie about the school that day, even before the first bell.

Queer things began to happen. Windows broke when no one was present; cracks appeared mysteriously where there were none before; nasty rumors spread throughout the school after strange messages appeared on the blackboard; and there were strange rumblings beneath the floorboards.

At first, nobody took much notice, but then in the SMILE SET ROOM a dreadful thing happened. Screams of terror broke out amongst the Grade 2's when a hairy shadow fell upon the northern wall. It was a bent shape, dark and sinister; it was the Hunchback, later to be known as the *Hunchback of Eudunda Area School.*

Only the children saw it. You see, only the sensitive eyes of the young could pick up the weird light rays. Those over eighteen saw nothing.

So when the children screamed, the teacher got very angry and decided to punish them by keeping them in after school. In vain they tried to explain what they had seen. The teacher simply thought they were making up excuses for their naughty behavior.

After that, the Hunchback really went wild. He pinched a teacher who had an innocent boy caned for the offense. He put his hairy paw through a window pane and the matriculation students got the blame. He made rude noises in English lessons, and, worst of all, he spilt ink on the Principal's best suit on visiting day.

The poor students were constantly in trouble, and the noise of the swishing cane became so frequent that everyone trembled in fear.

At last they could stand no more. Many had sighted the hairy Hunchback and they all knew they it was he who was causing all the trouble. He had to be stopped.

And so the children called an emergency meeting, with no teachers present, to find a solution. They were desperate. How could they combat the dreaded plague that was upon them?

Just when they were at their wit's end, a little girl in Grade 1 said, "Why not call on the Fantastic Four? They are our only hope."

Cheers broke out, and they decided to put out a call at once. Within minutes the mighty quartet had landed on the oval—Speedy Gonzales, Laughing Gas Leslie, Atom Ant (alias Catherine the Itch) and Simon the Super Skunk (the fastest smell in the West).

A quick council of war was called and the children told the Fantastic Four everything they knew about the horrible Hunch and his hair raising habits. They soon had a plan of action to trap the Hunchback the next day.

Not one student at Eudunda Area School slept that night. They were too excited.

It was a Tuesday morning and all the students were assembled in the yard when a shadow loomed over the school roof. It was the dreaded Hunchback and the students shrank in horror.

The Principal shouted for attention just as Speedy Gonzales whipped out from behind a tree and, quick as a flash, hit the hulking Hunch an almighty blow in the solar plexus. The students cheered and Hunch growled in anger, lashing out at Speedy who, slick as lightning, headed for the swimming pool.

Hunch followed and was just about to hammer a deadly blow onto Speedy's head when Atom Ant, flexing his nuclear muscles, gripped Hunch by a tiny hair on his little toe and whirled him round his head.

With one final whirl, Atom Ant threw the amazed monster into the pool just as Laughing Gas Leslie let herself into his lungs and began to unloose her hysteria.

The pool was soon rumbling with Hunch's forced laughter. Almost helpless now, Hunch was powerless to do anything as Super Skunk prepared for the final blow. With one breathtaking movement, Super Skunk emitted a paralyzing blast of odor which left the Hunch completely motionless at the bottom of the pool.

It was only left for Speedy to become a human shuttle and weave a net of rope over the pool. The Hunch was captured and, under the influence of the super stench, had become visible even to the Principal. Cheers broke out, and soon, back in the school, teachers were apologizing to students and praising their actions in the calling of the Fantastic Four.

After they had waved goodbye to their rescuers, the students went back to the pool to see the Hunch. To their horror they found their net broken and the monster gone.

Returning to school they found no trace of him except for one message scrawled on a blackboard: "The Hunchback shall return."

So far, Eudunda has remained a peaceful school. So far, no dark shadows have again entered the classrooms. But everyone remembers the day of the Hunchback and no one knows if he will ever choose to come again.

The End

Conclusion

I am convinced that storying by dictation is a "good thing." Admittedly, I played the game with four linguistically sophisticated children, but I can't say I see why it would not work with others with different language resources. These are the positive features I have isolated:

1. It seems to bridge the gap between talking and writing.
2. It demonstrates how writing differs from talking (e.g. encourages talking like a book).
3. It helps children imagine their audience.
4. It helps children to hold what they have already said in mind.
5. It presses children to elaborate, extend, and modify.
6. It gives indirect reading experience because it involves a good deal of "reading back" and "reading over." When it is completed it is, of course, avidly read and re-read by the teller.
7. It allows the child to break the barrier of inadequate productive syntax and brings performance much closer to competence.
8. It sometimes allows teacher (or secretary) to put words (and patterns) into the child's mind without tyrannizing over the meaning.
9. It subtly underlines the need for tense consistency, logical development of ideas, and appropriate closure of plot.
10. It is fun; it is cooperative; it is satisfying (and it isn't achieved without mental effort).

Response

STORYING BY DICTATION

PAULA DREW

I am convinced that storying by dictation is a "good thing" too! Not just for the creator of the written piece, but also for the "secretary." The Unit in which I work is an exciting place to be—there are 75 children varying in age from 5 to 12 years, three teachers and lots of parents, friends, grandparents and other interested adults who like to be around in the Free Choice Time, provided each morning. In this sort of environment it is easy for a would-be story writer (of any age!) to find someone who is willing to be scribe and mentor. The starting points vary—a 10-year-old who has been involved in an exchange visit to a country school and wants to write about the experience to the people with whom she stayed; a 12-year-old adventuring into the depths of "Dungeons and Dragons" with a fierce and frantic imagination but without the necessary handwriting and spelling skills which the situation demands; or a 6-year-old with "a gooder Cinderella story, called Cinderalla, about boys having to do work"!?!

The Unit places high emphasis on social interaction and development, and children of all different ages talk and play and dramatize together. As a natural progression, children are encouraged to write together, with a particular emphasis on the youngest children easing into writing, without fear of penalty. It is rare to hear a child say "I can't write"; rather "I'd like some help with this; who will write for me while I talk?" There is a more formalized language block each day (approximately 1½ hours) which may well involve personal, silent reading and writing, sharing, and group reading and writing tasks. In addition, each junior in the Unit has an older "Helper" with whom he/she spends about an hour a week—often engrossed in the production of an episodic story, e.g. Star Wars as it has never quite been told before, involving all the familiar "Unit characters." For me, as a teacher of language across a very broad range of ages, "storying by dictating" is a crucial facet of the language learning opportunities I offer. It is not an "extra" to be fitted in occasionally. In fact, there is a routine established with the Juniors that each Friday parents commit themselves for an hour to write with up to five children. It's exhausting, but the parents, whose initial commitment is for six weeks, keep coming back for more!

I believe that this process of interaction actively engages children in building confidence in their abilities to create writing, and extends understanding of syntactical structures, developing plots, and characters. How encouraging it is to hear a young or older reluctant writer say, after hearing his/her own writing read back, "Hey, that sounds good, doesn't it?" "No, that part about the robbers is a bit weak, but I know what I want to say." "I don't like that bit—what do you think? How can I say it?" It is essential in a classroom situation to make available many scribes, not just the teacher, but older students, parents, and other interested adults. It is fun, it is cooperative, it is satisfying for the person scribing and the child who is storying by dictating.

IV

In which the English teacher more deliberately sets out to pin down what happens when a sympathetic scribe interacts with a young storyteller. The playing described in Chapter III is translated into a serious experiment with the compliance of Simon, now nearly eight, who agrees to compose aloud in the presence of his father, as scribe, and a tape recorder. The recorder is soon forgotten as the story takes hold.

Significantly, the teacher-researcher stores the raw data for two years. Caught up in the crazy round of educational events to which change agents are often addicted, he seems to prefer to be nibbled to death by ducks than to discipline himself to some concerted and focused thinking.

When an invitation comes to address a national reading conference in 1979, he panics at first. It's an important engagement politically and educationally. The Australian Reading Association and the Australian Association for the Teaching of English have had little to do with each other. There seem to have been some deep ideological chasms between them (something to do with "skills" vs. "growth") and now, for the first time, there is a chance to begin communications. Reading theorists inspired by Frank Smith and Ken Goodman are revitalizing the Reading Association and there are signs that reading and writing are coming together as two sides of one coin.

The English teacher's panic recedes when the two-year-old data is revisited. The distancing of time allows him to approach the material archaeologically. He disassembles it and puts it together again, summoning some of his favorite theorists to help him interpret.

Becoming the Reader
Over One's Own Shoulder

An Experiment in the
"Conversation of Gestures"

"Only in terms of gestures as significant symbols is the existence of mind or intelligence possible; for only in terms of gestures which are significant symbols can thinking—which is simply an internalized or implicit conversation of the individual with himself by means of gestures—take place."

(G. H. MEAD, p. 42)

Introduction

An experiment was born when I began to wonder why Simon, aged seven years nine months, wrote so little so haltingly in his school "compositions." His formative years had been alive with the written word, read aloud with feeling in an atmosphere of warmth and mutual inquiry. We had bathed our child in language. He had also had a rich diet of television, devouring wildlife documentaries, "play school," cartoons, horse operas, space adventures, and the full catastrophe of advertisements. Surely, I thought, his head must be abounding with scenarios, plots, myths, characters, and words for all seasons.

Even allowing for the known gap between receptive and productive capacity, I hypothesized that there was an alarming gulf between Simon's suspected competence to write and his present performance at school. It was not a stunning feat of intellect which led me to consider the physical barrier of pen-wielding as the likely cause of blockage, assuming that there was a blockage. Any junior primary school teacher who had worked with "Breakthrough to Literacy" could have prescribed the experiment which I then set up. I decided to ask Simon to "talk writing," to tell me a story, to dictate a masterpiece while I scribed.

Few people would be surprised to find that I confirmed my suspicions. By this process, Simon dictated a story which, for his age, was quite an amazing creation, linguistically and stylistically sophisticated and with a secondary school "reading age." (See p. 51)

Both Simon and I were proud of the typed-up story about "The Killer Spider." Simon's teacher responded with some reserve according to Simon. I don't think she quite believed it. After all, Simon was the fidgety, untidy, reluctant writer who painfully etched out a few scraggly subject-verb-object sentences.

This introduction is not just to give me space for boasting. Nor is it to further the already proven power of scribing as a means of developing writing performance. It is to set the scene for the real experiment, which is the journey I have since taken in speculating about and analyzing the event. I had a tape recorder on the event between Simon and me. The tape lay dormant for two years. My mind, however, has often incubated on the significance of what happened between us during that storytelling. In talk with teachers, I have often, in broad terms, cited what happened to support my prejudices. Then, a few months ago, I decided to mine the quarry, asking the questions, "What is happening?" and "What is its significance?"

Eventually, I compiled a profile of strategies which Simon, as storyteller, seemed to be using and a parallel profile of strategies which I, as scribe, adopted. Instinctively, or so it seemed, I was going beyond the neutral role of writing instrument. Quite naturally, father and son weaved and danced around each other with their minds, carrying on what George Mead has called "a conversation of gestures."

All this speculation and analysis sent me back to revisit some of the more influential conversations I have had in the last ten years. In particular, I renewed acquaintance with L. S. Vygotsky, G. H. Mead, George Gusdorf and Michael Polanyi (see Bibliography). This convinced me that it was not instinct at all which led me to take that certain stance as scribe. It was a deeply embedded theory of language learning, resting on the insights of reflexologists, the social psychologists, and above all, on the seminal work of G. H. Mead. I, therefore, intend to cheat a little by writing up the experiment with its now articulate and explicit theoretical accompaniment, even though I was not being consciously theoretical at the time.

A Rationale for Child-Teacher Interaction in the Composing Process

Education is largely concerned with promoting the advance of mind for each student. "Mind" cannot be conceived of as an abstract entity. One conceives of the mind of another by observing how that other manipulates symbols (e.g. language) and tools in social interaction. The question lying behind the experiment which I conducted is "How does the child develop the mind of a writer?" or "How does the child learn to become a meaning maker with the written symbol?"

The brief answer is that the child internalizes what it is to be a writer through social interaction with readers, writers, and writing. Charles W. Morris neatly summarizes the position of G. H. Mead, upon which this answer is based:

> "Mind is the presence in *behavior* of significant symbols. It is the internalization within the individual of the social process of communication in which meaning emerges. It is the ability to indicate to one's self the response (and implicated objects) that one's gesture indicates to others, and to control the response in these terms."
>
> (MEAD, p. xxii)

So, if Simon is to become a writer, he must be exposed to the social process of communication through the written word and be encouraged to experiment with written "gestures." He will not have control of the medium until he can respond to his own "gesture" in the same way as the person or persons to whom the "gesture" is directed. He must become an object to himself, at one moment creating the "gesture," at the next responding to it, so that he may continue the communication. Without this dialectic of the mind, the written creation will not occur.

> " . . . Birds tend to sing to themselves, babies to talk to themselves. The sounds they make are stimuli to make other sounds."
>
> (MEAD, p. 65)

But the inner conversation is not accidental. It is the individual's internalization of observed social interaction, especially of the attitude of others toward self.

> "We are more or less unconsciously seeing ourselves as others see us. We are unconsciously addressing ourselves as others address us; in the same way as the sparrow takes up the note of the canary, we pick up the dialects about us."
>
> (MEAD, p. 68)

This leads me to a rationale for child-teacher interaction in the composing process. It is so easy for children to enter into the social processes of talk. Quite naturally, they enter into communication with peers and adults, gaining immediate feedback as to the effects of their vocal "gestures" and having access to the metalinguistic exchange of others about meaning and of the ways things are said. By five they have developed their own capacity to talk about talk and they have internalized a multitude of strategies for achieving effect and appropriate response through talk. The advance of mind with respect to this medium is miraculously swift.

But writing does not offer such easy access. The house of composition is poorly fenestrated. By comparison the child will even find it easier to internalize what it is to be a reader, because home and society generally offer opportunities for seeing other people reading, for listening to the written word, and for talking about the story or message afterwards. The five-year-old from a story-oriented home is likely to have a fairly well internalized notion of the rhythms and patterns of the written word and of the role of the recipient. By contrast, that same five-year-old is far less likely to have internalized much about what it is to be a writer, because people are rarely in the habit of talking about their own composing and also because adults write far less than they read in front of children.

My own observations over many years lead me to suggest that this state of affairs continues to prevail in our elementary and secondary schools. There may be more talk about *writing* as a medium, but I doubt if there is much chance for children to understand what it is like inside the head of a writer or what it is like to be on the receiving end of one's own meaning (in anything but a perfunctory manner). It is not surprising, then, that most children find composing a very difficult business and that even most adults are tentative, if not fearful, about the medium.

From this follows the obvious antidote. In the early stages of schooling, and perhaps throughout education, we should assist children in the learning of composition by opening up access to the inner workings of the composing/communicating process. This would involve adults and others "writing aloud" for children and children "writing aloud" for readers or scribes who undertake to give immediate access to the reader's response.

My experiment took up the strategy of "writing aloud" to a scribe/reader who is "thinking aloud." As will emerge, the reader in this case took on other roles besides that of the "thinking reader."

The Strategies of the Storyteller

Because Simon is dictating, many composing strategies which might normally be hidden become obvious. A teacher would be able to use similar techniques to the Goodman miscue analysis of reading in analyzing the composing process. I have isolated ten interesting aspects of Simon's "work."

1. *Finding a Way In*

   After a few preliminaries, and the activity of the scribe preparing to "take dictation," Simon eventually announces: "Now I'm ready" and immediately launches into a crisp opening sentence:

   > "Somewhere in this galaxy, there is a smallish planet called Delta III . . . fullstop."

   He says this with some satisfaction and one feels that he has a story inside him. Even though at the end he reveals that he had no specific details in mind, there is a sense of unfolding as Simon proceeds. The Killer Spider, which gives the piece its title, does not appear until over half way through the story, but the composer is obviously leading up to the revelation from the very first sentence.

   Two things are worth commenting on here. The first sentence of any writing is very important for the composer. If, as Mead suggests, each sentence is a "gesture" which calls forth continuing gestures, then it is crucial that the composer begin with a richly evocative sentence. Teachers know how many writers agonize over finding a way in.

   It is also interesting to notice the stylistics of the sentence. It is clearly "writing," not talk, and it very neatly encapsulates the story tone. The composer *knows* what a story is and how a story starts. The syntax and the rhythm of the opening invite us in.

No one has directly taught Simon this. He has naturally internalized it, from countless bedtime readings and from the "voice of God" narratives that accompany many television sagas. As the story continues, it becomes clear that Simon has learned much more.

2. *Dictating in Appropriate Clusters*
   An examination of the transcript reveals that Simon's pausation is rule-governed. He does not break at inappropriate places in his sentences. There are three kinds of pause:

   1. The break at a logical point syntactically ("Somewhere in this galaxy . . . there is a smallish . . . planet called . . . Delta III"). There is a neat choreography of dictation throughout, showing the composer to be aware of the amount of words the scribe can handle and the grouping of words which make sense.
   2. The pause before the revelation of a key name, noun or new element in the plot—" . . . set out for the distant planet . . . ." Eventually, after quite a bit of brain-searching, a name is invented.
   3. The pause before a difficult syntactic construction or when a "maze" has been noticed in what precedes: "It finally ended up . . . the trail finally ended up." Here the composer realizes for himself the ambiguity of "it." He pauses and corrects.

   The logic of the pausation is most interesting. It is a feat of some magnitude, showing a high degree of control of syntax and semantics as well as a deep empathy with the task of the scribe.

3. *Controlling the Poetics and Aesthetics of Composing*
   Robert Escarpit draws a distinction in literature between the poetics of the composer and the aesthetics of the audience

   "The artist creates according to a poetic pattern; the public perceives the creation according to an aesthetic pattern."
   (E. & T. BURNS, p. 360)

   There are many places in the dictation where Simon can be observed savoring his words, trying them out on his inner ear. In order to make poetic choices, he seems to need to become an aethestically sensitive audience to himself.
   The naming of the distant planet is important. Father is asked to help. Simon eventually proffers "The six moon planet." Father rephrases it, "The distant planet of the six moons." Simon then *whispers it to himself* (to find out how it sounds?). Then (and only then?), he incorporates it with satisfaction.

4. *Providing Corroborative Detail*
   From his exposure to "storying," Simon knows that fiction must present the illusion of life. Authenticity is aided by the proper sprinkling of dates, tiny details about scenes and about names. These aspects of journal writing and documentary are incorporated with facility. The immediate landscape of Delta III is quite acutely observed.

5. *Engineering*

Simon has decided that something must go wrong so that the space travelers can be moved towards the lair of the killer spider. He decides on a crash.

"Now, o, o, o (not going to land because it's going to crash) um . . ."

He is speculating about how he will engineer the mishap so that the routine flight can become an adventure.

The composer is at various points quite consciously a premeditating puppeteer, a "deus ex machina," with respect to his characters and his plot.

DAD: "What's happened to the others?"
SIMON: "I'm just getting to that part."

6. *Selecting Language Appropriate to the Scenario*

The reservoir of Simon's receptive vocabulary is obviously teeming with the words of Star Trek, Dr. Who, Adventure Comics, Space Documentaries and "Knowledge" books. His lexical choices depend on a knowledge of "space," "the past," and "crisis/adventure/mystery" scenarios. And so we have "cosmic storm," "exploding meteorite," "lunar dust," "ore sample," "time worf," "unknown planet," "blast off," "deadly space creature" (SPACE); "giant terradactyl," "two million B.C.," "hostile world," "abandoned cave," "monstrous fangs," and "prehistoric myth" (THE PAST); and "stranded," "teeth chattering," "crept," "trapped," "strange dots," "in the depths of the cave," "planned," "just at that moment," "there was no way they could escape," "then suddenly," "it was a slow death," and "pretty spooky" (CRISIS, ADVENTURE, MYSTERY).

In an older writer, one might begin to question the cliché. At this level, however, the selection signifies a most confident grasp of the "worlds" being explored, which is to be applauded, especially the ear for register.

I wonder why such a range of language had not previously emerged in Simon's school writing. It may have had something to do with a teaching stance that assumed words have to be given or suggested to the infant writer.

7. *Prefiguring*

Simon seems to be denying at the end that the story was prefigured. It may be that he was not conscious of his own unfolding plans. The title is "The Killer Spider." Well into the story, "eight smallish dots" appear in the lunar dust. Not until some paragraphs later do we eventually meet the black widow. Like any good mystery writer, Simon plants his clues. A close examination of the text shows that he skillfully builds up a tension which culminates in the confrontation with the spider. He does this by introducing a couple of minor tragedies on the way. My suspicion is

that he has so internalized such techniques from his reading and viewing
that he adopts the strategies without knowing it. (I think it was T. S.
Eliot who said that writers can only lie about their own composing
process.)

8. *Conducting Inner Dialogue*
Simon has engineered an attack by a swarm of giant "things." He asks:
"What would you say I should put there?" The scribe, sensing that this
is as much a question to self as to the scribe, asks a few returning questions but does not pre-empt in any way. Eventually, Simon solves the
problem by talking to himself.

"... Flying further? (laughter) ... No ... oh ... m ... giant? ...
m ... It can't be anything like earth ... it should ... make up some
funny name for it ... it's ... it's half mosquito and half ... wasp."

From this, one can get some inkling of the sort of inner debate which
must occur from time to time inside a writer's head when the problematic is confronted. The question is: "Do young writers know that this is
a necessary part of composing or do they feel that such casting around
is a flaw?"

Vygotsky has described how synpractic and egocentric talk eventually
goes underground to become "inner speech." This experiment leads me
to wonder whether allowing children to practice "outer writing" might
not be a most important strategy for ensuring that they become efficient
and effective creators of "inner writing."

9. *Sentence Building*
The syntactical complexity of Simon's dictation compared with his school
writing leads me to suggest that the dictator/scribe context by its very
nature encourages expansion of sentences. The enforced pauses while the
scribe takes down the words, coupled with the continual reading back,
seem to spur the writer on to make additional points by way of phrases,
subordinate clauses, or compounding.

"The giant killer spider ... which was just eating ... a terradactyl ...
which it had just caught ... with its monstrous fangs."

The situation almost enforces the writer to become as a reader and this
in turn seems to suggest to the writer the need for further information.

10. *Editing*
One function of the scribe was to present what had been said for critical
amendment. However, there are a number of examples of the writer self-
correcting without the aid of the scribe's "reading back."

"They went ... they went out of the ship ... and looked for signs
of ... any sign of life ... "

Anyone who has dictated writing is aware of the kind of subtle correction
made here. The "ear" and the combination of poetics and aesthetics mentioned before seem to be continually monitoring for infelicities following

in the wake of the composing. This subtle interplay between the composing "I" and the critical "me" appears to be one of the essential attributes of a good writer.

Taking Halliday's (Halliday, 1977) point about talk, that the role of adults and teachers is to track the developing language as it emerges, I have tried in the above analysis to tease out the composing strategies which Simon already "knows" and uses. Imagine devising a course in order to teach these "skills" directly. The feat of mind which has encompassed these skills through internalization and interaction is so complex and miraculous that no sequenced program could ever hope to induce it artificially. We, as teachers, need to know that these are the basics and we need to know all we can about the conditions which enabled Simon to learn them. Then we shall have the capacity to help children to compose.

Before dealing with the role of the scribe, it's important to note Simon's use of accompanying sound effects and bodily contortion. The dictation is punctuated with a kind of "rabbit" noise which seems to have been essential in keeping the brain ticking. The tortuous antics of body and face provided what may have been the mirror of a mind in tension. One wonders about the quiet and stillness so often prescribed for writers in school.

The Strategies of the Scribe

"A person who is saying something is saying to himself what he says to others; otherwise he does not know what he is talking about."

(MEAD, p. 147)

"I" learn what it is to be "me" by taking on the responses of others to the gestures I make. My spontaneous expression can only become communication if subjected to the monitoring and modifying of the "me" which has been formed in social interaction and has learned to read words as others read them.

Writers must continually compromise between invoking what is within themselves and involving the common experience of others. Writing is a subtle blend of liberation of self and denial of self.

"Men can agree only by avoiding difficulty; in other words by refusing to be themselves in order to play the role of soloists in the same collective choir."

(GUSDORF, p. 80)

In scribing Simon's story, I was setting up a context in which he could learn more about the nature of the compromises which writers must make in order to communicate. My task was to reflect back to him, as richly as I could, the effect he was having not just on me as his father, but also on the highly developed "generalized other" within me. In the unfolding drama, Simon's gestures called out in me a set of responsive roles. A brief examination of these overlapping roles may illuminate the highly complex task which teachers of reading and writing undertake:

1. *The Generalized Other*

> "The organized community or social group which gives to the individual the unity of self may be called 'the generalized other.' The attitude of the generalized other is the attitude of the whole community."
>
> (MEAD, p. 154)

Simon, like all children, is apprenticed to an articulate heritage or stored collective consciousness within the community. It is the teacher's task to help the child develop an increasing repertoire of "selves" at the same time as nurturing a unified and unique self.

The transcript of the storytelling shows that the scribe, apart from a couple of minor interventions, does not usurp the role of meaning maker. The writer's meaning is sacrosanct. The scribe's role is to help the writer communicate that meaning, not by telling but by reflecting what a general audience might be thinking:

SIMON: "They saw a patch of . . . of quicksand in the . . . in a hole . . . on the, on the ledge. It went straight through . . ."

DAD: "What do you mean it went straight through?"

SIMON: "It went straight through the bottom of the ledge."

In building up the sense of the generalized other, the scribe adopts a number of component roles taking the stance of various kinds of reader.

2. *The Restrained Editor*

The scribe does not directly edit or correct Simon's work. He does, however, play the role of a kind of "ghost" editor spotting points where changes may be necessary. By judicious selection of phrases which are re-read and by subtle inflections of voice, the scribe tries to activate the critical ear of the storyteller. If the strategy does not lead to self-correction, the scribe does not persist, in the belief that forced correction may inhibit the creative flow or place undue focus on techniques as opposed to meaning.

SIMON: "Then they setted out even further . . . "

DAD: "They they . . . ?"

SIMON: "Setted out"

DAD: "Setted out"

SIMON: "M . . . even further"

DAD: "Is that the way you say it? . . . Is it 'then they setted out' or 'then they set out'?"

SIMON: "Then they setted out"

DAD: "Right, 'then they setted out'."

Having assured himself that Simon is presently at the stage of generalizing the past tense rule of adding "ed," the scribe decides not to adopt the role of pedantic reader.

The role of the restrained editor is largely to shift the focus of the writer from meaning to mechanics when necessary. In Polanyi's terms

(Polanyi, 1958), the composing writer is first "focally" aware of the unfolding meaning with only a "subsidiary" awareness of the vehicle of language. However, from time to time the focus must shift to language while the story becomes part of the subsidiary awareness.

3. *The Aesthetic Reader*

The scribe, from time to time, takes on the role of the fastidious reader for whom infelicities in style can become such an annoyance as to spoil the story. A more mature ear and wider knowledge of which linguistic table manners offend allows the scribe to suggest adjustments to the writer:

DAD: "Lots of 'then suddenly's' "
SIMON: "Yeh, I know"
DAD: "Can we say anything else instead of 'then suddenly'?"
SIMON: "Then . . . just by chance . . . "

In this case the adjustment may not be much more pleasing than the original, but the writer is beginning to learn the art of finding the acceptable alternative.

4. *The Puzzled Reader*

It's very important information for a writer to know at which points the meaning is likely to be incomplete or misleading. The scribe, even when he knows, as confidant, what is meant, must continually adopt the stance of the reader coming to the story cold. Then by asking questions, seeking clarification or pointing out illogicalities, the scribe places demands on the writer which force him to re-cast, to amplify and to explain. Eventually, by internalizing the voice of this puzzled critical reader, the writer will become more and more independent as reader over his own shoulder.

SIMON: "The spider turned round . . . and saw them . . . It tried to go unnoticed."
DAD: "The spider tried to go unnoticed?"
SIMON: "No, the people."

5. *The Gourmet Reader*

The writer must be confident that others will savor what he is savoring. He must learn to call out in himself the same delights and fears that he wishes his readers to experience. A scribe can be very helpful in fostering this ability and in building up confidence. He acts as a kind of cooperating "word taster," sniffing the bouquet, holding the meaning on the palate, reflecting on the afterglow. He takes on a delicious complicity with the composer.

SIMON: "But it was really . . . a giant . . . black widow . . . the most deadly . . . space creature . . . "
DAD: "A, hah!"
SIMON: "Ever known . . . "
DAD: "Now the story's hotting up, now!"
SIMON: "I know, I know, I know, I know."

6. *The Indwelling Reader*

The scribe by imaginative empathy strives to become as the writer, at the same time as being the critical reader, because this is what good readers do anyway. By dwelling in the story as well as outside it, the reader picks up its music, its unfolding patterns and its tone. A crucial part of the scribe's work is to read the script with relish and understanding in order to reflect back to the writer what it might sound like inside the head of an engaged reader. The scribe flashes out the words and conveys the texture of the growing tapestry. He is a dramatist making whole and coherent the piecemeal dictation.

Writers must develop this ability to hear what they are saying. They must be able to see the future of their story rising in the matrix of what has already been said:

> "We are finding out what we are going to say, what we are going to do, by saying and doing, and in the process we are continually controlling the process itself."
>
> (MEAD, p. 140)

7. *The Anticipating Reader*

If the scribe is indwelling in the story, he must perforce be anticipating what is coming next and be considering the choices which the writer is making at every point. If the scribe can indicate to the writer what he is anticipating, then the writer can formulate continually more subtle moves to intrigue his reader.

> "A good chess player has the response of the other person in his system. He can carry four or five moves ahead in his mind. What he is doing is stimulating another person to do a thing while he stimulates himself to do the same thing. That enables him to analyze his mode of attack into its different elements in terms of the responses coming from his opponent and then to reconstruct his own activity on that basis."
>
> (MEAD, p. 243)

DAD: "What are they going to do, these things?"
SIMON: "Kill them of course."
DAD: "Kill who?"
SIMON: "Kill the people . . . "
DAD: "What about this black widow?"
SIMON: "They have to get the . . . they have to get past the shadow of the . . . survivor that . . . "
DAD: "Oh, so that this is before they get to the black widow. They've been attacked by something."

8. *The "Action Replay" Reader*

One of the hardest tasks for beginning writers must be to hold in mind the full sense of what has come before. They must learn the art of reading back in a variety of ways; sometimes back to the last sentence, sometimes to the beginning.

The scribe does all these things, in response to the explicit directions of the writer or to his perception of the writer's needs.

The transcript shows how the scribe and the writer continually "wind back" to gather the threads before going on. It is interesting to note the increasing tempo of the story. After tentative scene setting, the plot begins to roll with growing impetus. It seems that the process of writing fiction is, in this way, analogous to the reading of fiction where the tempo rises the more one gets into it.

The reading back seems to have helped the writer to formulate the next moves, because after each such reading, the writer plunges straight into the next sequence. It is as if the writer has found out where the story is growing.

9. *The Generous Reader*

The generous reader is related to the restrained reader.

> "But still, if writing is to be able to take on all its meaning, it is necessary for the reader to be able to receive this gift which is given to him. In the final reckoning, everything depends on his openness and his generosity."
>
> (GUSDORF, p. 115)

The scribing ends with a satisfied reflection on how it was done. Father is sincerely fascinated by the composing process and asks Simon, with admiration in his voice, how it happened.

DAD: "It's interesting how it comes isn't it?"
SIMON: "Mm. Just hits you."
DAD: "Just hits you! (Laughs) Bang. When does it come to you? Do you imagine it in your mind?"
SIMON: "No. I just say it."

Writer and scribe together celebrate both the process and the product. It is indeed "good stuff."

10. *The Collaborator*

The scribe talks of "we" while at the same time acknowledging Simon's role as creator.

DAD: "*We've* had that . . . *you* want to repeat that do you?"

Simon is learning that writing involves the collaboration of a reader. It can never be an isolated act. He learns that his effort must be met by similar effort from his reader.

> "The effort of the creator demands in reciprocity an analogous effort: Communication involves a sharing of difficulty."
>
> (GUSDORF, p. 87)

Alone, Simon, at this age, could not have constructed this story. But with the support of a persevering scribe, he becomes a persevering composer. The collaboration of the scribe allows him to indwell in the full reflexive act of communicating through writing.

The implications for the teaching of writing in schools are clear. Teachers should talk and write back. Together, children and teachers should build up shared meanings through writing.

Conclusion

"All monologue is by nature unkempt. Thanks to dialogue the soul of others penetrates into our own, as a comb digs its teeth into tangles of disordered hair. It penetrates it, straightens it out and tidies it up."

(EUGENIO D'ORS in GUSDORF, p. 101)

This experiment has yielded clearer insights into the composing process by allowing me to eavesdrop on a young writer at work. It has also strengthened my grasp of what it is to be a good reader. It certainly confirms the falsity of any pedagogy that would separate reading from writing.

The strategies of storyteller and scribe provide some useful clues about ways of improving the teaching of composition. I believe we have been guilty of keeping generations of students "in the dark" by placing emphasis on marking rather than on making and sharing.

There is a challenge implicit in the experiment. It is a challenge to teachers to enter into authentic dialogue with their students as fellow readers and writers. The teacher's voice and mind must be used in such a way that children are led confidently to take up the "articulate heritage."

"The [teacher's] voice is not limited to the role of accompaniment or mere echo. It becomes the educator of the first voice in this learning of co-existence."

(GUSDORF, p. 161)

Bibliography

Burns, Elizabeth and Tom (1979), *Sociology of Literature and Drama,* Penguin, London.

Gusdorf, George (1965), *Speaking,* Northwestern University Press, Evanston, IL.

Halliday, M. A. K. (1977) "How Children Learn Language" in *English in Secondary Schools,* ETA of NSW, Sydney.

Mead, G. H. (1962), *Mind, Self and Society,* University of Chicago Press, Chicago.

Polanyi, Michael (1958), *The Study of Man,* University of Chicago Press, Chicago.

Vygotsky, L. S. (1962), *Thought and Language,* MIT Press, Cambridge.

Appendix

THE KILLER SPIDER

by Simon Boomer

(as told to Garth Boomer)

Somewhere in this galaxy there is a smallish planet called Delta III. On 1 March, 1978, a space exploration team set out for the distant planet of the six moons. On 2 March they reached the planet of the six moons but they had to go back to Earth for supplies. On the way back they ran into a cosmic storm and their compass froze and they went off course and they headed for Delta III.

They crashed into a crater that had just been made by an exploding meteorite. It looked like a deserted mine shack that had been blown up. They went out of the ship and looked for any sign of life. They found some strange dots in the lunar dust. There were eight smallish holes in the ground. It looked like some sort of creature that had been made up in a fairy tale or some prehistoric myth.

They also found a dinted piece of metal or an ore sample. Then they set out for a trip around the planet following the dints in the sand. The trail finally ended up in an abandoned cave. It looked pretty spooky.

They heard something in the depths of the cave. It sounded like something's teeth chattering but it was really a giant black widow, the most deadly space creature ever known. They went even further into the cave. As they were going along a ledge around a gorge, they saw a patch of quicksand in a hole on the ledge and whoever fell in would have got dropped down into the gorge.

They tried to swing across the patch but someone slid off the rope and fell into the quicksand. It was a slow and quiet death as he fell into the quicksand and was sucked down to the bottom of the gorge.

The rest got over the patch of quicksand and headed into the center of the cave. The noise like chattering was still going on. Then suddenly, a swarm of giant ichynoccucus flew over them. These were half mosquito and half terradactyl. They had a giant sting and one of them shot its sting right through the heart of one of the men in the exploration team. He was then eaten whole by one of the ichynoccucus.

Eventually they got through the swarm of ichynoccucus and headed even further into the cave. Then, just by chance, they saw a small light at the end of the passage that they were going through. Without knowing it, they had walked through a time worf machine and they ended up in 2,000,000 B.C.

It was a horrible place to go to and they saw the giant killer spider which was just eating a terradactyl that it had caught with its monstrous fangs. Just at that moment the spider turned around and saw them. They tried to go unnoticed but the spider saw them too quickly and started running after them. As soon as they found a small cave they would rest but as long as the spider saw them there was no way that they could escape.

Then one of the men had an idea. He said: "Why don't we split up and meet again at the cave we started from?" The people thought that it was a brilliant idea but one of the men did not. He said: "We don't know what is in this hostile word. There could be many dangers when we go back to the cave entrance." But the people thought he was crazy and they didn't listen to him.

So they went on as they had planned. The man that they thought was crazy they left behind to let him find a way out himself. This guy was a scientist and he knew the most logical way to get out. So he worked out the plan and followed it, as it was made.

So finally, he found the entrance. The spider was still waiting at the entrance of the cave and he wanted food very badly. And so the man camouflaged himself as a bush and crept into the entrance and made it through the time worf and back to the ship in time.

The other members of the team had not thought that the spider would have been still at the entrance. One person tried to run across the path to the entrance but he was trapped by the spider's huge legs and was eaten within a minute. Meanwhile, the scientist was ready to blast off for planet Earth. The other people finally made it through but they were too late. He had left the planet before they could reach the entrance to the rocket. They were stranded on an unknown planet.

The End

Response

MAKING MEANING TOGETHER

JENNIE COGGAN

"How come she's doing your work for you?"
"She's not. She's just being my secretary."

Christine stayed for a little while after Paul's adamant retort, just to make sure I wasn't doing Paul's work for him. She watched as I read over what Paul had dictated and together we made changes. All three of us were quite impressed with the result.

I have found that students rarely query what is happening once "scribing" or "cooperative writing" becomes a normal part of classroom practices.

Most of the scribing I do with students occurs in the regular classroom. I use the strategy with individual students, when I can manage a few quiet minutes alone with them, mainly to help them overcome a physical and/or psychological "barrier" that makes it difficult for them to get what's "in the head" down on paper. I also regularly set up cooperative writing tasks with the whole class and with small groups. The major purpose of these activities is to "open a window on the composing process."

These practices are perhaps best illustrated with some examples from my high school classes.

Cooperative Poetry Writing

After several lessons reading and talking about "bullying," we were all busy writing on this theme. I always write too during the initial stages of any writing activity because I've found it a most effective way to encourage all students to write. It also helps me to appreciate the difficulty of the task and forces me to resist the temptation to intervene before I'm really needed.

I had decided to write a poem about "bullies" on the board. After three lines I paused to read over what I'd written. A voice behind me made a suggestion about what should come next, then several more were offered. Before long most of the class seemed to be involved in my writing, calling out words or just watching. I wrote rapidly in response to the noisy and contagious flow of language. It was no longer my poem—it was ours. Some changes were suggested and argued about each time I stopped to read aloud what we'd written. When it was finished and we had read it aloud together several times, there was an almost tangible feeling of surprise and excitement at what we had created. In response to the students' suggestion that we write another poem, this time about "victims," I handed the chalk to one of several volunteers and retreated to the back of the room to watch while another poem noisily took shape.

Cooperative Letter Writing

Another scribing activity with the same class didn't work quite so well initially. They had spent twenty minutes in groups planning the contents of a brochure on "Handy Hints for High School" for the Year 6 students who would soon be coming to the school.

Three students had recorded on the board as a member of each group reported their group's suggestions to the whole class. There had been several heated discussions along the way about why things such as "which teachers to avoid" and "places where you can smoke and not get caught" couldn't be included. We now needed the Principal's approval to go ahead. We could have sent a delegation to his office, but I felt this was too good an opportunity to miss for some genuine letter writing and also for some composing together. We talked a little about what could go in the letter; then I told them I would do the draft on the board if they would tell me what to write. They were much less enthusiastic about this kind of writing and very few participated. The group up the back soon became involved in a discussion about the injustices of the lunchtime touch footy match which the staff had won, and numerous others became engrossed in "decorating" their books.

I decided to abandon the activity as a whole class effort and sent them back to their original groups with felt pens, large sheets of paper, and the instruction that one person in each group should act as scribe. This appeared fairly chaotic as they spread out on the floor in the classroom and corridor, but resulted in much more individual involvement and lots of good talk about what should and shouldn't be included and the appropriate wording. One member of each group then took the group's rough draft to write up ready to be given to the Principal.

Cooperative Story and Play Writing

The students were working in groups of two or three writing stories or plays. Sarah, David and Amanda were working on a comedy about Roman times. Sarah was acting as scribe but couldn't keep up with the flow of ideas. Amanda came and asked for a blank tape and the cassette player. I saw them later in the corridor listening to the tape as it played back the ideas they'd recorded. They completed their first "draft," including quite a few changes, all on tape. They then took turns at taking the tape home to write up sections of it. They read, discussed and revised each part of the written draft as it was completed. When satisfied, they made a final tape with sound effects and shared this with the rest of the class.

Whenever students write cooperatively, they seem to be able to unconsciously teach others a great deal about writing and how to make it better.

Cooperative Essay Writing

From the amount of fidgeting, I could tell that many of the students in my Year 10 class were having difficulty with their essays. I asked what the problem was. "Don't know how to start."—"Don't know how to organize it." After some more discussion I decided to use the overhead projector to show them how I would approach the task.

I spoke all my thoughts aloud as I wrote, read over, and revised my writing. I asked occasionally "What do you think I should write next?" We talked about their suggestions; then I began to write again. When I read over all I'd written, they could see that the first draft was not only messy, but also somewhat lacking in clarity and coherence and would need quite a bit more time spent on it if it was to become a significant piece of writing.

Occasionally I ask another teacher to join the class for part of a lesson. We both then write on the same topic "in public" on the board, or on large sheets of paper. The students watch, then listen while we discuss and reflect on what we've written and the process of writing it. From this the students can see that whilst the writing process remains basically the same, the approach to the same writing task may vary from one individual to another.

Some of the more confident students in all my classes are now also prepared to work on their first draft "in public" using the board or felt pens on large sheets of newsprint taped to the walls.

The students gain a lot from discussing their work with other students or with me while it is still in draft. Sometimes I will take drafts to read later when I can't give them the attention they deserve in class and record my response on different parts of the draft. This provides a starting point for discussion with the student when we next meet.

When I'm involved in a writing task of my own, I bring in the drafts to show them how I revised my writing and cut and paste to save rewriting (oh, for a word processor!).

Scribing for Individual Students in the Classroom

It was the fourth lesson of an eight lesson "writing workshop." In the earlier lessons we had read quite a few pieces of student writing published in the school magazine, shared the results of several "short burst" writing activities, and talked a lot about writing—the process and the product.

Most of the students seemed to have really "got going" on their own writing the lesson before, but Leanne still couldn't think of anything to write about (Leanne worries about her spelling and is a reluctant writer most of the time). She had talked with others, tried a few things, and doodled a bit. Now she sought my help because she said her "imagination had dried up."

The room was very quiet. (When everyone is writing we usually have at least twenty minutes of "quiet time" to accommodate those who don't like noise around them when they're writing and to enable me to talk with individual students without distractions.) Leanne sat down beside me and we began to talk. I was trying to tap something in her own experience which she would feel was worth writing about. It didn't take long to trigger "the incident in the stormwater drain." As she recalled the event with great delight, I wrote rapidly. I asked a few questions because I was genuinely interested and her answers generated more writing. I read aloud what I'd written to check that I'd recorded the details correctly. Using arrows we changed the order of two sentences and inserted some more information. We then sorted out a pronoun referral confusion, found alternatives for some words that had been repeated too often and fixed the misspellings I'd made in my haste to keep up with her. I left her then to read it over and decide where the paragraphs should go and then write the story out herself before sharing it with others in the class.

A similar effort with Tracey didn't work out quite so well. Tracey was adamant that there was nothing in her own experience that was worth writing about and had her mind set on doing a ghost story. I recorded the few ideas she had but these were soon exhausted. I made a few suggestions which appealed to her. I now found that the story I was scribing was more mine than hers. I had become the "meaning maker." I was almost relieved when I had to leave Tracey to sort out a disturbance that had broken out over a pencil case. Tracey abandoned the ghost story completely the next lesson. She lost interest I suspect because she'd lost "ownership" and control.

Scribing for Individual Students in the Library

There are many opportunities to work one-to-one with students during library based units of work, especially if the librarian is also able to join the class. It's also often easier to find a place to work without interruption or distractions in the library.

Occasionally I will help a student take notes by recording the information the student gives me as she scans the pages looking for answers to specific questions and headings we have listed prior to the reading.

More frequently I will scribe after a student has spent some time reading and note taking and is having difficulty using the notes to write a report, essay or story.

Paul was having trouble getting started on his story about a visit with the Sherpas of Nepal. The class had been researching the effects of a mountainous environment on the lives of people. When I noticed Paul beginning to stir others (a much less demanding task than writing), I offered to scribe for him. He didn't know where to start so I began asking questions about the things I would want to find out if I was reading a story about the Sherpas of Nepal. It soon became clear that his difficulty writing on this topic resulted from his lack of knowledge on it. I wrote my questions on some computer paper with a space under each and left him to see if he could find the answers from reading and studying pictures.

It was much easier to scribe for Nick. He has been reading about the various forms of transport used in S.E. Asia. His task was to write a story about a journey through S.E. Asia using many different kinds of transport. I offered to scribe for him. He has trouble with spelling and believes he's "no good at writing" because he's "dumb." I didn't need to ask questions. The information just poured out. One and a half pages were recorded before he drew breath and we could stop to read over what I'd written. After we made a few changes, he took the draft home to write up and illustrate. He told me later it was the first assignment he'd handed in in two years, and I began to think how marvelous it would be to have someone available full time to scribe for students like Nick, who know so much but fail so often, because they lack confidence in their ability to write.

When discussing drafts with students I sometimes find that what they have written represents only a fraction of what they know on a topic. When this happens I usually record in note form the student's answers to the questions I ask, or I simply list the questions. We then decide together where this additional information should be inserted. At the end of a library-based unit their work is usually read by other students so it's important that they record all they have found out for their own satisfaction and for the benefit of other students.

Scribing in a Withdrawal Situation

There are some students who, because of their specific needs, will benefit enormously from cooperative writing in a one-to-one situation in an area that is free from distractions and interruptions.

I have found that locating such a place to work in a large high school can be difficult, but it is less a problem than finding a person to do the scribing. I have approached teachers from all faculty areas and found that a few are prepared to spend an hour of their time away from "face to face" teaching helping to provide the additional assistance needed by these students. I have also trained volunteers from the school community. They each come for one hour a week to work with:

- students who have very limited reading and/or writing skill. (The scribing that the volunteer does helps the student with writing and also provides material that the student can read with confidence.)
- students for whom English is a second language. (Writing cooperatively about pictures, objects, things read, and real experiences helps to expand the student's knowledge of English vocabulary, sentence structure, and pronunciation.)
- capable students who have a specific problem with spelling and/or handwriting.

I have also approached parents of this latter group of students to encourage them to act as a scribe when the student has a home assignment involving writing. This has worked well when there has been a good relationship between the child and the parent.

In all composing together activities, whether in a one-to-one situation, in a small group, or with the whole class, there's a considerable amount of valuable interaction which helps students to internalize reading and writing behaviors and to gain confidence as "meaning makers."

V

By now, 1979, our English teacher's focus is turning from what children do to what teachers do. He is required, for his sins, to assess secondary teachers for promotion and this means that he spends long periods of his life sitting at the back of classrooms watching teachers at work.

Working in secondary schools with their forty-minute enforced periods, he realizes what a comparative paradise the elementary classroom must be where there is opportunity for flexible use of time and where language learning and teaching can go on all day.

And yet, when he goes into primary schools or listens to his own children talking about "language arts," he finds that most teachers, emulating their secondary colleagues, are making their own prisons, teaching by patchwork, slotting themselves into boxes called spelling or reading or comprehension or dictation rather than ranging boldly across an unfenced territory.

At this point our English teacher is becoming worried about his lack of exposure to the "real thing." He still teaches the occasional lesson or conducts limited experiments with classes, but he has not gone "the full distance." And yet, he is convinced that his own fantasies could work. He imagines what he would try to do if he took up teaching again.

His fantasies are the product of privileged spectatorship on those who are perhaps too caught up in the drama of teaching to see inherent contradictions in what they do from moment to moment. He recognizes both his presumption and his vulnerability, but there is an incorrigibility about the imagination.

Why not see what teachers make of the fantasies? A dance begins with teachers. He watches and reflects. Teachers respond to his reflections and tell him where the flaws are. It's a productive partnership.

Writing Fair Dinkum in the Primary School

Take a thousand pieces of primary school writing and I'll bet you can immediately pick out those written in composition lessons or for "creative" writing. Of those you pick out, some will be formal essays, others free verse. But all will have something in common.

What is it? You're right. All of them will be phoney. All of them will be written to impress. All of them will be written to a dead letter office. Sad, but basically true. They are destined to be marked, or ticked, or "good work" stamped, or pinned on the walls, or corrected. That is, whether or not grades are given, they are destined to be judged in some way. They are transactions with the teacher, seeking approval. No one is going to write back anything but lip service. There isn't time. Just occasionally, you'll come across a piece where authentic excitement or intent to say something true begins to break through. Sad again, but quite understandable when you consider how we generally go about stimulating writing. And that's just where the rot sets in. In the beginning is the stimulus.

Can you ever recall going back to the staffroom glowing with pride because you managed to get some good work out of them? The vicarious thrill. Their work is all your own work.

You may have done the following:

1. Filled the blackboard with good words they have offered on the set topic.
2. Had lots of small group talk on aspects of the current theme.
3. Showed them a picture and talked excitedly.
4. Played them evocative music.
5. Led them through the latest topic in the structured composition laboratory.
6. Had them produce little impromptu plays around the topic or theme.
7. Given them possible sentence beginnings for each paragraph.

8. Shown them a film, followed by sound effects and slides, accompanied with experiments in tasting and touching.
9. Taken them on an excursion.
10. Stood on your head.

You motivate them. You are the coach. And they lift their game. Usually they all write at the same time, on the same topic (though it may be nicely open-ended) for the same audience—you. You may be of the "old" school demanding neat presentation, correctness, and etiquette or you may be of the progressive "slack" brigade allowing them to let it all pour out oozing with emotion. Either way they'll do their best to oblige by producing an acceptable writing surface. Underneath the various surfaces the same disease is probably at work. No one is really listening to the message and there is no personally felt intention to write. So they go through the motions. At its best it can be a happy game. At its worst it is sheer purgatory. Usually it's somewhere in between.

You may object that you do care about their messages. But do they think you care? Ask them what they're doing and they will not say, "I'm writing to teacher about X because I know she'll be interested." They're more likely to say, "I'm writing this *for* teacher because this is writing time."

So what? *We* all had these kinds of composition lessons and look at us. We can all write. Well?

But there is another way, a way that will produce fair dinkum writing, a way that will produce writing conventionally correct but also alive with vigorous, direct meaning, conveying the personality of the writer. It's a way I want to explore with you briefly. It's based on common sense and an understanding of how writing works in the "real" world outside schools.

In the real world:

1. People write to other people in order to convey information, or to persuade, or to describe, or to order, or to entertain, or to express love, sympathy, concern, excitement, etc.
2. That is, they write for a reason and they expect some response.
3. They write usually when they feel up to it or when it's absolutely necessary.
4. The people they write to generally write back or do something as a result of the writing.
5. If the writing is important they usually do it twice or a number of times and they ask other people (or use a dictionary) if they are worried about spelling or correct usage.
6. Sometimes people write to "nut something out" on paper; other times they write diaries that nobody else sees.
7. A few people write books and poems and plays for publishing.
8. Only students write essays and compositions.
9. Lots of people fill in forms from time to time.
10. Lots of people leave notes, write shopping lists, and enter the lottery.
11. Almost no one writes anything to anyone if that anyone already knows about it. (In schools it's different.)
12. If you can't write very well, you go for help to someone who can.

OK, let's translate this into the school setting and see what sort of writing program we get, keeping in mind that kids are at school to learn how to write, which means we have to provide instruction and guidance. Let's remember also that we learn to write by writing, not by doing exercises.

We'll need a program in which kids can take up their own intentions to write to somebody for some reason. And we'll also need to ensure that certain situations make it necessary for kids to write. We'll need to provide people who can offer editorial advice on such things as spelling, construction, and presentation. We'll need people to write back.

Shazam! It is done. Listen while Lotta Common-sense (grade 5 teacher) describes what happens:

> I took all the time formerly allotted to formalities, Active English, Dictation, Spelling and Compositions, added it together and came up with the notion of four "quiet times" (Tuesday, Wednesday, Thursday and Friday) in which kids would get on either with their writing or their silent sustained reading or their reflective meditation (thinking).
>
> On Mondays we talk about all the things that are going to happen this week, what happened last week, and about any other experiences inside or outside the classroom that seem to be of interest. Then all the kids decide (sometimes, I must admit, with a bit of a nudge from me) who they'd like to write (oops, to whom they'd like to write) this week and what they'd like to write about. (Sometimes this is decided later in the week if inspiration or intention is not around.)
>
> On Mondays we also nominate the five editors of the week. I am, of course, always editor-in-chief. The job of the editors is to read each draft in the final stages before it's sent off to the intended audience. They are not to alter the meanings but they are to help pick up spelling errors, run-on sentences, faulty construction, and such like. They may also comment on the contents if they wish. They are never to indulge in rubbishing, sarcasm or one-upmanship. If the editor is not a good speller, he or she is still responsible for checking out suspect words. I am the final arbiter.
>
> When it comes to "correctness," cheating, or rather, cooperation is encouraged. They can ask Mum, Dad, Auntie Freda, Mr. Bloggs, or the school cleaner but they are also warned to seek a second opinion. This is how I teach grammar—by making them askers, so that, if necessary, I can be a bona fide teller.
>
> Our audiences are varied. For instance, this week, John, Marcia and Kate are writing to some of the people in our "parents and citizen" pool, people who volunteered to be correspondents from time to time. They pop in occasionally to talk with some of their pen pals. Another group is busy writing a story for the Year 3 class. They'll take it down and present it when it's ready. A couple are writing to other teachers. Most, however, are writing to me, which is flattering but not good for my fast developing writing bump (I hold my pen too tight). At least the writing comes to me one piece at a time, as it's completed, and at least they're all different. I

must admit that I don't always write back at length, but there are usually six or so that get back a fairly long screed, not always in my best hand-writing. I do most of it in the quiet times while they are reading and writing, in between the occasional appeal for editorial umpiring. When the final form of the writing comes to me, I *never* mark out mistakes. If I find some, I simply make a note that the editing process needs im-proving. But there are surprisingly few. Three cheers for cheating. And you'd never believe how my writing has improved.

Every now and then when I'm in full extrovert mood I write a letter (on the fordigraph) to all of them. Replying is not compulsory but I usually get a good response.

I've got two kids who, for reasons unknown but guessed at, have been totally turned off writing. I showed them Neil Sachse's *Sunday Mail* col-umn and convinced them that there's no great shame in dictating what you want to say and having someone else write it. So they tell their messages into a tape recorder and a couple of the high-flying whiz kids transform it into writing. They then give it back to the authors for final approval. I'm hoping that they'll eventually take up their own pens, but I'm play-ing it cool for the moment.

I used to have them put their writing in envelopes and address them. At that time we had a class postie. Now, because envelopes are expensive I leave it up to the kids to devise their own method of delivery.

We spend quite a bit of time talking about the various kinds of writ-ing and in subtle, I hope, ways I nudge them to try new kinds (like short stories, poems, letters to the editor, magazine articles). Many of them, to my surprise, write about things they've learned in social studies or about their art. Inevitably some write very personally and this is where I find the greatest difficulty (you know, firmness vs. sensitivity and the keeping of confidence).

I don't insist on one piece of writing per week because some are in-volved in great continuing sagas, but I do keep on reminding them that you learn to write by writing. You might say that my classroom is one great writing workshop. Whatever happens (a poem, a dead frog, a visit, a book, a math lesson) is potential fuel for writing. Nothing is going to lead to obligatory writing.

Our writing is fair dinkum. It's also good by anybody's standards. If I gave you a thousand pieces of Primary School writing, I reckon you'd be able to pick the ones from my class.

Response

FAIR DINKUM WRITING—FAIR DINKUM TEACHING

PHIL CORMACK

"Fair Dinkum Writing" outlines three principles for an effective writing program. First, involve the children in choosing what and why to write; second, provide the writers with help when and where they need it; third, ensure their writing reaches its audience and gets a response. Sounds straightforward, doesn't it? At least that's what I thought when I embarked on such a program in my classroom. I was, however, soon to discover that these principles could not be applied like a new coat of paint over the old. What happened was that the new principles of the writing program clashed with my previous teaching practice. This led to many setbacks, doubts, and challenges which had to be overcome before the program could work. In retrospect I can see that the first months, and to some extent years, of the new program faced me with three major challenges:

1. How to establish a classroom which encourages and supports real-life writing.
2. How to *teach* writing (rather than expect it!).
3. How to overcome my own and others' insecurities about the new program.

1. *Establishing a classroom which encourages and supports real-life writing.* My new writing program struggled because I was planting it into the arid environment of the old. Children need more than a "composition" book and some time to write. I soon became overwhelmed by many unforeseen problems.
   - Lack of materials for the variety of writing forms being tried.
   - Children running out of time to complete their writing and audiences to write for.

These turned out to be problems of organization, which were the most easily resolved. The lack of materials was overcome by establishing areas around the room where implements were stored. The children's writing books became personal journals and reams of computer paper were made available for their rough copies and "cut and paste" drafts. I also bought stamps and aerogrammes and sold them to many letter writers in the class. Above all, the children were encouraged to improvise with materials in the classroom and bring from home those they could not find. We set aside art time to make a puppet theater, a small sound studio (a tape recorder in a decorated refrigerator carton), fake televisions, and a writers' information and publication display board. All of these changes were designed to make the classroom a place where the tools of the writer's trade were close at hand.

In the old writing program I had established myself as the sole source of information and help. That was fine when the children all wrote on the same topic at the same time, but now I found myself besieged by children needing help on everything from research to radio plays. Overcoming this problem is more difficult because its solution lies beyond the organization of the class. It means a change of attitude on the part of the teacher and the children. Primarily it involves an acceptance that the children are capable of helping themselves and each other. I worked with the children to establish rules and guidelines on what to do when help was needed. Many children found it difficult to share their expertise—probably because they had been rewarded for keeping it to themselves in the past: "No cheating children!"—and were often very negative about each other's writing. In the face of these problems, I found a number of strategies that helped to make the classroom environment more supportive.

- With the class watching I would run a writing conference with one child, modeling ways of responding to drafts. I would listen attentively and usually respond with questions of clarification about the content of the writing.
- We established writer's workshop groups where children met for 10 minutes a day to discuss their writing.
- We did group writing of stories, plays, and research studies where children worked together from topic decision to publication.
- I invited parent helpers to be editors and advisers.
- Children were encouraged to "have-a-go" before asking for help (e.g. they invented the spelling of an unfamiliar word and underlined it for checking during a polishing conference).

2. *Becoming a Teacher of Writing*

Soon after initiating a real-life writing program, I realized how little teaching of writing I had done in the past. Previously I had given grammar exercises and corrected spelling and taught punctuation. These issues were still taught—although I was amazed at how few children needed my concentrated assistance—but they were overtaken by the children's real writing needs:

- "I want to write to the author of my favorite book—what should I say?"
- "How do you write poetry?"
- "This story isn't spooky enough!"
- "I don't know what to write."

Such questions quickly revealed that I was far from being a writing expert and that I had been expecting rather than teaching writing. The challenge of becoming a teacher of writing fortunately did not require me to undertake a college course or months of reading. In fact, I did much of my learning in the classroom alongside the children. I wrote with the children and discovered the true meaning of the terms *rough* drafting, writer's block, writer's cramp, and various other writer's ailments. A significant event was being cajoled into writing a short article about my experiences for other teachers. This helped me discover the importance of getting help along the way from friends. It also helped me to see how much awareness that writing was to be read by a real audience guided and restricted what is written. Both these experiences enabled me to talk with the children, not as an expert but as an equal who was faced with many of the same problems.

Some of the teaching strategies I tried were:

- writing in front of the children on large sheets of paper or the overhead projector. This enabled me to demonstrate the process in action —where my ideas came from, crossing out, using arrows, re-ordering the writing, using punctuation.
- bringing some of my writing drafts from home to show. This helped legitimize making drafts messy and using scissors and adhesive tape as well as the pen to write.
- having "fishbowl" writing conferences where I modeled talking with a child about his/her writing while the class watched. By doing this I was able to demonstrate how they could respond to each other's writing in helpful ways. Typical conference questions included:

  "Why did you choose to write about that?"
  "Do you like what you've written?"
  "Is there any part you're unsure about?"

  I encouraged responses like:

  "I liked the beginning, ending, etc. of your story because . . . "
  "I don't understand . . . "
  "Why did you say . . . "

  These responses helped the children focus on what they were trying to achieve in their writing and became questions they could ask themselves as they wrote.

- setting up a table where I held editing conferences with 4 or 5 children a day to prepare their writing for publication. My big breakthrough came when I decided to work on one teaching point each time rather than trying to fix everything. This was a wonderfully liberating experience for the children and me. Now conferences became 3 or 4 minutes long rather than 20. Typically I would tackle the one aspect of the writing that the writer and I agreed was the most important and then do a quick editing job myself. The edited draft would usually go to a parent helper or teacher aid for typing, or the child would write out the polished version.

3. *Overcoming Insecurities*

In my first months of teaching writing as a process I had to overcome the insecurities of the children, the parents, and myself in ascending order of difficulty:

The children After years of writing programs which took responsibility for selecting what to write about, who to write for, and doing all the correcting, it isn't difficult to see in retrospect why many resisted the new approach. At the time, however, I was at a loss to explain why they were so wary of this "wonderful" new approach. Problems which arose were:

- not knowing what to write about.
- resenting the fact that they, rather than I, had to decide what they liked or didn't like about their writing and whether or not to publish.

Some children needed help for months to find topics for their writing. Usually the breakthrough came when they were taken under the wing of other children and shared the writing task. Often the problem was that these children did not believe their own experiences and interests were important. I spent much time listening to these children talking about what they liked and relating personal experiences. The idea was to tell these children that what they thought and did was important and hope the next step would be the confidence to write about it. Publication proved to be the key for many—when the children saw the response others received to their writing and the obvious self-satisfaction of having published, the writing bug took hold.

The parents This, at least, was one challenge I anticipated. I moved early on to court the parents into the new writing program. I wrote a letter to the parents explaining the most important changes—children choosing what to write and the emphasis on publication. In that letter I asked the parents to help their children at home with anything they needed, from spelling to ideas for writing, but most importantly to ask their children to take their writing, rough drafts and all, home for sharing. At a class parent meeting later in the term, when the children's enthusiasm was high, I explained the reasons for the new program and demonstrated some of the ways I taught writing. Finally I invited parents to the classroom to help the children as they wrote, or to be pen-pals with children in the class. Not everyone was convinced as I was of the benefits, but its overall acceptance was, I believe, due to the enthusiasm of the children and the fact that I had shown I was still teaching writing.

The teacher I was my biggest critic. At times I would worry about children who seemed to be getting nowhere, or not being able to give enough attention to every child, or wonder if anything was being achieved. I often remembered my quiet classroom and the neatly packaged certainties of set topics and drills. A number of factors helped me stay with the program so that it had a fair chance of working:

- The children, their enthusiasm and ability to amaze me with their learning when I least expected it. I noticed that while there were always some children in the doldrums, there were also those charged with energy and growing and that over time children moved in cycles —just as I do in my teaching.
- The records I kept, mainly samples of the children's writing, enabled me to see that the children were improving. However, I discovered

that it wasn't a steady growth—most were erratic in their achievements, having one good piece followed by others seemingly several steps backward. I learned to accept the fact that all children would not be improving all the time and to take a long term view.

- I was fortunate to be able to meet with a group of teachers about once a month who were trying a similar approach. It was such a relief to know that my problems were not unique and a joy to have people to share the success with. Having just one other interested teacher in the school often helped me to recharge when my energies were low.

I can remember very clearly the first day (about 3 months into the program) that I was able to stop for 5 minutes and actually survey the classroom because everything was happening without me. There were children talking and swapping writing, a group rehearsing a play, others writing alone or staring into space. It didn't last long, of course, but it was the time I first realized how all the energy I had previously put into motivating and deciding for the children had now been released so that I could teach writing. Fair dinkum writing, it seems, had led me to some fair dinkum teaching.

VI

In which the English teacher/researcher/change agent, encouraged by teacher response to his piece on "Fair Dinkum Writing" (Chapter V), takes up the challenge offered by a group of teachers to say what "all this theory means in practice."

It is now 1980 and the centralized system of education in South Australia has begun to produce revolutionary new guidelines for the Language Arts curriculum. These guidelines are strong on rhetoric and exhortation. They advocate activity methods, integration, individualized teaching and "process" approaches.

All these things have profound implications for the structure and organization of classrooms and schools. Unfortunately, the central guidelines are not at all explicit about how the rhetoric might be translated into a workable program. By his own principles, the English teacher/change agent knows that teachers will not take up a new mode of teaching unless they can imagine themselves doing it with some pleasure and effect.

By talking with many successful teachers who have managed to turn rhetoric into practice (or rather practiced that upon which the rhetoric is based), he is able to empathize both with the presently paralyzed traditional teacher and the dynamic, engaged "front-runner."

He decides to write a reality-based fantasy which might help teachers to construct reasonable pathways into the new territory. At the back of his writing there is a gradually developing theory of curriculum composing.

Some Thoughts on Programming for the Language Arts

(In this article, I have taken on the role of an elementary/primary teacher to present my vision of programming.)

The Security Blanket

At the start of a year, I find it very helpful as a teacher to have worked out, preferably with other teachers, the broad territory that I hope to cover in reading, writing, speaking, and listening. I don't want this to become a straightjacket, but it is a "security blanket" to clutch whenever I feel that my curriculum is starting to "splatter" out of control.

These are the lists of things I like to have:

- Kinds of writing we are going to tackle this year (diary entries, free verse, narrative, eye-witness report, etc.)
- Kinds of reading experience we are going to have this year (reading story aloud to class, free "library" reading, prepared reading aloud by children, diagnostic sessions with individuals, etc.)
- Kinds of talking we will engage in this year (informal one-to-one conversation, task-oriented talk in small groups, reporting, informed debate, simulation and role playing of various characters, etc.)
- Kinds of listening we will engage in this year (listening to stories and talking about them; listening to instructions and carrying them out; listening to a film or video and recalling the information, etc.)
- The things I want my children to know or be able to talk and write about this year.
- The major *content* of my Language Arts program this year (e.g. three novels/short stories; 20 key poems; two play scripts; a one-week camp; three integrated topics involving drama, social science, art and music).

- A checklist of specific abilities that we have agreed to as important in reading, writing, and group behavior in this school (not just for this year level).

Leaving Room for the Children

I don't try to put this into week-by-week sequence or even into term-by-term sequence at this stage, although I have a reasonable idea about the kinds of units I will be trying for the first half of term one. Other teachers may want to be more tightly organized, but my teaching depends on leaving a fair amount of room for the children to shape my planning and for topical ideas to be included. My main concern is to be sure *on looking back* that I've covered most of what I set out to cover.

Now, armed with my broad map, I can look at programming my first, say, four week's work. I need to know how much time I've got and so I add up *all* the time that our school provides for language arts (reading, writing, speaking, listening, spelling, dication, "English," drama, grammar, etc.). This fills me with confidence. We have well over ten hours per week for our language arts work.

Towards Sanity

In the past, I've gone a bit crazy trying to keep all the "bits" of language arts on the simmer. My program used to be like a patchwork quilt with 15 minutes of vocab development followed by 30 minutes of composition and so on. These days I'm trying to work in bigger units which have fairly concrete *content* and *focus.* My growing insanity in the past was partly brought on because the children and I could never really get our teeth into something as we could do in a social studies topic or a health education unit. And so I've rediscovered literature, good stories, poems, plays and articles which can be a starting point and something to explore, in all sorts of ways, over a period of time. Sometimes, of course, an excursion, or a school happening, or a project working up to a performance, or a topic in social studies or religious education or science can provide my *content.*

Using this content I then try to cover some of the activities which I have on my "things-to-do-for-the-year" lists. For instance, in my first four weeks of work, I might decide to feature some story writing, paragraphing, small group talk and vocabulary development (spelling) of words related to the ideas in the content. But it might be a little clearer if I gave you my rough recipe for making a program.

Recipe for Making a Short-Term Program

Starting

My program ideas can start anywhere. I might start with a specific skill I want them to try using. I might start with a really good story I want to read to them. I might start with the idea of getting them to work up a drama performance.

Incubating

I like to let the idea simmer a little, maybe even ferment, as I think about the children in my class, the sorts of activities we did last time, the sorts of ideas that children at this level could deal with profitably, the general demands that the school policy and parents make on me and what resources are available to me.

Deciding on the Content (or Territory)

Wherever I start I eventually have to decide *what* it is we are going to be learning about and exploring as we use language. I have learned by failing that language activities have to be about something worthwhile. This means deciding on a story, or some poems, or some content material from another subject, which will challenge the children and provide lots of opportunity for the whole class, small groups, and individuals to explore. For instance, I might decide that over a period of four weeks we will read (much of it with me reading aloud) *The Lion, the Witch and the Wardrobe* and that as many activities as possible in reading, writing, speaking, and listening will be used to help the children understand what the novel is about, what they think about it, and what other books are like it. While doing this, I have to be able to justify this work. It has to generate important questions about life and society. It must not be some slick but superficial theme or "busy work."

Deciding Where and How to End

When I have worked out the major content, I then like to imagine a good set of conclusions for the journey we are about to take. I call these "outcomes" or "products"; that is, what I would like children to be able to say and show at the end. And so, I might decide that I would like them all to have written their own story in response to the novel, that I would like them all to be able to talk about what the novel is about in reasonable depth, that I would like small groups to compose and act a small play based on one of the incidents, that I would like all children to have compiled a list of new words found during the unit (and be able to spell them) and so on. Now I am fairly secure. I know what will be the territory and I know where we are going. I don't know specific details at this stage.

Imagining How to Get There

What happens next is a kind of story which I have to tell myself. I think of the children (the highly skilled and the less able, the conformists and the rebels, etc.) and try to imagine them going from the challenge which I will present through to the final making, doing, and saying. Without tying myself down at this stage to day by day planning, I need to get a fairly clear idea of what activities will occur and in what order. We might start with three or four days of just reading the novel together and then negotiate individual, small group, and class contracts. I might imagine introducing some poems at a certain point. I certainly have to decide how and where to fit in some regular spelling and vocabulary discussion. I also have to decide what things can't be fitted into this "story." For instance, I probably won't be able to program for the "basal reader" sessions. These would have to be separate.

Listing the Media and Skills to Be Used

Once I have an idea of the story and the outcomes, I can list the "media" that children will be most likely using during the program of work. By a "medium" I mean a vehicle children use in order to learn and do things. The following "media" are common in my programs: talking, reading, writing, listening, acting, making models, painting, drawing, filming, taping, moving. Music, dance, mime, making collages, etc., are also used from time to time.

I can also list the specific skills children will be practicing (and possibly needing direct instruction in) as they go about meeting the challenges. If I want to include a specific skill not yet on my list, I can modify or add to the planned activities to ensure that it will be used.

Taking the Plan to the Class and Inviting Suggestions

Depending on how well I know the children and how used they are to making contributions, I now like to unveil my "plot" and offer the children the opportunity to add things, change things, ask questions, etc. I will, of course, make quite clear those things which cannot be changed or altered. The degree of negotiation varies but I have found that all classes, even year ones, can contribute. Here are various ways in which children have contributed to my programming:

- Children suggest some resources they can bring (e.g. a book, a picture, etc.)
- Within the general framework, small groups or individuals decide on a product they would like to work towards (in addition to my demands).
- The class makes suggestions about learning activities.
- The class arranges deadlines and timing of the activities.
- The class brainstorms with me on possible methods of evaluating how well we have done.
- The class suggests modifications or extensions to the content.
- The class convinces me that they already know much of what I have planned for them to learn.
- Individuals convince me that they should be allowed to draw up their own alternative program.

With new classes unused to collaborating in programming, I usually start by discussing what I intend and then inviting contribution of resources. It's also important for me and the class to establish what we already know and can do and what we do not know and need to be able to do. It's inefficient to cover unnecessary ground.

Preparing a Tight Plan

At this point, after negotiations have led to understandings of the tasks ahead, I usually use butcher's paper at the back of the room to draw up a fairly tight contracted (day-by-day) program with deadline and structures clearly stated. Our program is composed in the presence of the class as part of the preparation for learning. I find that this is an excellent means of encouraging children to "own" the program, and it certainly pays off in terms of their (and my) sense of direction. It also helps them to explain to parents what is happening at school and where it is heading. The time invested is not wasted. I find that children work with greater tenacity and energy when they know what they are trying to achieve. My old programs were rather like magical mystery tours where, like a conjuror, I revealed exercises and lessons one by one while the children sat waiting for their instructions.

Performing the "Script"

What is on the butcher's paper is like a score or script waiting to be performed. My task now is to "conduct" the curriculum, organizing, monitoring, calling meetings to clarify or improve the performance, helping out with information and demonstrations, etc. There's an understanding that the plans can be changed if things are not working, but I demand a good deal of tenacity before agreeing to any alteration to the contract.

Reflecting on the Journey

My old programs used to be fairly dishonest in that they were a set of good intentions which weren't often achieved. These days I do my pre-planning fairly roughly and spend far more time writing up a formal record in note form of what happened, what was achieved, where it was successful and where it could have been improved. This helps me to plan better next time and it makes a useful document to read in a year's time. I usually invite the class to assist me in evaluating the strengths and weaknesses of the program and their own learning. Once again, this is not time wasted. All travelers like to tell and savor the story about the journey. It's their way of making sense of it all and keeping it in their memories.

Tests and assignments are, of course, other ways of evaluating achievement. I have found that the tests are more exciting and better accepted if the children have helped to set them (usually before they start the journey).

Some Things to Be Careful About

Gradual Change

I didn't develop this recipe in one hit. Gradually over a couple of years, I changed from a tightly structured but fragmented approach to this equally tightly structured whole unit approach.

Themes

For a while I got sidetracked into doing superficial integration. Taking a theme like "Animals," I would program a host of ingenious activities. It worked well for me, but the children soon got bored with this kind of work, because I didn't go deep enough and I didn't have some gutsy content to challenge them and stretch their minds.

Now I've learned that "Animals," if I choose a theme like that, has to be tied to a good story or some poems or an anthology of new information. Collecting anecdotes and examples of "Animals" is little better than busy work. And I've also learned that I don't have to use a theme to generate a coherent unit of work. The generator and focus can be a text, an excursion, a drama project or any topic "across the curriculum." Sometimes, I can treat a whole range of subjects in one unit.

Individual Difference

In programming for individual assignments I have to take account of the "gifted" and the "retarded" learners, and all those in between. And so my butcher's paper has to allow plenty of space for me to set up small-group teaching sessions directed towards special problems. And so while we all collaborate to explore aspects of the same topic at our own best level, each individual must have the chance to concentrate on aspects of language which are presently not under control. I can't say that I'm brilliant at finding the balance between whole class work and individual electives but I do try.

Separate Sections

As I said earlier, I don't try to fit everything into whole units. Certain aspects of the Language Arts program are still separate, although I've successfully jettisoned separate Word Power, Comprehension, and other exercise work. I can cover these in the course of real writing and talking that the children are engaged in. But some basal reader work, some specific information about language rules, and some diagnostic testing, etc. usually fall outside the unit approach.

The Work Load

As I've seen the improved quality and volume of language coming from the children, I've lost the cold feet I had when I first started. The best part is that *it requires no more work* once you get the knack. You simply spend your energies differently. I work fairly hard in the negotiating and establishing stage and fairly hard again when we are evaluating. In between, I work solidly but happily on a wandering, helping, trouble-shooting, teaching-when-needed basis.

This contrasts with my old approach where each week I had to gather my ammunition to keep the work up to them and then spend great energy in presenting, urging, controlling, and directing. Sometimes at the end of a week I felt like a tired sheep dog.

A Challenge

But don't take my word for it. Start a few small experiments for your-selves. Maybe you could begin by planning *one lesson* following the recipe. Even then it might not work immediately because the children may be taken by surprise.

Response

TAKING UP THE CHALLENGE

HELEN CAMPAGNA

My perpetual teaching challenge is to make learning in my classroom real, relevant, purposeful, and productive. "Getting the knack" of Garth's program-ming structure has given me some power over ways of doing this.

Initially, I found it difficult to distinguish much difference between his recipe and my ideas about theme work. It reflects my beliefs that:

- language is learned while being used for real purposes and audiences;
- skills must be developed in meaningful contexts;
- learning is an active process;
- children are individuals, with differing needs, interests, and levels of development.

Because of these beliefs, I too abandoned the "patchwork quilt" approach. Now I have also come to see my old theme work in a similar way—a patchwork quilt in one color.

Two aspects of Garth's programming ideas are central to me: the role of content and learner negotiation. Together, these have had a profound effect upon the nature of teacher and learner responsibility in my classroom.

I reflected upon the analogy between programming and story writing. Stories have structure. Very simply, they go like this: Setting—Problem—Episodes (interrelated and focused upon solving the problem)—Resolution. An overall Theme is also evident. In my old thematic programs, I provided the setting, theme, and a diverse collection of loosely connected episodes (learning activities/lessons). The problem and resolution were missing. Although the children were using language for a wide range of real purposes and audiences, there was no clear, overall purpose connecting and focusing what they were doing. Often such work did "splatter out of control" or slowly dissipated and dissolved through children's flagging interest.

Now I emphasize content. This doesn't mean stuffing irrelevant facts down children's throats, nor does it mean that children's needs and interests aren't pursued. It means ensuring that the content, what children are learning about, challenges them and defines a problem to be resolved. Thus, for all possible content, required or otherwise, I ask myself:

Why is it worth learning about? What has it got to offer my students in terms of developing their knowledge and understanding of self, others and the world?

I then pose some key questions related to my answers. These become the problem for my curriculum story. (Good literature abounds in worthwhile content. It does much more than entertain. Stories, poems, novels, and plays deal with real life themes and issues, offering readers models for coming to terms with them in their own lives.) The story's resolution, answers to the key questions, are embodied in the products and outcomes Garth includes in his recipe.

Having a clear idea about the problem to be solved, why is it worth solving, and what will be produced if it is resolved, enables me to consciously select learning activities which have mutual purpose and direction. I select them so that they have some sequence, interrelate, and build upon one another. I never artificially force in any aspect of language or the wider curriculum which doesn't contribute to solving the problem. As Garth suggests, I teach them separately at other times. At this stage I have found it important to be very aware of the skills the children will require to successfully engage in the activities. Some will be familiar, others new to the children. The latter will require some intense input from me, so I need to ensure there's a balance between familiar and new tasks.

This entire story writing process is a rigorous, professional challenge to consider the children's needs, interests, past experiences, level of language development, and specific skills. It means taking responsibility for setting a context for children's learning which clearly reflects many factors.

A negotiation time before embarking upon a unit of work is when children start taking up *their* responsibilities. It's a much more complex idea than simply asking the children what they want to do, or if they like what I have planned. I have invested some hard thinking and I want them to develop skills for doing likewise. Ideally, this session(s) is a time when children can connect with, and make sense of, my ideas about what's important and worthwhile, and I with theirs. It's a time for them to become involved in the story, see themselves as the characters, take up the challenge to solve the problem. It's not easy.

Children often have completely different expectations about what teachers do, want, and value. At first, they are tentative, suspicious and inexperienced in seeing alternatives and making contributions. I've learned that children need lots of support, models, and guidance in developing the skills for engaging in this process. They need to grow from dependence towards independence. It takes time. Garth's suggestions for starting are worthwhile in this regard.

I try to set up a specific context for children's contributions to my plans. Rather than just dumping my plans on them (and risk unceremonious dumping myself, by their lack of interest), I try to have a strong opening experience, related to the content, first. For example, a good story, film, video; a visitor; excursion; problem solving activity. I find this gets the children's minds "on track" and offers them a framework for looking at my plans and ideas. I use it as a strategy for bringing to the fore all that the children already know about the topic and to expose them to, and spark their interest in, new possibilities they may never have thought of previously.

I never cease to be surprised at what children offer, given the information and opportunity. The more I show that I value and will use their contributions, or explain in their own terms why some are inappropriate, the more willing and adept they become. As a result of children's contributions, I do change the story to varying degrees. I always clarify where their ideas fit and why certain points are not negotiable.

What results from my preliminary story writing and the children's negotiated contributions is *shared* responsibility for learning between teacher and learner, much understanding and mutual support. The children have a sense of ownership and control over what they are doing. We all have an overall sense of purpose and direction. We all know where we are going, why we are going, and how we plan to get there. Finally, we will know when we have arrived and can look back and ask ourselves how well we set about solving our problem.

Some other practical considerations:

- I find it hard to generate tight plans on the spot, before the children. Consequently, I take them home to ponder in relation to my broad map and specific aims. I then explain to the children precisely how I have used their ideas and mine in the final program.
- It's easy to get carried away and program too many activities. Scaling down and starting small makes implementation manageable for the children and me. It enables us to see an end and use opportunities which arise to learn new skills.
- I treat each learning activity as a mini-story, with the same structure as the overall program.
- Regular, whole-class sharing times are vital for pulling things together and setting short term goals along the way, especially when a lot of small group work is involved.
- I always tie the outcomes/products of each activity into a final, public, culminating activity: a display, performance, bookmaking. Something which enables children to share their learning and celebrate in solving the problem. This also enables us to engage others in our evaluation process.
- I continue to run my individualized reading and writing programs. Inevitably, these ebb and flow into and out of various units of work, but I rarely drop them completely.

VII

Some are born great, some achieve greatness, and some have greatness thrust upon them.

Andrew Wilkinson, due to be keynote speaker at a national conference on "Oracy," falls ill and cannot come to Australia. It's a fairly academic gathering to which the English teacher is called in as first reserve. He knows how the battle lines are drawn. It will be a fight to the death between the taxonomists (divide talk into its constituent parts and practice) and the functionalists (develop authentic contexts and talk to make sense for a purpose). Indeed, the opening platform is to be shared with a speaker from America who will advocate a tightly sequenced repertoire of instruction in "communication skills."

He is nervous. He abandons his usual populist style and goes rather academic. He is beginning to discover in himself an analytic streak or rather a drive to sift until he finds principles in things. This is his attempt to make an academically respectable case for what he believes. He is grateful that an action research grant some years ago allowed him to find some gutsy local data about what is happening in Australian schools.

Incidentally, he finds that he has made links with the "Halliday school" of linguists. Another barrier has been broken down. There is really no need for trench warfare between "literature" and "language" people. The differences of emphasis are healthy. At base, both sides are fighting for human minds against the reductionist predator.

Oracy in Australian Schools
(Or Doing What Comes Naturally)

Introduction

Australian five-year-olds have not yet come under public attack for failing to talk. Mothers and fathers seem generally pleased with the progress that children have made at this stage. Ten years later these same children are likely to be the object of "high" public and, in particular, academic disapproval as they allegedly mangle, mumble and muddle their way through spoken Australian English.

If such allegations have any substance, then it might be argued that schools not only exacerbate continued learning to talk but even cause talk to atrophy. On the other hand, it could be argued that learning to unlearn talking is a culturally induced phenomenon which has little to do with Australian schools. Yet another argument, more cynical in spirit, might contend that it is politically expedient to produce massively inarticulate electorates.

It is certainly customary, and has been customary for as long as I can remember, to caricature Australians as terse, even monosyllabic, speakers bordering on the inarticulate. This is actively cultivated by those who wish to promote a John Wayne/(Chips Rafferty?) type myth of the Aussie battler spitting out a hard-bitten word to settle the bulldust. Indeed, while the civilized may long with anguish for a more articulate generation of young Australians, it seems that the average citizen equates fluency with palaver. We are on our guard against the spiel.

And yet our five-year-olds love to talk. It seems that by doing what comes naturally, tuning in to what is going on and trying it out for themselves, they have learned to talk without the benefit of formal teaching.

And so, somewhat wryly, I come to my theme.

In preparing for this talk, I thought I should establish the ingredients for an "on to basics" movement in oracy by searching for those conditions which seem to promote talk in the preschool years and by hypothesizing that these

80

same conditions might continue to promote oracy if they could be replicated in schools. Having established these basics, I might then speculate about more formal, planned and "unnatural" elements which could be adopted in schools to make them less accidental and incidental teachers than life. Such an approach should also take account of the present conditions in Australian schools.

And so, this paper has three parts: one, an investigation of the conditions most likely to promote growth and progressive realization of meaning-making potential in oral communication; two, a summary of the findings of two pieces of South Australian research; and three, an attempt to tease out implications for teaching oracy in Australian schools.

I The Conditions Most Likely . . .

Parasitically, I made a quick journey through selected writings of Stratta, Wilkinson, Halliday, Britton, Novick, Waters, Bernstein, Sapir, Vygotsky, and Bruner to find out what might happen if schools tried to replicate the best features of language learning before and outside school. In brief, this is what I extracted.

Tracking

" . . . One can see that the baby is leading the dance. The mother is slightly behind, tracking his movements and responding in kind. By an analogous process, for months and even years the mother, and possibly others too may continue to track the child's language development . . ."

(HALLIDAY, 1977)

Halliday points to a secret teachers need to learn. The mother and the close-knit early "meaning" group of the child do not actively set out to pump new language into the infant. They delicately and sensitively tune-in to the meanings which emerge. They attend and respond.

"To understand another's speech, it is not sufficient to understand his words—we must also understand his thought. But even that is not enough—we must know his motivation."

(VYGOTSKY, 1962)

Caring and Sharing

Wilkinson and Stratta talk of the need for "imaginative empathy" (1977), a similar notion to tracking. Halliday calls this "intersubjectivity" (1977) a term he borrows from Trevarthen. Collaboratively, the child and the "meaning" group build up the language to represent and refer to things held in common. The picture that emerges is one of caring adults kindly licking language into shape by their responses. But the meaning maker's meaning is sacrosanct.

The Means-End Tie Up

"Here in the home, then, there is a direct means-end tie up between speech and what it achieves for the speaker. Can we preserve that direct relationship throughout the years of schooling?"

(BRITTON, 1977)

The hypothesis is that children learn language so brilliantly because it so powerfully serves their needs. Britton and others isolate the following functions of
talk.

- *Synpractic and egocentric talk as it serves cognition*
  The work of Luria, Vygotsky and Ruth Weir suffices to convince us that
  talk helps children get their minds around things.

- *Communication through conversation*
  "Though some of this conversation will consist of an expression of wants
  and needs, most of it will be by way of comment: in Susanne Langer's
  words, "Young children learn to speak . . . by constantly using words to
  bring things into their minds, not into their hands."

  (BRITTON, 1977)

- *Expression*
  This includes delighting in what Croft calls the "auditory imagination,"
  celebrating what Britton calls the "me-ness of things," enacting, sym-
  bolizing and making sense of the subjective life of the mind. It is the artis-
  tic function, every bit as satisfying as conversation about the "thingness
  of things."

Britton argues that home is a near perfect language workshop:

" . . . the give-and-take, the rough-and-tumble of language as it is unself-
consciously used for work and play in the home, constitutes a better
learning situation than would anything more deliberate."

(BRITTON, 1977)

The Mature Speaker as Conversationalist

Novick and Waters (1977), cite Brodbeck, Irwin and Goldfarb (1945, 46)
as gatherers of evidence that "children cared for in institutions and hospitals
have considerable deficit and this is presumably due to the absence of verbally
oriented interactions between a significant adult and a very young child." In
their own study Novick and Waters see the adult as a very important bridger
of misunderstandings, promoter of compromise, and giver of rulings. Halliday
emphasizes the role of the intimate adult as socializing agent helping the child
to get "socio-semantic" and "socio-semiotic" perspectives on the life of the
community (Halliday, 1977). The work of many researchers into language
acquisition (e.g. McNeill) also draws attention to the role of the adult as ex-
pander of elliptical utterances, thereby assisting the gradual unfolding of a
syntax approximating ever more closely to the adult model. The more varied
the interactions with adult speakers and the more responsive the language environment, the more likely it seems that the child will develop into a powerful
meaning maker.

Bernstein throws further light on the likely harmful effects of institutions
by examining the difference between "person-oriented" and "status-oriented"
interactions with children. The "person-oriented" home as Bernstein depicts,

or caricatures, it encourages elaboration and the making of implicit meaning. In the "status-oriented" home the child is more acted upon than acting.

The Play Way

Transcripts of pre-sleep monologues by Weir (1962) and Boomer (1976) show quite dramatically the child's strong drive towards metalinguistic playing around with what Britton calls " . . . patterns, ploys and routines" (1977). (I would add "intonations.") At times the play on and with words is followed by reflection and appreciation, suggesting that the child is engaged in an almost calculated exercise in code-cracking, pattern finding, and verbal aesthetics.

> "A piggy back
> A piggy back on me . . .
> We had a piggy
> A piggy nick . . .
> A piggy nick?
> Oh, that's another good word"
> (BOOMER, 1976)

Bruner underlines the value of this kind of activity:

> "Play has the effect of drawing the child's attention to communication itself, and to the structure of the acts in which communication is taking place."
>
> (BRUNER, 1975)

Challenges and Transactions

> "We did find that transactional language doubles in quantity out of class . . . . Children seemed to find the need or the opportunity to linguistically influence others more often in the schoolyard than in the classroom. The data suggest that in the schoolyard the children have a more personal stake in what they say."
>
> (NOVICK AND WATERS, 1977)

In playing "The Carpenter Game" in their research, Novick and Waters established a context in which children had to discuss choices throughout in order to complete a task cooperatively. They found a high degree of negations in the transcripts and suggest that this seems to indicate a high level of challenge and involvement.

Anyone eavesdropping on young children at play is likely to find a similar high level of negations.

Conceptual Growth

Sapir sees the child's language growing "in constant association with the color and requirements of actual contexts." (Sapir, 1961) Wilkinson says "one learns language by being in a situation that calls language forth" (Wilkinson, 1971). Novick and Waters stress that conceptual growth through having to deal with the demands of new contexts and linguistic challenges is at the heart of language growth. Oversimplified, the formula might read "the wider the range of contexts and challenges in which the child has a personal stake, the more profound will be the language development."

Exploratory Talk

Stratta and Wilkinson (1977) have documented some excellent examples of children engaged in using language exploratively and in listening with tolerance while others explore. "Meaning for each individual is being accumulated and modified operationally in the course of the discussion. Furthermore, each individual makes what he can of the discussion in the light of his own individual experience, which, although having common touchstones with others is, nevertheless, unique."

Britton makes a similar point when he underlines the need for children to have the opportunity "to match new meanings of words and utterances with what is already known about the world." (Britton, 1977)

Gusdorf nicely summarizes the role of the ideal listener when such exploratory connections are being made. "Like a comb through tangled hair," he says, "the words of another can help bring order." (Gusdorf, 1965)

This kind of talk is crucial to cognitive development, which is in turn essential for continued linguistic growth.

*   *   *

I do not pretend that these eight features extracted for comment represent all the conditions likely to promote oracy. I do suggest, however, that they make a good starting point for any search for the "basics" of oracy. How might Australian schools fare measured against such criteria?

II   And So to School . . .

Official system's curriculum guides say many of the things outlined in Part I. Most are, however, very thin when it comes to offering operational strategies, maps, or suggested structures for an "oracy" program. Consequently, many teachers are easy prey for pseudo-taxonomists and laboratory vendors who invent plausible sets of sequenced sub-skills and then offer guided tours at a price. Others who instinctively sense the toxic qualities of such programs may be content to rely on the truism that we learn to talk through talking. But this can so easily degenerate to the recycling of present ignorance. Others, still, suspicious of the new commercial curriculum package but needing to appease nagging guilt, bring out the remedies of antiquity to make a program of traditional bits and pieces of show and tell, language games, debates, mock councils and listening "comprehensions" without a great deal of thought to sequence, purpose, or principles of language development.

At the risk of seeming presumptuous, I hazard a guess, based on widespread observation of Australian schools at all levels over many years, that few have a clearly articulated policy (in action) or a functioning plan for "oracy" in the curriculum. Many junior primary schools are adopting certain naturalistic approaches, but often this is a veneer over deeply entrenched views of the child as "deficient," in which case it is easy to detect patronizing relationships and pseudo-attentiveness. In primary schools the fragmented approach may be giving way to integration around themes, but I suspect that this is often an ingenious and tenuous ploy for taking the old fragments and packaging them in a new way. As for secondary schools, talk is rarely part of the official assessment and so the reality is that few teachers and students take it seriously. Perhaps, I can defend this fiction by referring to two pieces of recent South Australian inquiry, one at the lower primary level and the other in four secondary schools.

Novick and Waters (1977) in their intensive study of children's talk at years 1, 2 and 3, are scrupulously careful not to draw glib conclusions or to offer neat answers about strategies for the future. I shall try to be equally careful in extracting from their work.

They confirm what people like Flanders and Barnes have shown in other places that teachers do talk a lot (up to 70% of the time) and that when teachers join groups of children at talk they usually reduce the language flow. "When teachers participated, the children's utterances were reduced by 40% at year 1 and 27% at year 3." It is also interesting to note that in this situation more than half of the teacher's utterances were questions.

At the same time Novick and Waters repeat a number of times, in a number of ways, that wise mediation by mature adults is a key element in language learning, and that there is a need for more conversation on a one-to-one basis in the early years of schooling.

A fascinating aspect of the Novick and Waters findings is that SES (Socioeconomic status) differences cannot be easily detected at year 1 but are becoming more apparent by year 3. It is also interesting to note that working class children gradually withdraw over the years from initiation of conversations with the teacher, although at year 1 they initiate twice as often as higher SES children. Such information makes it hard to refrain from asserting that schools actually teach SES language differences or, to put it another way, that children gradually learn to behave according to the teacher's perception of their SES.

Novick and Waters remark on the constricting nature of much teacher questioning which forces the classroom response to be compressed to one or two word answers. Their radio microphones confirm that longer utterances are elicited in the playground. They suggest that children in schools don't seem to have the same *stake* in what is happening inside.

In comparison with Bernstein's work in England, it is interesting to note two conclusions from the South Australian study:

- "While the working class child may not perform as well cognitively (certainly as measured by school success), there is no indication that this failure is produced by his language."
- "Differences in the language performance of social class groups are less marked in Australia than in Britain or the United States." (Novick and Waters, 1977)

This research is teeming with information that could suggest ways of improving the conditions for oracy in schools. I will confine myself to just a few observations based on this work.

It is imperative that we develop ways of training teachers in how to *organize* for new structures conducive to talk. This includes the fiddliest of details in terms of instructions, seating arrangements (the presentation of space is crucial), and intervention strategies. Above all, we need to discover ways of increasing one-to-one conversation with mature speakers (this includes ways of using vertical grouping, interclass visiting, etc.). The importance of issuing challenging tasks which will promote negation and concerted collaboration emerge as does the critical nature of concept development (children must be continually put into new territory and assisted to formulate understandings).

With respect to curricula, teachers must be helped to define the crucial processes, activities and situations which will continue the language growth of the first five years.

The way to do this, say Novick and Waters, is not through exercises where no person-to-person interaction is involved, and it is certainly not through the kind of "misguided" programs that Engleman and Bereiter popularized in America, nor through the patronizing "talk reform" techniques of Gahagan and Gahagan (which grew out of an overzealous response to the early Bernstein).

*   *   *

At the secondary level, my own work with the Language Across the Curriculum Project concentrated on individual teacher inquiry into perceived language and learning problems. It did not focus on specific "oracy" programs within the subject English. What it produced was a picture of schools as environments for languaging.

Before the project started, we asked teachers in the four participating schools to comment on perceived language problems and their causes. With respect to talk, the predominant complaints were about "laziness," "slang" ("they relax in class areas and their use of slang annoys me"), and "careless language" ("they almost seem to delight in it"). The causes were variously seen as lack of concentration, lack of clarity, "constant exposure to television," and "insufficient grounding in the basics." Only three teachers out of 172 indicated that the schools or the teachers might be in any way contributing to the perceived problems.

After many inquiries and seemingly endless tape recordings of classroom interaction, the project officers made these concluding remarks about talk after citing a number of documented cases:

Thus the norm was—

1. Teacher controls the input of knowledge.
2. The lessons are tightly structured around content.
3. Teacher has a definite pathway in mind and rejects discussion that is an excursion.
4. Teacher talks most of the time.

5. Teacher is the initiator.
6. Teacher language is very subject-specific.
7. Teacher questions are information-seeking and do not invite open exploration.
8. Student participation is minimal and limited to short utterances in response to closed questions.
9. Student answers must be precise.

We found situations involving any of the following extremely rare—

1. Teachers having an end point in mind but allowing students to walk a variety of paths.
2. Teachers being colloquial and hence allowing students a point of entry into the knowledge.
3. Teachers asking lots of open questions.
4. Teachers allowing the language of home and playground into the classroom.
5. Students thinking aloud.
6. Students initiating sequences.

> We have tape-recorded several teacher-student exchanges in a one-to-one situation and have found little variance from the above. The teacher still has a preconceived end in mind and carefully drops hints to maneuver the student towards that end. The language resulting from this is limiting and very task-oriented, and it is doubtful the student reaches a clearer understanding of the subject.
>
> (BOOMER, RICHARDS AND ZUBRINICH, 1979)

This leads the team to remark:

> It is only when the language of the classroom is flexible and serving many functions that students will make new meanings. Imagine a classroom that allows all these things to happen: storytelling, use of personal anecdote, hypothesizing, wondering, passing on information (telling), reflecting.
>
> What we have said so far has wider implications, of course. If the kind of talk occurring in the classroom is to change then such things as—
>
> - teacher-pupil relationships,
> - the balance of power,
> - teacher perception of the curriculum,
>
> will also have to change.
>
> (IBID)

When it comes to the subject of questioning in schools, the concluding comments are pointed:

> It appears as though students rarely feel inclined to question teachers and teachers rarely feel inclined to encourage them to do it. This situation has been well-documented and commented on by the likes of Barnes, Bellack and Flanders, but it is nevertheless a rather peculiar phenomenon.

Why is it that teachers spend much of their time asking questions when they already know the answers, and students who are ostensibly seeking answers ask far fewer questions?

We find this paucity of student questioning rather disturbing, particularly when a search through all our transcripts yielded only one example of a speculative question asked of a teacher. Almost as rare were teacher questions which invited students to speculate. . . .

It would be foolish of us to suggest that students do not ask searching questions, or engage in exploratory talk in schools, but we do wonder where this sort of activity occurs. There was certainly very little evidence of it in full-class discussions, and little more in small group discussions. Presumably questions are asked in children's heads, or perhaps they are sometimes surreptitiously aired behind a protective hand when a child is driven to question a peer. It is almost as if schools are deliberately trying to inhibit learning.

(IBID)

Another section of the conclusion looks at linguistic registers used by teachers and textbooks. Sections of transcripts of lessons and extracts from texts are quoted to show the kind of bafflement which occurs in schools. The team is not impressed by some of the "simplistic" attempts to overcome this by replacing "big words with smaller words," or by teaching the "meaning" of the big words. With an obvious debt to Frank Smith and Kenneth Goodman, the writers assert the following:

Words do not have meanings which dissolve in children's cognitive structure—it is the children who bring the meanings to words. The most important information in these processes lies not in the print or in the sounds, but in the children themselves, in the knowledge which they bring to the task. Both reading and listening are predictive processes: when listening to or reading an utterance the child is constantly utilizing his knowledge of the language and of the subject of the utterance in order to predict what will come next. That is, he is constantly processing information as he reads or listens. If the complexity of an utterance is such that s/he is unable to utilize this knowledge s/he is forced to rely only on the information in the printed page, or in the sounds heard. This means that the child reads or listens almost on a word by word basis; thus his/her memory is overtaxed, his/her information processing apparatus becomes overburdened, and the utterance becomes incomprehensible noise.

(IBID)

Now after many years of wondering about schools as institutions where there are unwritten laws about what can and what cannot be said, after examining our impressive evidence that the talk in classrooms is overwhelmingly teacher talk, after looking at evidence from elsewhere, and after thinking about unburnished, rusting swords, I understand why ours is not a particularly articulate society. In *Negotiating the Curriculum*, a paper based on the Language Across the Curriculum Project, I conclude that it all revolves around the uses of power:

Now my specific concern is to promote more open communication, more talk to exchange and seek information, and more questioning to relieve mystification, because one of our basic assumptions in the South Australian Language and Learning Unit is that learning is vitally connected with the language resources which can be brought to serve it.

A more equitable distribution of power, or at least a more healthy exercise of power, which we know can be used either benevolently to let in or maliciously to exclude, will not come while those *in* power monopolize the talking space, thereby keeping other people in relative ignorance.

III So What? . . .

We think a child learns his native language systematically and naturally, without any formal tuition or formal testing. This learning, we think, can continue in a similar manner throughout the period of formal schooling.

(NOVICK AND WATERS, 1977)

I support this view, but I believe that schools should also be able to intensify the learning process, increase the repertoire beyond what might be naturally acquired outside, and add to the students' power by helping them to understand how language works in the world. I also believe that schools have a specific function to teach the "language of schools" as well as subject specific languages and metalanguages. However, the principles for learning these things should be the same as those which apply in the learning of the basic mother tongue.

If we were earnest in our intention to promote oracy in schools, we would set about developing a taxonomy, not of sub-skills, but of situations which would make certain language demands related to the language demands of the real world (including the real world of academia). Then we would try to arrange these in some sort of developmental sequence without claiming divinity. Having done this, we could then consider how to translate the known principles (Part I) into a pedagogical recipe which, I suggest, might go like this: "Expose the learners to plenty of examples of the register (or language task), challenging them to "crack the code" and to begin to produce their own version. Then provide ample opportunity for trial, error, and feedback. As proficiency develops, allow plenty of time for reflection on how it works. Put the emphasis on a workshop-type approach and make sure that the learner sees purpose in the endeavor. Throughout the sequence, make sure that the teacher role is consistent with the best practice of mature adults who nurture the growth of the preschool child. The learner should be convinced of the need to guess, to take risks and to bring previous knowledge to bear on the new challenge. It would be of great help if the teacher could show, where appropriate, how she does it herself, giving access to her own thoughts about it. Avoid fragmented exercises. Concentrate on whole tasks. Teach component skills where needed. Learn how to organize the class into groups and how to negotiate without degenerating into chaos.

Once we had this straight we would need to look to the tone of the institution. If it were formidably an Institution the odds would be against one teacher trying to establish free flowing language. It might mean that compromises would be needed. If most of the other teachers do not share the frame of mind, it is likely that the students will try to tyrannize the individual teacher back into the norm. The very strong will make it work.

Biblography

Boomer, G. and Spender, D., (1976), *The Spitting Image,* Rigby, Adelaide.

Boomer, G., Richards, N. and Zubrinich, R. (1978), *Language Across the Curriculum: An Experiment in Learning,* unpublished MS., Adelaide.

Boomer, G., (1978), "Negotiating the Curriculum" in *English in Australia,* (no. 44, June 1978).

Britton, J. N. (1977), "Talking" in *English in Secondary Schools,* English Teachers Association of NSW, Sydney.

Bruner, J. (1975), "The Ontogenesis of Speech Acts," *Journal of Child Language,* Vol. 2, no. 1.

Gusdorf, G. (1965), *Speaking,* Northwestern University Press, Evanston, IL.

Halliday, M. A. K. (1977), "How Children Learn Language" in *English in Secondary Schools,* op. cit.

Novick, D. and Waters, D. (1977), *Talking in Schools,* Education Department of SA, Adelaide.

Sapir, E. (1961), *Culture, Language and Personality,* University of California Press, Berkeley.

Vygotsky, L. S. (1962), *Thought and Language,* MIT Press, Cambridge.

Weir, R. (1962), *Language in the Crib,* Mouton, The Hague.

Wilkinson, A. (1971), *The Foundations of Language,* Oxford University Press, London.

Wilkinson, A. and Stratta, L. (1977), "Listening and the Teaching of English" in *English in Secondary Schools,* op. cit.

Response

GROUP WORK AND ORACY

PETER FORRESTAL

This chapter speaks to me powerfully of the need for classrooms to preserve the best features of the natural process of language learning, and the need for rigor in short- and long-term planning. What happens in our classrooms should give students greater control over their lives by enabling them to understand how language works in the world.

In my own teaching I have responded to the work of the theorists by accepting that:

- student talk needs to be encouraged and valued;

- students have to be given opportunities to think aloud and use their own language to learn;
- learning needs to be viewed by teacher and pupils as a process involving several stages in which students move from tentative beginnings towards carefully articulated conclusions.

I have found that using small groups of four students as the basic unit of classroom organization enables me to put these things into practice. Furthermore, small groups offer the *opportunity* for the full range of talk contexts and situations related to learning.

Some of the problems that teachers will face in operating a classroom where small groups form the basic unit include:

- the fact that most teachers have few or no models in their own learning on which to base this approach to teaching. (This, in itself, should be a compelling reason for teachers in tertiary institutions concerned with teacher education to operate in the way they believe classrooms should work.);
- the fear that students will waste the time they are given in which to talk;
- the worry that not being able to control class discussion will lead to a loss of control of the class;
- not being sure how to structure lessons so that student talk focuses clearly on the task at hand and students are moving towards an understanding of the work being tackled.

Garth's call for a pedagogical recipe to translate the known principles into classroom practice is a call for a structure that will help teachers overcome many of their concerns about using group work. The following practical guidelines that I have developed may help other teachers in developing their own planning structures. They are also important if the work we do in schools is to intensify the learning process:

1. The classroom atmosphere must be a supportive one which values the contribution of students and enables them to see that their language is an important learning tool. They need to understand that talking helps learning.
2. Students need time for exploratory talk (or writing) after reading or listening to literature—or any other information that teachers wish to share with them. This time for exploration should be short and unstructured with the students' focus being on trying to understand more clearly what they have read. Increasingly I believe that teachers should give students any instructions *before* they read so that nothing else comes between the literature and the student.
3. The question of time is vital. Students should have enough, but not too much, time to complete tasks in groups. There needs to be some tension for the best learning to occur.
4. We need to consult students more and more about the learning process. We need to be sure that *they* understand what they are doing, how they

are going about it, and why. By asking them constantly to reflect on their learning processes, we can learn much that we need to know to refine our teaching. They can give us valuable feedback about structuring groups, the amount of time they need, and how to make the learning process more effective.

5. Students need to know exactly what they are to achieve when they work in groups. Their tasks must be clear as well as appropriate to both their interests and abilities and the teacher's purpose.

6. Just as we accept that writing needs a real purpose and audience so does the talking students do in groups. Students need the opportunity to present what they have been working on to others. This can be done by combining groups, joining two students of one group with two from another, or forming new groups with one representative of four separate groups.

The teacher can achieve much by carefully structuring groups at this stage.

Group tasks and group situations inevitably are talking tasks and situations, as well as whatever else they might be. Most of the features that play a significant part in language learning before and outside school are possible in a classroom where the students work primarily in small groups, where the teacher structures the learning process in such a way that students accept a degree of responsibility for their own learning and have the opportunity to become engaged in making meaning.

Such a classroom

- places an emphasis on students making meaning;
- can be a place where students see that language serves *their* ends;
- can give students the opportunity to have a more personal stake in what they do and learn;
- places a value on exploratory talk.

Because a classroom that focuses on working in small groups changes the role of the teacher,

- situations such as Garth describes where "caring adults kindly lick language into shape by their responses" are more likely;
- there are more opportunities for students to engage in conversation with the teacher on a one-to-one basis;
- because students have more power and more responsibility they are more likely to have a high degree of involvement in their learning and more likely to be challenged by learning activities.

We do still need to plan regular opportunities for one-to-one (or even one-to-four) interviews with concerned adults—either the class teacher, another teacher, administrator, or parent—possibly to discuss such things as reading lists or extended pieces of writing. Likewise, we need to stress to parents (perhaps in our homework policies) the value, in students' language development, of discussion with interested adults.

The quality of our planning will determine the level of challenge that students find in the tasks we set. Our ability to structure learning experiences and plan worthwhile activities will likewise influence the quality of students' language growth.

In looking at ways of giving students opportunities to use talk for learning we have focused on the question of how we can best teach. While we still have to grapple with this question, and refine our practical-theory as a result of our teaching experience and what we learn from students, I believe it is now time to focus on another issue: the issue of sequence in English teaching.

I support Garth's call for a taxonomy of situations that would make language demands related to the language demands of the real world—in an attempt to arrange a developmental sequence. No one wants or needs a prescriptive lock-step syllabus, but English teaching in this country could be transformed by rigorous and thorough attention to the notion of sequence in the English curriculum.

VIII

The *Language and Learning Unit* in South Australia (1980) sees itself more and more as a base for informing parents about language development. Many schools and teachers are resisting the system's invocations to lay down their drill worksheets and take up reading, writing, talking, and listening with their children. A compelling reason given is that "the parents" will not allow it.

Now, the obvious retort to this excuse is to ask, "How do you know? Have you asked them?" Invariably, the answer suggests that only one or two vocal agitators have been terrorizing the school council. No concerted attempt has been made to justify new methods to all the parents. There is a well-founded suspicion that mythical "parents" are being used as scapegoats by teachers who are themselves frightened of or opposed to a new regime in language arts.

Growing impatient with such pusillanimous sheltering behind the cardboard replica of the parent body, members of the *Language and Learning Unit* plan a subversive document which will give information to parents and lead them constructively to unsettle the tardier teachers of their children.

Christine Davis joins Garth Boomer to produce a letter to parents and a set of answers to questions which parents allegedly ask. The cheeky part is a section called, "What to look for in your child's school." The paper has never officially been released and yet it has had a widespread effect on schools in South Australia.

How? It was stamped "draft only" and let out to a few people for response. Somehow it came to be photocopied and soon had a widespread circulation on the "underground." Some schools included sections in newsletters home to parents, unthreatened by its frankness.

Indirectly, it got into the hands of parents. One parent sent it along to school via her daughter. The principal of the school was incensed and wrote to the Director-General of Education complaining that the *Language and Learning Unit* was deliberately and unfairly undermining the authority of teachers and principals. He demanded a full inquiry. The inquiry revealed that the paper had never been officially released to parents.

The document still circulates. It was last seen in Canada.

A Parent's Guide to Literacy

Dear Parent,

This is a time when teachers are often under attack in the press, and in the street, especially when the topic is literacy. Some employers tell tales of job applicants who can't spell and you yourselves may have grave doubts about your own child's progress in reading and writing. You may even be tempted to go to the Principal and ask him or her to tighten up and "get back to the basics" of reading and writing.

But remember that teachers may be feeling a little misunderstood and battered at this time when it seems that open season has been declared on schools. It would certainly be a pity if your approach to the Principal resulted in some of our finest teachers being pressured to "pull their horns in" and return to a brand of teaching which used to produce children who were seen and not heard.

You want your child to be able to read and write well, but I feel sure that you also want your child to be able to speak up and to struggle in times when it is easy to go under.

So when you go to your child's school, make a point of emphasizing that you want literacy *and* self-confidence. You don't want your child turned into a meek follower who can understand simple instructions and write dull compositions.

I am writing this letter to you because as a parent and an "educator" I think I am in a position to see both sides of the coin. Too often schools defend themselves against criticism by saying that the public is "uninformed." Too often the public is indeed uninformed, but not always. The teaching profession has been too often silent and unprofessional in not making clear what it is doing and has always done to teach children how to read and write.

We need to clear the air but at the moment I think that parents may not have enough information to put their point of view on an equal footing with teachers. Millions of words have been written about literacy by educators, often in a language that is as remote as quantum physics. And yet when you squeeze all these words there seem to be some simple common-sense conclusions which we can all share. I want to share with you some things that are commonly understood among experts in language development. Of course, my colleagues would want to quibble on some of the details, but I'm confident that they would support most of what follows.

At least, this parent's guide should convince you that there is nothing mysterious about teaching children to read and write and that parents can do a great deal to help. The real mystery is something to delight in—the complexity and brilliance of the human mind.

Yours sincerely,

Garth Boomer

The Guide

1. *Question*

    How do children learn to read and write?

    Answer

    This is still very much a mystery because it is not possible to get inside a human mind. However, it does seem that it happens in much the same way that children learn to talk and listen. Gradually, through wanting to read and write, children will try things out, ask questions, play around with words, try to make sense, watch others reading and writing, listen to their teacher's (or parent's) advice and eventually start to get "the hang of it." It does not come quite as naturally as talking but it seems that the more children are surrounded by reading and writing and the more they want to learn the skills, then the quicker they will learn. Many different methods of *teaching* seem to work although there is growing evidence that working exclusively from letters to sounds to words is not the best way to approach reading. The most vital factors seem to be self-confidence and a desire to learn on the part of the children and encouragement and wise advice from the teacher. It is quite clear that if children are constantly taught *about* the rules of reading and writing and never get to try the real thing they will not learn. (It doesn't work for bridge either.) Once children have learned the rudiments of reading and writing it's a matter of having someone around to help them if they get stuck.

    ### What to Look for in Your Child's School

    You have reason to be worried if your child seems to be doing more *exercises* in reading and writing than actual reading and writing to make sense. In the early stages, the child will need to practice forming letters and recognizing words, but as soon as possible the school should be encouraging "the real thing." The so-called "remedial" readers and writers who enter secondary school are often children who have continually been sent off to practice isolated bits of reading and writing. Sometimes it is too late to get such children out of the habit of reading aloud with no understanding, or writing with a kind of paralysis because they are frightened of making a mistake. And so, you should be looking to see how much "English" is just exercise work (filling in blank spaces, un-jumbling jumbled words, correcting incorrect sentences, etc.) and how much it is real reading and writing with help and encouragement from the teacher. The school which concentrates too heavily on exercises may be producing crippled readers and writers. You should also be worried if your child is constantly being chastised for making errors. The children who boldly and confidently "have a go" and then receive kindly advice from the teacher will do much better than those who see reading and writing as a kind of booby trap where you must tiptoe tentatively in fear of being blown up. It may mean that the school is too fond of penalties. It is disastrous for children to learn how to fail.

Be concerned, too, if your child never seems to read anything except the basal reader. Be delighted if a new library book comes home each day.

2.　　*Question*

How can parents help to prepare children for school?

　　Answer

By reading and writing themselves and talking about *what* they do and *why.* By reading stories and news items and signs and packet labels to children and encouraging them to ask questions such as "What does this mean?" By encouraging children to play at reading and writing.

　　What to Look for in Your Child's School

Particularly in the Junior Primary School, you should look to see whether the teachers carry on what you have started. Do they have lots of signs and labels and books around for children to read? Do they read aloud to the children? Do they encourage children to guess what the signs say? Do they show children how their own stories can be written down? Do they talk about why people read and write?

3.　　*Question*

Should children be taught phonics?

　　Answer

Many children have learned to read without being taught phonics (how letters are combined to represent various sounds). Many more children (including most of us) have learned to read in a program based on phonics. The children who weren't taught phonics must have eventually worked out how the letters represented sounds, and the children who were taught phonics had also to learn that sounding out words was not reading until you could also make *sense* of the sounds.

We now know that the child learning to read cannot rely solely on phonics and that there are real dangers in teaching reading by building from letters to sounds to words because this can produce terribly slow, halting readers who try to decipher every mark on the page. This forces them to go so slowly that they cannot understand what the marks are saying.

A healthier approach seems, right from the start, to be "reading for meaning" where the child is required to use all sorts of clues to guess at the message. The teacher does not ignore phonics but teaches such things when it will help the child unravel a difficult word. The danger with an overweighted phonics approach is that it may make reading far more difficult than it needs to be.

But the fact still remains that many methods of teaching reading seem to work, especially if the teacher is enthusiastic and obviously cares. In such cases, children may eventually nut out how to read for themselves in order to please teacher.

What to Look for in Your Child's School

Take the sentence "The cat chased the *mouse.*" Imagine a child is stuck on the word "mouse." One piece of advice may be to "sound it out" m - ou - s ("o" and "u" make "ow"). A better hint could be "Guess what the cat could be chasing which starts with "m." You can then use other clues to get rid of words like "maybe" because "maybe" does not make sense in that position of the sentence.

Look for such a rounded approach in your child's reading program. Try to find out if the child is being encouraged to use all kinds of clues to work out the meaning. Try to find out if your child attacks all reading as if it is going to make sense. Get worried if the program seems to consist of a lot of laborious reading aloud of material which doesn't make much sense. Certainly be concerned if your child is not doing most of his or her reading *silently.*

4.   *Question*

Has grammar been thrown out?

Answer

There is a great deal of confusion, even among teachers, about grammar. Some people refer to the ability to put full stops in the right place and to spell; some think of "parts of speech"—verbs, nouns, adjectives, pronouns and so on. Still others think back to their own school days when for the old Q.C. you had to be able to analyze sentences into subjects and predicates, subordinate clauses, and adverbial phrases of time and place. Many grandparents and parents remember long hours of instruction which led them to be able to explain why "It is me" is a grammatically incorrect sentence. Some may even recall that they got 10/10 for grammar and only 6/10 for composition.

If we mean by *grammar* formal study of the structure of sentence, then we can say with certainty that this does not help children to write better. (Seventy years of research have shown this over and over again.) This means that we who were taught this kind of grammar must have learned to write in some other way, even though we may be tempted to believe that we owe it all to grammar.

Unfortunately, a good deal of this kind of grammar teaching still exists in our schools—more out of habit, I think, than out of any real belief that it works. Children are kept busy picking out verbs and adverbs when they could be better employed *writing* and then discussing the effectiveness of their writing with others. Indeed, if large numbers of our children are bad writers, it could be due to the simple fact that they have not done enough writing. Grammar, as I have defined it, should be thrown out. *But this does not mean that full stops, commas, spelling, and effective expression are no longer important.* It means that there are more powerful ways of helping children master these things.

The best recipe is to learn to write by writing with plenty of opportunity to discuss what you have written with the teacher and others and having lots of talk about *how your own language works.* Teachers need to write themselves so that they can explain their craft to children. This could be called the workshop or practical approach to writing, where full stops and spelling are learned *on the job.* Terms like "verb" and "noun" will eventually arise as naturally as "carburetor" and "clutch" do in a garage.

What to Look for in Your Child's School

Judge the effectiveness of the teaching of writing in your child's school by the *amount* or real writing done (as opposed to exercise work), by the interest in saying something worthwhile, by the way in which your child can talk about his or her own writing, and by the amount of help your child gets in editing and polishing pieces of writing.

Be concerned if your child thinks "English" is just correcting sentences or doing comprehension exercises, rather than learning to write.

On the other hand, be just as worried if your child writes *creatively* all the time and is never encouraged to polish and to discuss ways of doing it better.

5. *Question*

How can children be taught to spell correctly?

Answer

No one really knows and so you should be skeptical about anyone who pretends to have the answer.

One way to look at the problem is to consider what good spellers do and compare this with what bad spellers do. Good spellers are, above all, confident that they will get it right and they are not afraid to tackle words they have never seen before. Bad spellers are likely to panic, to avoid using "difficult" words and to behave rather like someone who has bad breath and knows it.

Good spellers may write the word down and then change it because it doesn't look right; bad spellers may try to remember whether you double the "l" when adding "ing" or whether it's "i" before "e," and in the process become confused. Bad spellers tend to be ashamed of themselves. Somewhere in their schooling they came to accept their inadequacy, and since then they have lived up to their reputation.

Of course, there are some people who seem to be congenitally destined to be awful spellers (though perfectly capable in other areas), but it's probable that most people could learn to spell correctly if they set their hearts on it and were given sound advice.

Without claiming anything divine about it, my formula for a good spelling program would be *confidence, curiosity, practice,* and *reading.* I'd keep the number of rules to a minimum because I can only now remember two rules myself and because there are exceptions to every rule anyway. The only rule I would insist on would be: *never avoid a word because you can't spell it; have a guess and then get help afterwards.*

Words, what they can mean and how they are spelled, should be a constant source of curiosity in any classroom where literacy is valued. Lessons might be spent talking about words that children are using or want to use. Families of words can be discussed and a healthy spirit of inquiry can be nourished by urging children to guess how words might be spelled. Eventually, after guessing, they can be shown the correct spelling. This seems to be a more sensible approach than exacting penalties when children get words wrong in tests or in compositions by making corrections a punishment.

Once again, the most powerful way to teach spelling would seem to be by means of the workshop approach where children keep note of words they misspell in their own writing. The "Friday Test" can be on their own word list.

If you also read a lot it seems likely that you will be more able to spot the words that don't look right.

In the case of the incorrigible misspeller the only sensible thing to do seems to be to teach the child where to go to get the correct information. If you are an incurably bad speller you need to know it and what to do about it without feeling ashamed of it.

What to Look for in Your Child's School

You don't want a school that gets hysterical about bad spelling and treats misspelling like leprosy. Nor do you want a school that believes spelling will look after itself.

Look for a program where there is excitement about words, encouragement to "have a go," opportunity to get it right, and plenty of reading.

Be suspicious of a school where spelling is taught largely by drilling twenty new words a week and where corrections are seen as a form of punishment, not learning experience.

6.   *Question*

Should teachers mark out all the errors?

Answer

It is irresponsible for teachers not to help children polish or edit writing that is important and about to be handed up or sent off to an audience. But this is a different process from marking out errors *after* the work is handed up. Traditionally teachers have done the latter, but research has shown that this may not be a very effective way to help children write better. If the energies used in doing this kind of marking could be diverted to helping the child "on the job," it is more likely that the child's writing will improve.

In the case of the child who finds writing difficult, it could be very deflating to have red marks all over the page. A better approach would be to point out one or two areas for improvement rather than to reinforce feelings of hopelessness.

So, the teacher should not be expected always to mark out all errors. Each case must be treated on its merits. Sometimes we write rough notes for ourselves and as long as we can understand them it's nobody else's business. It's different, however, when we are writing a job application or an important letter. When children try these kinds of writing, they should be expected to come as close as possible to a "perfect" product. Teachers should ensure that they stick at it until it has quality. This will also teach that good writing does not come easily.

What to Look for in Your Child's School

Teachers who write back to children sometimes are teaching something else that is very important, that in the real world people respond to your messages. Look for a workshop approach to writing where children are encouraged to improve a piece of writing until it has quality (in much the same way as one might do in woodwork or art).

Look also to see the kinds of comments teachers make on a finished piece of writing. If the comments are always cryptic (like "good work" or "spelling needs improving") ask yourself whether this is really helping your child to do better next time. If the teacher sometimes writes back in response to what has been written, this is a sign that the teacher cares about the meaning as well as the surface features of the writing.

Don't immediately attack teachers if you find a spelling error not marked out or a faulty sentence uncorrected. There may be a good reason for not doing so. On the other hand, if the teacher always marks out errors and insists on corrections, look at the quality of your child's writing from the point of view of interest and lively use of the language. Correct writing is not necessarily good writing.

Overall, look for a program that encourages a variety of writing tasks and gives the child a chance to do a good job by allowing for rewriting and editing.

7. *Question*

How much time should be spent on reading and writing?

Answer

Schools used to frown upon children talking too much. Some still do. And yet, experts in language development tell us that ability to talk confidently and freely has a very positive influence on literacy. Children should spend a good deal of time talking about new ideas, helping each other to solve problems, and asking questions of clarification. This is not the sign of a slack classroom as long as rules of politeness and co-operation are followed.

As children gain power over the spoken language, they are building up a source of knowledge that will help them read and write better. So time spent on good talk helps to promote literacy.

It is impossible to say exactly how much time should be spent on reading and writing, but it should be remembered that in *all* subjects at both primary and secondary level children should be asked to read and write. The time spent in "English" is only the tip of the iceberg. Good teachers will therefore be teaching reading and writing throughout the day whenever children are using language in this way.

Some studies in America found that despite an enormous formal allocation of time to reading on the timetable, the children only did an average of four minutes of real reading a day. Most of the time was spent on exercises.

To come back to an earlier point, the real test is not what time is allocated to something called reading or writing, but rather what time children actually spend reading or writing in any one school day. The more you do it, the better you are likely to become at it.

What to Look for in Your Child's School

Look for a school that knows the value of good talk, because the confident speaker has a better chance of being a confident reader and writer.

Look for a school where talking and reading and writing are going on for a purpose.

Look for a school where "English" is taught in science and social studies, in art and mathematics.

8. *Question*

How useful are reading-age tests?

Answer

They can be useful broad guides if handled with sensitivity, but they can also be very dangerous and misleading.

They vary in quality but even the best are not very valid scientifically. Perhaps the most reliable way to find out how well as child is reading is to ask the child, find out what the child is or is not reading, and listen to the child read aloud.

Blanket tests of a whole class or a whole school can yield a rough picture of reading capability as "remedial." There is ample evidence to suggest that a child's so-called reading age varies with the reading task and the intensity of the desire to get the information.

A child may fare badly in a test situation, but quite capably when faced with a *T.V. Guide* and a desire to find out what time a favorite program is on. A basal reader with a reading age of nine years might prove difficult, while a book on dinosaurs, reading age twelve, might be read with quite a deal of understanding. Similarly, a student whose reading is well-developed might be attracted to an "easy" book and will browse through it briefly.

Some schools, with the best intentions, group children for reading according to their measured reading age. This can have most unhappy consequences for the "poor" readers, because there is a very strong tendency for children to live up to their labels. (Even if teachers try to hide the labels, children soon work out what is going on.)

Parents should not get over-anxious and alarmed if they find their child is below his or her reading age. In fact, parental anxiety can too easily be passed on to the child and result in the child having more negative attitudes to both self and reading.

There is a strong case for not disclosing a child's reading age, and my personal opinion is that it is often dangerous even for teachers to have this information.

What to Look for in Your Child's School

Look for a school where reading-age tests are used sparingly and certainly not as a sorting mechanism so that children can be grouped for reading.

Make sure that your child is not just a reading-age score waiting to be improved.

Look for a program that encourages a positive attitude towards self and towards reading.

Be concerned if the books in your school are graded or color coded to suit groups separated by age, sex, or reading age. If your child is prevented from reading a book because it is too hard *or* too easy, be perturbed.

9.   *Question*

What materials should my child read?

Answer

This question is important when your child is first beginning to read and after as s/he broadens the range of what s/he reads. There is evidence that many of the graded readers, designed to make reading easier, may actually make reading more difficult because they tend to contain lifeless, meaningless language and often don't have a story. So, many junior primary teachers are using a "language experience approach" where children dictate their own stories and picture captions and then read them to themselves, their teachers, and other children. This approach means that children do not have a reader (which worries some parents) but do have the chance to learn to read *more quickly,* as they already know what they have to read and *more soundly,* as they start reading by expecting it to make sense. Other teachers are using all those lovely books published for children which are in school and local libraries as the readers for their classes.

As children grow up, they will be reading a very wide range of materials—both at school and at home. They will probably go through various phases as their taste in reading is being established: the comic phase, the Enid Blyton phase, dinosaurs Star Wars phase, the science fiction phase, the romantic phase, etc. There is nothing wrong with any of these provided that eventually your child moves into a new phase. A ten-year-old reading Enid Blyton is no problem; an eighteen-year-old who still reads her has not developed mature reading habits.

Children's librarians report that very often children choose from a limited range of material because they do not know about the variety that is available and they are too unsure to experiment for themselves. An enthusiastic adult saying "Have you tried this . . . ?" is usually enough to encourage a child to try something new. On the other hand, there is no need to be ashamed of returning to a well-loved book or author.

As your child matures, the school will demand the reading of books thought to have merit—either because of the way they are written or for the ideas about life they present. The discussions which are part of "studying" novels are an important part of your child's developing literacy.

Sometimes your child is attracted to books, magazines, etc. which you do not approve. You might be inclined to ban them, but it is worth thinking of an alternative strategy. Such material often loses its appeal if it is not banned (the deliciousness of forbidden fruit!) and if its limitations, by your standards, are discussed openly in your home and alternative literature is offered.

What to Look for in Your Child's School

A junior primary school where interesting books are the basis of the reading program, where children write their own books, and where boring readers are sent away to be recycled.

In your child's primary and secondary schools be delighted if your child is reading widely and excitedly and if s/he is obviously engaged in challenging discussions regarding the worth of what s/he is reading.

10. *Question*

Why don't the children do comprehension exercises like they used to?

Answer

Most comprehension exercises of the type we all remember doing are disappearing from our schools. So children are no longer doing comprehension, i.e. reading a paragraph and answering questions set by the teacher or choosing the correct answer from several alternatives.

One problem with these exercises is that they test comprehension instead of teaching it because if you already know, you can get the answer right—if you don't know, the test won't help you get any better.

Another problem is that usually only trivial information is the sort that can be right or wrong, e.g. "Is the girl's dress blue or green?" "What is the dog's name?" The most important aspects of an author's meaning are a matter of opinion and need to be shared.

The real rigor comes in working out your own understanding of something written, in hearing other people's understanding, in going back to the text to evaluate yours and others' responses, in learning that sometimes more than one opinion is possible, in changing your opinion if appropriate and in knowing just what meaning you have taken from the point and why. This seems to be best achieved by purposeful discussion which can then lead to writing if necessary.

What to Look for in Your Child's School

If your child is doing lots of written comprehension exercises, you probably have cause for concern unless there is rigorous debate during the process.

If you child has a *real reason* for finding out what the author means, e.g. a question about the world that the science textbook is supposed to "answer" or the responsibility for finding out in order to teach someone else, etc., you will find your child prepared to struggle with difficult meanings, to talk it over, to go back to the text and sort it out to his/her satisfaction.

Be pleased if your child's school includes time when the students struggle with meaning until they've got it by allowing for lots of discussion. Be concerned if they spend their time answering trivial questions in reading laboratories or grammar books.

13.　　*Question*

Should children read silently or orally?

Answer

Little children love reading to adults because that is the type of reading behavior they know best, because it is exciting to show off new accomplishments, because books are good to share, and because it is a sure way to get approval from adults. It might also be necessary for beginning readers to hear what they are reading before they can read silently—although no one is sure of this.

The problem with oral reading is that it is a different skill from reading and it demands a different approach. To read orally successfully you have to concentrate on getting each word correct and on phrasing, expression, etc. Adults who are asked to read aloud in the real world (news readers, public speakers, actors, politicians, etc.) usually *preview* their material and *understand it before* attempting to read it to an audience. They are then able to correct themselves when they make the inevitable slip because the monitoring device in their heads says: "That doesn't make sense," or "That doesn't sound right. Go back and sort it out."

This does not happen when children are reading meaningless language (as in early readers) or when they read new material with no chance to preview it. So they often struggle on, reading word by word, understanding nothing. Their own monitoring device is not able to work so they don't go back to sort it out—they go on and become used to the idea that reading is meaningless. Children who do read a passage aloud with expression and relatively few miscues do so because they already know how to read that material, not because they are learning from the experience. Silent reading teaches children the real art of reading, of selecting enough material from the page to capture the story line without letting the brain become overloaded with an excess of information. Good readers expect print to make sense: they sample the page, they go on or go back if something doesn't make sense, they guess well about what is going to come next, and they operate at a faster rate than the oral reader so they can concentrate on making sense.

What to Look for in Your Child's School

Be pleased if your child's reading program includes some silent reading from the very beginning and is almost entirely silent after a year or so. Be delighted if the oral reading which occurs in your child's school stems from a real reason to read aloud, e.g. to share a story, to perform a play, to share a riddle or limerick, etc. Teachers need very occasionally to monitor what children appear to be doing with reading by listening to them, but to do this frequently or with unprepared material is not very useful.

Be concerned if your child has to read everything to her/his teachers before being allowed to "go on," if your older reading child has to regress to reading aloud at school or for homework, if parents who go into the school to help with reading do nothing but hear children read instead of talking about the story.

Above all, be worried if your child is not allowed to *tell about* a story read silently and has to read it orally to "prove" that it has been read.

Response

THE CLASSROOM AS A LITERACY SHOP

CARRIE HERBERT

"Terrific," I thought at first glance when I read this article. "It's down to earth, it makes sense, and it is being directed at that large group of people teachers call 'the parent body.' At last here is an 'expert' prepared to give some information about what to look for in schools. He is challenging parents to find out how and what their children are learning."

Surely it's about time the client had a say; and parents will only begin to ask questions, to challenge old methods, and to support new approaches if teachers and educational experts allow them "in" to the mysteries of the classroom. But as a teacher, I am also aware that even with this information, the parent still will have little say about which classroom their child will go into.

I think schools should be moving towards a system of explicitness that encourages diversity of methods and content, where individual teachers put up-front on their classroom doors the kinds of education experiences they are offering youngsters. For example, if we saw each classroom as a specialty shop, which advertised its wares appropriately, then only the customers wanting those particular "goodies" would enter that shop.

You wouldn't go into a shoe shop for chocolate. Neither would you go to a classroom in which spelling drills and dictation played a large part, if you were looking for leadership qualities, problem solving strategies, or decision-making abilities. If you wanted those things, you would search for a classroom which displayed evidence of lots of lively discussion, honest opinion-giving, a sharing of ideas, and the students taking responsibility for their own learning.

Such "up-frontness" agrees with my own ideas about learning, and it is something I do when I work with learners. They know what I intend and why I do what I do. Similarly, I try to be equally open and honest with parents. Teachers must take time out to make sure parents know about the subject areas, the new methodologies, and the evaluation procedures we are currently using. (Education has moved forward some twenty years since they were at school—behind desks.) Parents who have such information will be more likely to support and encourage us. At least that is my experience.

But on second reading of Garth's paper, I thought, "Wait a bit! I don't think that Garth is actually serious about giving this paper to parents." Can you imagine the dissension and anger it would cause? Far from bringing teachers and parents together it would, in fact, cause division and hostility. So, Mr. Boomer, with you and your dangerous little paper, what could we teachers do?

Quite clearly, the paper as it is written has been aimed at an audience with a fairly sound background in education. Most schools would need to rewrite this document, to use it in a context of a parent education program or to pick out parts and use them as discussion points for parent meetings. They would also, I think, want to remove the combative style of the piece which could quite seriously undermine parental confidence in teachers and in turn cause many sound teachers to feel unduly guilty about their present teaching.

At Magill Primary School, I ran a five-week parent education course which covered the basic areas of Language Arts. The sessions were based on discussions and compared the traditional methods with the different approaches we are now using at Magill. For example, the "conferencing" method with children's writing and the drafting, editing and publishing phases were all new to the parents and they loved it when it was explained and demonstrated. They also found the idea of using "real" library books as the basis of the reading program a far more logical thing than color-coded basal readers.

Following the five-week course I gave the parents Garth's paper. They thoroughly enjoyed it. In the context of the course just completed they didn't see it as ammunition and they didn't want to rush into classrooms brandishing swords. It just confirmed their views about the teaching of Language Arts.

So, to conclude, this paper is an exciting and innovative one, but rather naughty and provocative. If given to parents at random, it would probably encourage confrontation and hostility between parents and teachers. Since this is certainly not the appropriate way of operating, I hope Garth would not be advocating it.

Parents and teachers need to get together, to respect one another, and to know from where each is coming. This can only be achieved if both parties are prepared to communicate, to be honest, and to listen to one another. Roll on the day when all parents are welcomed as co-educators of children.

IX

It is not only parents who need to be convinced that new methods of teaching in the Language Arts are soundly based. Right wing elements in the university sector, media barons, and employer groups continue to delight in implying that sheer anarchy is being or about to be loosed upon our schools. "Drafting compositions today, heroin tomorrow."

The English teacher is becoming increasingly politicized. He realizes that if classroom teachers are to have room to move, they need national legitimation of what they are doing. They also need parental support and access to resources which are not permeated with behavioristic exercises that devalue both teacher and child.

The chance comes at a national seminar to take up the public fight. The seminar slogan is: "Are our standards slipping?" On the platform are four panelists: the English teacher, a tertiary lecturer who has carried out research into alleged illiteracy (these two on the side of the angels), a Director-General, and a prominent ex-politician (these two asking "serious," "searching" and "responsible" questions).

The delivery by the English teacher is confidently assertive. There is danger that the embedded iconoclasm will do the cause some harm, but the researcher is in the wings with figures that make nonsense of the "decline" theories. The paper is well-received. Indeed the public forum ends in a palpable victory for good. A national reading journal further cements the arguments by publishing what follows.

Literacy
Where Should Australia Be Heading?

What Is Literacy?

Literacy is the ability to make good-mannered sense in reading and writing to the satisfaction of those who have power over you with respect to the task you are attempting. Thus, if I cannot make sense of a memorandum from the Director of Education, he may call me illiterate. If I write a report full of faulty punctuation, he may also call me illiterate, not because he cannot understand but because I have been ill-mannered, judged by what is considered to be good taste in educated circles.

Literacy is almost always defined and diagnosed downwards. Very rarely does a less powerful or less prestigious community group accuse a *superior* section of the community of being illiterate. When *ordinary* people come across, say, lawyers or academics who do not make sense, they usually shrink from accusations about illiteracy or ill-manners.

And so when we look at society, we find that it is the relatively powerful who are presently making the accusation or statements about illiteracy with respect to the relatively powerless, upon whose continued servitude they often depend for their continuing power. Employers, tertiary teachers, professional groups, chambers of commerce, newspaper editors, and some politicians seem to have the loudest voices in what I have termed *the illiteracy scare.* And of those voices, the middle-aged and elderly would, I suggest, predominate. I certainly have not heard the young suggesting that the adult community is illiterate, though one Australian survey at least indicates that there is a higher rate of *measured illiteracy* among those who have left school than those in the upper secondary school.

Measured Literacy

If a power group wishes to appear more certain of its accusations of illiteracy, it may commission a measuring agency to conduct an *objective* survey using test items. In setting up the test items, the power group and the measurers have to decide what they consider to be indicators of literacy. That is, they must decide what tasks it might be reasonable to expect those being measured to be able to do.

And so they set arbitrary standards and a selection of tasks designed to test how well these standards are being met. The measurers are, of course, quite ready to admit the arbitrariness of their selections, and they put it in writing that any results are simply handy indicators (not ultimate truth). In this way they can be absolved from any misinterpretations or biased reporting of their findings. They are usually less ready to admit that performance in a test is not necessarily a good indicator of actual competence, even though it is well-known to all who have gone through schools that some people are superb test takers while others are thrown into quite traumatic disequilibrium at testing time.

Measured literacy is, then, highly suspect, and should be treated with caution if not irreverence. In fact, it is not. It is worshipped by most of the power figures, for its usefulness, and swallowed by the gullible masses who humbly accept the divinity of those who measure.

Is literacy a ticket to all the sideshows?

If I were to read motor manuals but not newspapers, I would probably do well on a literacy test based on motor manuals but fail a newspaper test. Similarly, I might write a superb story about my childhood but find myself quite useless in writing routine orders (having never been an army officer).

Contrary to prevailing mythology, neither reading nor writing is like riding a bike. When you can ride one bike, it is highly likely that you will be able to ride any bike. But to read *Nip and Fluff* is not necessarily to be able to read a cartoon.

The language rule is this. You learn to do tasks by doing the tasks. If you have never done a particular task before, you are likely to be measured as illiterate if tested on that task.

The poor showing of Australian children on the newspaper reading item in the A.C.E.R. literacy and numeracy survey is an indicator that few fourteen-year olds read newspapers intensively in school or out. If we wish to improve that ability, we must get children doing that task. Giving them brain-muscle exercises in some so-called basic skills will make them good at the task of doing basic skills. Newspapers will continue to be misread but with more muscularity.

What Are the Basic Skills?

The quite erroneous view of most people in society is that there is a magical set of basic building blocks in language and, once these have been cemented into a foundation, one can go on adding rooms forever. This is dark-age nonsense, as ludicrous as flat earth theories, in the light of what we now know about language.

Learning to talk is the single most miraculous learning achievement in our lives. A highly complex art, which is still defying the world's greatest linguists to analyze satisfactorily, is learned without the benefit of basic skills teaching. It is learned in use and interaction with real people for real purposes. Indeed, one wry commentator has estimated that if we set out to teach talking by analyzing component skills and teaching them sequentially, human beings might still be stammering at eighty. As it is, they teach themselves before the age of five.

When it comes to reading and writing (literacy), the myth of basic skills really comes into its own. A first list for reading might go something like this:

letter recognition
sound blend recognition
word recognition
sounding out words
syllabification
recognizing word families

For writing, a list of basic skills might be:

ability to make letters
ability to translate sounds to letters
ability to make words
ability to write a sentence
ability to punctuate
ability to use appropriate capitalization
knowledge of the parts of speech

These are, in fact, illusory basics. Teachers could teach these things forever without ever getting children to read or write. What, then, are the real basics?

The Real Basics

To consider what the real basics are we should first ask two simple questions:

- Under what conditions are children most likely to become literate?
- How do reading and writing work in the real world? (Or what is it that literate people do when they read and write?)

Here are the basic conditions for talking as I see them:

- Children are constantly surrounded by people talking in contexts which give clues about what they are saying.
- Adults respond to children's early sounds as if they make sense and respond always as if the child is trying to make meaning.
- Talk always serves a purpose for the child (it works for the child).
- Adults tolerate truncated talk but encourage children to expand and approximate more closely to adult models.
- Adults answer children's many questions about names of things.

How does talk work?

- Talk goes on between people and is reciprocal (people talk back).
- Talk serves many purposes.
- Talk is accompanied by gestures and is often intelligible only to the participants (the context gives clues).
- Talk varies with audience, purpose, and context.
- Talk is modified by the feedback the talker gets.

By analogy, we could identify the basic imperatives for reading and writing:

- Ensure that children have a good reservoir of confident talk.
- Surround the learners with many examples of reading and writing and show them how it works in the real world. (Read aloud a great deal and examine lots of writing.)
- Help the child from the start to read and write *whole* messages for which there is a clear purpose.
- Avoid meaningless exercises in the early stages.
- Reduce physical constraints to a minimum.
- Allow learners to use every available clue (context, pictures).
- Insist on making sense and on children saying what *they* think.
- Encourage guessing and don't exact penalty for error.
- Give lots of feedback and answer questions.
- Make sure that the learners do a lot of it.

How does reading work (or what are the essential abilities necessary)?

- The reader needs to be able to recognize the kind of message (and world) being conveyed.
- The reader needs to marshall all the resources of experience and language relevant to that message (or world).
- The reader needs to begin predicting and to continue predicting throughout.
- The reader needs continually to relate what is being said to what he or she knows. (Tie it in with experience.)
- The reader needs to guess and use all the context clues when meaning is not clear.
- The reader needs to understand the style or convention adopted (e.g. newspaper versus tax form).
- The reader often needs to go fast and skip over the unknown word rather than stop and attack.
- The reader sometimes needs to be able to attack difficult words (break them down into parts).
- The reader needs to be able to flesh out words with all their music, associations, nuances (reading behind and between the lines).
- The reader needs to be able to talk about the messages received to confirm or disconfirm understanding.

How does writing work (or what are the essential abilities)?

- The writer needs to have a reason for writing.
- The writer needs a known audience (including self).
- The writer needs to be able to formulate talk into writing (by being very familiar with the style and *music* of the written word).
- The writer needs time to incubate, compose, and polish (or edit).
- The writer needs access to editorial assistance.
- The writer needs the audience to write back.
- The writer needs to know the conventions and style appropriate to the occasion.
- The writer needs to talk about and know various alternative ways of saying things.
- The writer needs to be able to imagine the response of the reader (and become the reader over his or her own shoulder).
- The writer needs to know how to spell (or where to get information) and how to follow the *rules of the road.*
- The writer has to *know* what he or she is writing about.

Alongside the mythical basics, these *basic* basics show much of the teaching for literacy in our schools to be highly suspect.

Threatening of the Real Basics

I do not believe that past generations of Australians were more literate than the present. I do believe that the products of today's schools are far more exposed to real world tests of literacy than their mothers and fathers. There are fewer and fewer unskilled jobs with the advent of automation. There is more and more printed material (forms, reports, instructions, guidelines, rules). In other words, there are greater demands on literacy.

Now, while passionately defending schools against charges of going to the dogs, I wish to subject them to a critique designed constructively to suggest ways of lifting the game.

To go *back* to the mythical basics listed above would be catastrophic. Indeed, for many schools it already is catastrophic. Unwittingly, taking up half-baked cries for primitive remedies, many parents and employers are directly or indirectly bullying teachers into prescribing toxic medicine for children. In droves, all over Australia, teachers are taking up excruciatingly boring and harmful language exercise texts in the name of *back to basics.* These texts deny the basic basics; they cut children off from the real thing and take time away from the activities which will really promote literacy. They deny the basic principles of language learning. You may well respond by pointing to your own experience with such texts, asserting that it did you no harm. Are you so sure? Are you a confident reader and writer? And if you are, did you possibly learn in the end despite the exercise books, by doing the real thing?

When I go into a primary or secondary school wanting to know if it is likely to produce literate adults, I have one simple test: How much of the time is spent doing real reading and writing (with help from teacher) and how much time is spent teaching *about* reading and writing, doing exercises, practicing bits and pieces and writing about writing? The higher the percentage of the first set of activities, the more literate will be the students; it is as simple as this.

What Are the Negative Aspects of Schools Today?

What follows must be seen in the context of the many positive and effective measures being taken in Australian schools. The critique is based on research by the Language Across the Curriculum Project Team (1975–76) in South Australia.

The following appear to be some features which need remedying:

- overuse of language laboratories and kits as opposed to reading and writing for real-life purposes;
- overuse of project work which too often involves copying strips of other people's words;
- inordinate amounts of time in some schools spent on formalities, comprehension and other exercises as opposed to on-the-job help with actual writing problems;
- underemphasis on the power of reading, hearing, and talking about good literature (stories, poems, plays);
- failure of many teachers to take a pragmatic approach in explaining things to children and *showing* them how it is done (e.g., demonstrating their own skills);
- insufficient emphasis on the importance of personal experience and knowledge as a basic condition for *languaging*;
- proliferation of individual worksheets requiring short answers rather than extended prose;
- underemphasis on children's choice of reading material and writing topics;
- overemphasis on marking at home as opposed to editing in the presence of the writer;
- lack of range and variety of reading and writing challenges (too much of the monotone—e.g. the essay); and
- failure of schools to take account of the linguistic demands of the real world (unlifelike assignments).

In addition, it is fairly clear from data gathered by the project team that children are doing very little writing of extended prose in secondary schools. One-word answer tests and worksheets abound. It is also clear that few teachers outside English have accepted the responsibility of teaching the language tasks of their own subject, for instance how to write a history essay or a science report. Few schools have a clearly formulated literacy policy which is understood and acted upon by all teachers, with the result that children are likely to be exposed to quite differing approaches to language from year to year, or even from lesson to lesson.

Concluding Comments

In summary, I suggest that there are some simple strategies which could be applied effectively in our schools to ensure more powerfully literate graduates. These include:

- a workshop approach to literacy where children roll up their sleeves and sweat over crafting various kinds of writing which they need to master and where the teacher is master to the apprentice, showing, helping, criticizing, guiding;
- continual emphasis on making sense;
- continual effort to make schools more lifelike (taking children out into the community, bringing the community in); and
- an emphasis on learning to do it by doing it (not by practicing something else).

All this presupposes that the learner intends to learn *and sees the need.* You can lead a horse to water but it will not drink if it is not thirsty. Our first task with any learner is to take this attitude: *When you feel that you would like to learn to read and write, I know how to help you.* Especially with the senior secondary student, we should refrain from imposing the breast when there is no hunger. We have to use our highest faculties to arrange conditions whereby the learner will come to realize the need. Then, following such basics as spelled out above, teachers can come into their own, helping the learners make language work.

Response

YES, BUT—OR YES, AND THEREFORE . . .

PAT SHEPHERD

These ideas cannot be easily or quickly actioned in the classroom. On the contrary, despite the continuing literacy debate about what ought to be taught and how we should teach it, the majority of teachers remain mesmerized by the lockstep beat, seemingly convinced of the magic of the sequential-component skills-building-block approach to literacy. In fact, most of these teachers would suffer extreme, if not dangerous, withdrawal symptoms if denied the reassuring sounds of chants from Nip and Fluff, or the staccato throb of letter-by-letter analytic phonic decoding. After all, there is an element of certainty, of tranquility and permanence about it all, and historically, teachers have not been favorably inclined towards change, especially the type of change implied in Garth's paper.

As a school principal, I used Garth's paper to explore the implications for whole school planning and practice. I used it first with my former staff who had spent four years experimenting in an attempt to unify theory and practice, and who had developed a healthy language program which reflected an awareness of the reality of children's needs, of how children learn, and a management system that allowed lots of different kinds of doing and learning to take place.

These teachers literally cheered in response. They agreed that the paper provides an overview of the most pressing issues and ideas facing today's teachers. As was their wont, they began to examine their current practices from the perspective of the author, they began to search again and to try to tie ideas together, and they were re-energized by the whole process. This was a group of teachers who had spent four years trying to make sense of learning and language, and to share with the learners the control of what is learned, how it is learned, and why.

I used the paper also within my new school with my new staff, and, in a quite different context, I realized again the powerful force of conditioning and blind tradition. These teachers had been programmed into a system that was incompatible with the ideas presented. Garth's paper spelled "CHANGE." It caused immense disquiet. It asked teachers, as power holders, to yield some of their power, and this threatened them.

Responses, though varied, generally reflected their rejection of the paper. Some showed a lack of awareness of the reading and writing process. Many who said that they agreed with some of the views hastened to add, "but not applicable for my grade level." Others said that class sizes would have to be reduced to "fifteen" if these ideas were to be implemented. The "yes, buts . . ." abounded. Many mouthed remarks about throwing the baby out with the bath water, and many prophesied sloppy habits, anarchy, and sloth. However, a feeling of uneasiness prevailed.

All this is a perfectly normal response to change. Teachers who for many years have trivialized instruction and isolated instruction from purpose grow to doubt their ability to handle something like this. The change implied is closely tied up with the teacher's status, self-worth, and role acceptability in the eyes of the community. They begin to feel deskilled. The reorganization, the management, and the reordering take ownership that many of them don't want. It is easier to blame if there is no ownership. We are asking them to be learners, to be open, and to work in a gradual trial and error, risk taking, collaborative way which is quite foreign to them.

Nevertheless, despite the attitude of disbelief, Garth's paper had challenged my people. There was now a feeling of disquiet. I am ready to work alongside them over the next two to three years as they work their way through the familiar stages outlined below. All will move through the same stages, but at their own individual pace. There will be different interventions for each stage and much support. The important thing is to keep working from where each teacher is. We must avoid falling into the trap of trying to create a new system or to replace the old system with a system that is supposed to be the ONE right approach.

Garth's paper was timely. It has stimulated my staff to begin to examine and re-examine ways of doing our essential task, helping our students become better readers, writers, speakers, and listeners, rather than better test takers and exercise doers. It has stimulated us to begin to experiment. A time of reflection and renewal is upon us.

From Resistance to Celebration

Developmental Stage of Teacher	Likely Indicators Manifestations Responses	Facilitator Strategy
1. Rank disbelief	"This is a complete waste of time. We have important things to do. How can you read unless you know the letters . . . ."	Accepting and giving feedback in an open-minded way.
2. Disbelief yielding to fear of consequences i.e. deskilling, threat to security.	"But we've always taught this way. . . . Parents want it . . . . Kids want it." Plenty of evidence.	Accepting the person but still saying, "We've got to look at this. It can't be brushed under the carpet. It won't go away."
3. Some openness to ideas.	"What would happen if a child did not have to read a reader?" . . . "Let's consider it as a possibility." . . . "What if it is right? . . . Let's take time and look at at it."	Stresses that this is the only rational base. Comes on strong. Reduces risk. Shows false assumptions of old methods. Recognizes the underlying values clash and clarifies it. Provides information.
4. Drafting an action research project and controlling the experiments.	"What if it's right?" . . . "I wonder if . . . ." "Maybe . . . ."	Strongly supporting. It's O.K. Recognizes the "cold turkey" withdrawal symptoms. Also says "If it is disproved after a fair trial, we can go back."
5. Adopt, Monitor, Trial, over 2–3 years	"How do you tell other people—the parents, other teachers—of the value of this?"	Assembles resources and materials. Is supportive.
6. Celebrate Redefine	"How did we fail to see this before? I want to find an even better way to . . . ."	Helps refocus . . . . Cycle starts again.

X

South Australia, through a "language across the curriculum" project carried out in 1975–76, is acknowledged as the state which pioneered and confirmed action research by teachers as a means of professional development.

At that time action research was not academically respectable, but it made sense that teachers would only move to new understandings by systematically trying new methods and reflecting on what happened. Because the term "action research" was daunting to many would-be participants, the "language across the curriculum" project preferred to use the term "teacher inquiry."

Thus, upwards of fifty teachers conducted inquiries into such things as the effects of students rewriting science and mathematics textbooks, the strategies of peer-to-peer teaching, methods of student self-assessment, and the efficacy of journal writing.

Advisory units in other states of Australia took up this mode of professional development and for a number of years until 1980 teachers were contributing to a new kind of literature, based in the reality of schools and written for their colleagues. But then "the cuts" came and all of the advisory units and bases for "language and learning" were wiped out. Action research suffered a setback because inquiring teachers need the outside support of facilitators and publishing houses.

Ironically, at the same time, action research had been made academically more respectable thanks to some fine work emanating from Deakin University. In 1981, Dr. Stephen Kemmis of this University obtained a national research grant to call together leading practitioners in the field of action research to a seminar which would lead to a publication. Thus, the Australian gains in action research were consolidated and celebrated.

Now, in 1984, education systems acknowledge and advocate action research. Indeed there is something worrisome about the facility with which it has become a popular slogan. Is it anything to do with the fact that funds for in-service are drying up and that action research conducted by teachers, in addition to their normal workload, is relatively cheap?

Addressing the Problem of Elsewhereness

A Case for Action Research in Schools

To learn is to research. The practice of "action" research for many teachers and students is a reacquainting of themselves with certain parts of their brains; a repossession of the "secrets" of research with which they were born. This paper puts a case for developing the school as a "community of thinkers." It is based on the considered view that, by and large, schools are not presently institutions of learning and thinking and that big "R" Research will not significantly contribute to educational change until this is so.

If I were to begin with a lament about the struthious behavior of many "big R" Researchers and the alienating effects of the stirpiculture which they have created, I might temporarily turn the more tenacious and curious of you into researchers. Those of you less curious and tenacious would most likely become alienated because of the stirpicultural bias of my lexicon and my deliberately adopted struthiousness with respect to your vocabulary and experience.

Basil Bernstein argued at a Conference in Canberra in 1978 that schools breed citizens with two distinctly different consciousnesses and world views. One group, those who succeed, tend to believe that they are capable of seeking, possessing, and banking on knowledge. The other group, those who fail, tend to believe that knowledge is "elsewhere," not to be possessed, to be deferred to, rebelled against, or distrusted. Thus, a kind of knowledge capitalism is reinforced from generation to generation.

I would be more confident about education if even this were so. Then teachers, those who have succeeded, would at least teach that knowledge can be actively sought, possessed and acted on, if you agree with me that, enduringly, when all the surfaces of the curriculum are stripped away, teachers teach what they are. It is my fear, however, that most of those who succeed merely learn the social and economic advantages of "academic" knowledge and how to *show evidence* that it has been possessed. Few, I think, learn how to seek out knowledge and to test it in action; that is, do *research*. I base this on my own experience of secondary and tertiary education and the quite remarkably similar tales which generations of graduates have told me. Research in education is a postgraduate luxury.

I submit that it is a relatively rare teacher who can teach children how to be researchers, because it is a relatively rare teacher who *is* a self-conscious researcher. The science teacher tends not to be a scientist; the English teacher tends not to be a writer; the Maths teacher tends not to be a methematician. The scientist, the writer, and the mathematician are self-conscious and deliberate learners. They must continually seek out solutions to problems and test their findings in order to be what they are. Their trades, while differentiated at the surface level, are at base the same. They are professional generators of hypotheses and seekers of solutions.

Now, teachers teach science and mathematics and English. To do this they, too, must generate their hypotheses and test them, hypotheses about how best to teach the next concept, how best to provide materials, how best to control, how best to arrange and order the syllabus and so on. They are to this extent action researchers in teaching. This is where they have knowledge beyond that of any outside student of education. They are applied educationists. What they are likely to teach students best, then, is what teachers do: how to be taught, how to deal with school, how to be a scholar and so on. But usually they do not do this *deliberately* and *explicitly*. Unlike the scientist, the writer, and the mathematician they tend not to be *deliberate* and *self-conscious* applied scientists or artists. If they were, then school staff rooms would be alive with theories and the intercollegial hum of reflection on, and surmise about, the ongoing work in the "laboratories."

Three tiers of education have progressively alientated many teachers from their own craft, the craft of teaching and learning. It is as if the medium in and through which they work is invisible to them and therefore inaccessible to theorizing. The established acts of education have become taken-for-granted. Such teachers tend also to have been alienated from their own heads, having been so constantly challenged in their schooling to accommodate other people's heads. They are therefore chronically prone to teach alienation.

I can see, at this point, that I am in danger of confusing the issues through over-generalization and caricature, through lack of definition (e.g. "research"), and by leaving the notion of "self-consciousness" unexplored. Let me come at it another way.

*   *   *

Having been invited to a seminar on "action research" I tried to clarify for myself what this term means. If you include "eventual action" research in the definition of "action research," then I contend that you no longer need the term "action research." All research worthy of the label is action research. "Research" is not "research," of course, when it is the onanistic pursuit of academic simulacritude, unless it can be seen as a working hypothesis on how to get a further degree.

What, then, is the special nature of the term "action research"? I think it has something to do with ownership. Most "big R" Research, as I call it, could be defined as institutionally legitimate inquiry into problems which exist in their chronic form elsewhere than with the researcher. The problems become the problems of the researcher, but they usually relate to somewhere or someone else. The researchers are, therefore, to a degree *detached* from the problem. Even though it may be presently a crucial element of their lives, they can usually remain aloof from the central "action" consequences of what they find.

The "action" consequences for them personally are more likely to be in the form of modified strategies for their next piece of research, a refinement of research methodology, rather than a modification of their own lifestyle, belief systems, or behavior related to the problem they have addressed. The required action is usually for others to decide or divine. This is not exactly "disowned" research (although there are many examples where researchers have publicly disowned the consequences of their work), but it is, I think, clearly distinguishable from "owned" research, that which is more commonly differentiated and named as action research.

I must hasten to qualify "owned" because big R Research is usually also well and truly "owned" by someone. By "owned" *I* mean "owned" by the person or the group doing the research. This is their *own* research into their *own* problem so that the consequent action is also *"owned."* The resultant action will be a modification, however minimal, of their *own* behavior. The research cannot be disowned.

Big R Research may, in the first instance, be aimed simply at the generation of knowledge. The problem, in this case, is to find out more. Personally owned research is always oriented towards a solution to the *present* problem with respect to the act, although its effect may be to create new knowledge, new problems, and new questions by the way.

I am nearing a definition of that which I wish to discuss. Only the word "research" remains in my way. We cannot remove the semantic dye into which "research" has been plunged. It is almost impossible to give it the "small r" meaning. It has accumulated connotations of validity, generalizability, objectivity, and control which get in the way of those of us who want it simply to mean "finding out in order to act more effectively." Therefore, while tempted to cash in on the prestigious ring of the word, I favor putting it aside in order not to complicate things with superficial debate. "Inquiry" or "investigation" will do as a substitute.

One last point and I have a definition of "action research." Teachers, for instance, may subconsciously work on day-to-day problems and incidentally pick up solutions from time to time. I do not include this kind of serendipitous problem solving in my definition. Thus "action research" is *deliberate, group or personally owned and conducted, solution-oriented investigation.* And this coincides precisely with what I consider "learning" to be if one omits incidental and accidental learning from the definition. My logic leads me to conclude that research is deliberate learning.

Since schools and universities are institutions for the promotion of deliberate learning, all teaching, if you accept my reasoning, should be directed towards the support of deliberate, personally owned and conducted, solution-oriented investigation. All teachers should be experts in "action research" so that they can show all students how to be "action researchers." That is, all teachers should be experts in learning so that they can remind all students how to learn.

Therefore, I do not offer the modest proposal that teachers might bravely encourage a little more small scale research among some of their students; I offer the bold injunction that all students at all levels must be researchers and all teaching should be based on the methods of research, if we are serious about learning. Whenever people decide to learn, they undertake research. If teachers wish deliberately to learn about their teaching they must do research. If children wish to learn about electricity they must research. Learning is defined as understanding in such a way that one can say it in one's own words and be understood, or do it and be effective.

Quite patently, whether one observes schools casually or examines the growing body of phenomenological studies, classrooms, with few exceptions, are not places of research, that is, learning, as I have defined it. Learning tends to take place despite the teaching.

* * *

The argument so far goes like this: Schools promote different attitudes to knowledge according to success and failure, but even those students who succeed may be alienated from knowledge if they have not learned how to "own" their own investigations; if they still believe, at heart, that knowledge resides "elsewhere." Teachers who have not learned this will perpetuate and strengthen the belief that knowledge is "elsewhere."

"Action research," as defined, is personally owned learning. It is, if you like, the antithesis of, and antidote to, "elsewhereness." Schools must be institutions of "action research" if children's heads are to come into their own.

Now, to make the connection between research and learning clearer, I need to address the workings of the human brain.

* * *

With the caveat that we are all capable of rigging our own experiments, I wish to report that ten years of investigation and reading have confirmed me in the view that human beings are born scientists. We come into this world hypothesizing. The human brain is biologically the same instrument across all but physically brain-impaired humans, and it goes about "processing the world" in the same way. When you boil down all the psychologies, including all but the most banal behaviorism, you are left with the basic human processing formula: problem $\rightarrow$ observation $\rightarrow$ hypothesis $\rightarrow$ testing $\rightarrow$ evaluation. The surface manifestations of this basic formula are infinitely varied, the vehicles and media of learning vary from case to case, "messiness" and non-linearity may be observable features, but there is always a common underlying "brain strategy."

In order to write this I must overcome massive educational and social structures. Is it not presumption thus to reduce the massive psychology industry? Is it not almost the holy writ of democracy that we are all different? What is my evidence for such totalitarianism?

In the past five years hundreds of teachers, students and parents at conferences throughout South Australia have been asked to tell anecdotes about a recent piece of learning (learning to do, or to "know"). In small groups they compare and contrast each other's learning, looking for patterns and dissimilarities. Unerringly, the classic scientific method emerges: problem observation $\rightarrow$ hypothesis $\rightarrow$ testing $\rightarrow$ evaluation. The learner runs back and forth across these "phases," but each and every piece of learning can be accommodated within the model.

I have discovered to my present satisfaction that the human brain is a classic instrument of research. Research is simply institutionalized and formalized thinking. It is doing self-consciously what comes naturally.

I can go for comfort and reassurance to the cognitive psychologists, who depict the brain as a kind of aggressive, rule-inducing computer, or to the great educator John Dewey, who has been rediscovered and reinvented in different ways for fifty years. Perhaps the most powerful illustrations of what I say can be found in the now superbly documented studies of early language acquisition. We may not be born with a "language acquisition device," but we are able to invent rules and try them out. This is what most distinguishes us as humans.

Another way to put it is to say that we are born with the capacity to imagine what it might be like. From observing humans around us reaching and grasping, it seems that we begin to imagine doing it ourselves. Bruner tells us that even before we practice actual reaching out, appropriate muscles at a subliminal level begin "to intend." Within ourselves we are role playing being a reacher and grasper. Eventually, through trial and error, we come to reach and grasp. Throughout life, imagination leads us to reach and grasp. When imagination dies, we are to all intents and purposes dead.

There will be argument and qualification about what I say so simply, but I find my simplification to be powerful, devastating, and liberating when I shine it on the education industry. And therefore I shall not abandon it lightly.

What happens to intents and purposes in schools? What do teachers intend and purpose? What do children intend and purpose? I find perhaps the greatest enemy of learners' intents and purposes to be "motivation" as it is understood and practiced in schools. Schools, if you like, tend to have the wrong motives when it comes to learning.

Novick and Waters in their book *Talking in Schools* show that working class children come into school firing questions in excess of middle class children, but within a year they have become alarmingly quiescent. The authors remark tentatively that schools, with seemingly the best of motives, may work against language development. In preschool years the interrogative abounds.

Progressively, through school it seems to wither. The work of Barnes and other observers of classroom interaction confirms that teachers talk at least two-thirds of the time and that child-initiated questions are rare.

Bernstein and many others argue cogently that schools have to become more congruent with the culture of the children who attend them. I want to go further and say that schools must become more congruent with the workings of the human brain.

In order to bring this about, I believe that teachers must become students and practitioners of learning. This would lead them to abandon "motivation" (a concept which generally means in practice "something that teachers do in order to get students to learn") in favor of arranging for and ensuring the basic conditions for learning, the most basic of which is that the learner be able to recognize a problem and can imagine what it might be like to have solved it. I submit that there is a world of difference between the classroom based on motivation (where a deficiency model of human brain is at work—"If I don't, they won't") and that based on arousing the learner's intents and purposes (where the teacher assumes an aggressive brain and arranges problematic matter for it to attack).

Between the preschool child and the adult researcher, there is schooling where teachers traditionally tend to pose the problems and set the tests. Schooling is therefore likely to result in some atrophying or retardation of the learner's brain power, because most of the school answers are already known and known to be already known.

Fortunately, it is almost impossible to stop the human brain from learning. Action research still abounds in classrooms as students investigate such problems as how to get an "A," how to get away with the minimum labor, how to disrupt the teacher, how to be a good student, or how to think of other things while appearing to attend. The challenge for teachers is how to harness this rampant brain power and get it to engage with those problems which society looks to schools to address—such things as how to read and write. This is unlikely to occur consistently unless teachers are prepared to negotiate the curriculum with their students.

*   *   *

I have now reached a point where I can be a little more practical; where I can consider what happens when teachers believe that their task is to arrange for deliberate group or personally owned and conducted, solution-oriented investigation among their students.

You may have rejected some of my supporting arguments, but my conclusions about ideal practice may still be valid. It is simply, or rather profoundly, a matter of doing deliberately and formally what comes naturally.

Looking back on this paper so far, I am aware that I have painted a bleak picture of schooling. Of course, there have always been some brilliant teachers who Socratically or by sheer exuberant example inspire students to intend and to inquire. Of course, there are lessons, or at least moments, in the daily life of almost every teacher where the teacher's and the student's intentions coincide.

Ask teachers to reflect on their most memorable and effective teaching sequences, and you are almost certain to hear about occasions where teachers, students, and subject matter together produced mutual excitement. I am interested in deliberately planning to make this happen most of the time.

In a paper, "Negotiating the Curriculum,"* I explore in some depth the problem of warring intentions in schools. I argue that depending on such things as charisma, sanction-making ability, and reward systems, teachers will have more or less success in getting their intentions to prevail over the intentions of the students. I believe that enormous amounts of energy are expended by teachers in making their intentions stick. My metaphor of "sheep dogging" indicates what I believe so often to be the state of the learner's mind when teacher's intentions are unremittingly pursued.

I propose that any learning sequence should begin with a negotiation of intentions to the point that both teacher and student intend in the same direction and mutually *own* the curriculum as *jointly planned.* Under this model, the unit of curriculum is itself a piece of action research into learning which can be reflected upon and evaluated by both teacher and student. There are then many action-research "plays" within the "play." The whole class may set itself a certain "product" goal, groups within the class may negotiate inquiry options, and individuals may contract to conduct personal investigations.

Under this scheme, the teacher is a supporter and collaborator with the students with respect to deliberate class, group or individually owned and conducted, solution-oriented investigation. Time is not wasted on what is already known. This is established before the journey. The teacher's role is to make sure that the learners have the opportunity to clarify the problem, to make observations in potentially profitable areas, to form and test hypotheses and to reflect on the results. To omit any of these opportunities would be to jeopardize the learning.

The principle of ownership and personal intention is crucial. This separates what I am saying from much of the pseudo-inquiry which is now in vogue in schools. I refer to such institutionalized "inquiry" materials as the Australian Science Education Project (where the experiments are set up by the textbook writers and imposed), and even Man: A Course of Study. (Admirable as it is, this material rests on the premise that a remote teacher can organize the material for the students, a serious flaw which Bruner now recognizes). Current social studies courses in South Australian primary and secondary schools advocate an inquiry approach but they actually list the questions which the learners will investigate. In the name of humanity, a blatant act of cognitive imperialism is perpetrated.

I contend that the curriculum itself must be problematic for the teachers *and* the students. What shall we teach and learn? How shall we teach and learn it? Why is it worth doing or why are we compelled to do it? What is of such minor significance that it can be told (facts, information, background)? What

---

*Boomer, G. (1978), "Negotiating the Curriculum" in *English in Australia,* No. 44, June 1978.

is of such major significance that it must be experienced and investigated in order to be owned?

Acting on these principles, teachers are obliged to think aloud about their intentions, their theories, and the ideas which they wish to teach, genuinely inviting students to do the same. In such a "community of thinkers," intentions become shared, thinking power is increased, and, through reflection on the learning, teachers and students progressively learn more about how to learn. They increase their knowledge, or their knowing, at the same time as they become more talented in deploying the capacities of the human brain.

Students are protagonists in the created drama. Teachers are both deuteragonists (in the students' drama) and protagonists (in their own ongoing experiments in education). The whole is a recipe for dispelling the mists of metaphysics that cling to education. There is probably no other human endeavor beside religion itself where there is such a gap between espoused theory (metaphysics) and practice. Action research will bring theory and practice together, *here* in the classroom. Answers will be sought *here* rather than *elsewhere*.

The big R Research which occurs elsewhere will become potentially vital information *here* in the classroom now that the local problem is defined and owned. Big R Research will be picked up, as appropriate, by thinking heads. It will, in this way, become a bona fide participant in the quest to improve action in schools.

Response

TOGETHER

MARIE BRENNAN

Most of the time I don't need this article; I take your points for granted. But when I'm "running low" (e.g. doing something I thought I'd grown out of years ago!), then this article is precious. It's articulate about things I know and hold dear. When relationships are scratchy, a class sour, you remind me of essential questions for my reflections, e.g. "What do the students intend and purpose?" Quite often this question is overlooked in a search for what I, as teacher, did or intended. Then the question "Where has our joint planning and research come unstuck?" is relevant and able to be explored.

In learning to help students (and myself) become active learners together, perhaps the hardest part for me has been learning to share the identification of problems with the students. This used to be part of my concept of the teacher's role: to smooth the learning path for the students, to find strategies for them, to overcome barriers. Now that's all shared. I still have to come up with strategies, articulate what topics/methodology/timing could be most fruitful, but the responsibility is not all mine. I no longer expect that I'll be able to solve others' learning problems—a great weight off my mind, because no one can do that in reality; but also a much more difficult job as teacher to create the time to work closely and build up an equality-of-learning relationship with students. When things are difficult or frustrating for them, they want me to give an answer, speed things up, take the blame. It's difficult not to respond in kind. I've learned to build in reflection time about the process of learning as well as about the topic. Very quickly students learn new vocabulary to describe what up till now has been hidden curriculum. The problem is not mine, nor even one student's, but a class one. We have to identify it and solve it together. Many teachers I know have been through that "progressive" stage of asking students "what do *you* want to do?" Most of them rejected the approach because it tied students to their past ignorance and to mediocrity. The role of the teacher was peripheral. Your arguments here make teaching and learning vigorous and forward-looking. "What's important to know?" is a much better starting point and one in which teachers, parents, and students can participate. Negotiating real curriculum is possible; negotiation means that teachers have a more central role in students' learning.

But how do teachers come to the stage of achieving this? From my reading and experience, it's rare for teachers to share their learning. There's a dreadful social and professional amnesia, enlivened only by the odd apocryphal tale. Our learning is slow—perilously so in an age where change is so fast.

I've learned a great deal with my students. That's our strength. But I suspect that I'd not have been able to take so many big steps in changing teaching style without the support of, and joint learning with, my colleagues, other teachers. That's the area of your "case" which is weakest. Action research for teachers almost has to be a group activity; otherwise the pressures and myths can get too strong.

Action research undertaken by a group of teachers not only offers moral and personal support, it also speeds up the learning process and creates useful theories about teaching, learning, and schools. In the groups in which I've worked, we question each other's plans, look over data and help interpret what it means, and suggest resources and strategies. Our documentation makes it possible to move our learning on into the public arena and out of the folk-history category. (Admittedly, we all still have trouble making time to write.) Now there's more interest in the approach; courses and rationales are being written up and shared. Students have done a great deal to help document classroom work. Late last year a group of students organized, ran, and gave input at a conference attended by teachers and consultants. Even two years ago that would have been an aberration, almost inconceivable. Now it's exciting, but possible.

We're getting there. We just have to keep on keeping on—together.

XI

English teachers who continue to push out the frontiers of their knowledge need to support and protect each other because riding the professional boundaries can get fairly lonely and frightening.

The *Language and Learning Unit* in South Australia was one means of keeping a club of inquirers together. But even units themselves are vulnerable. By dint of some good lobbying, the national *Curriculum Development Centre* provided funds from 1978–80 which allowed similar units in five states of Australia to meet and collaborate regularly. On a more informal basis, links were forged between a South Australian group interested in writing and the "Narrative Working Party" sponsored by the Victorian Association for the Teaching of English. These two groups decided to continue to present papers on work in progress to the linguistics section of the national conference of the Australian and New Zealand Association for Applied Science.

Adelaide and Melbourne are only five hundred miles apart. Mt. Gambier is halfway between, on the border between South Australia and Victoria. As part of the preparation for the conference, Christine Davis, Michael Dilena, Gunther Kress, and Garth Boomer from Adelaide drove to Mt. Gambier to meet for a weekend with Mark Garner, Marie Brennan, Jenni Haynes, and Bernard Newsome of Melbourne.

It was a time of great intellectual stimulation. The focus was on a wide range of children's writing. The speculation was about both process and form. At the end of the weekend various tasks were allotted. Garth Boomer took up the challenge of pulling together knowledge about the composing process. It was certainly a good exercise for him, but his more critical readers of the piece that follows suggest that he had not fully digested the information.

Towards a Model of the
Composing Process
in Writing

Introduction

There are tacit assumptions about the composing process behind the teaching of writing. I suspect that these assumptions are rarely articulated, examined, and tested against developing theories about what writers do when they write. I suspect also that both at the primary and secondary level, the teaching of writing has not changed appreciably over the past fifty years. The teaching sequence or model might look something like this:

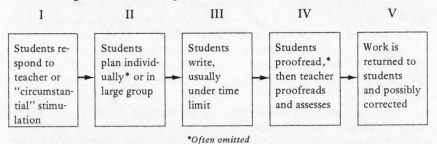

I	II	III	IV	V
Students respond to teacher or "circumstantial" stimulation	Students plan individually* or in large group	Students write, usually under time limit	Students proofread,* then teacher proofreads and assesses	Work is returned to students and possibly corrected

Often omitted

In the seventies the work of James Britton, James Moffett, and Michael Halliday had considerable impact on the contents and spirit of official departmental curriculum guides, but it is doubtful whether more than, say, 10% of teachers have internalized these new insights into the nature and functions of writing sufficiently to change their writing programs in fundamental ways. Taking a national view, at best, or at worst according to your point of view, certain features of the theories of Britton, Moffett, and Halliday seem to have been welded onto existing deep-seated assumptions, often with a disturbingly faddish enthusiasm. And so we may see some schools assiduously providing a wide range of audiences, or requesting the students to practice a spread of writing functions, or deliberately incorporating time for editing activity, or insisting on a balance between expressive, poetic, and transactional writing, or teaching new functional grammars and so on. At least this is a sign of growth and exploration. In my view, however, this growth may prove cancerous unless teachers can transform their emerging *teaching theories* into *learning theories* which take account of the writer's intention and the complex strategies which writers must apply in making a piece of writing.

The history of education yields notorious examples of feverish alliances between educators and the models developed by researchers to explain phenomena but never meant to be applied directly in teaching. Children are often the bemused Hamlets who suffer under such illicit weddings.

" . . . O, most wicked speed, to post
With such dexterity to incestuous sheets.
It is not, nor it cannot come to good"
(HAMLET I ii)

So it is with more than some reserve that I set out, as a teacher, not as a researcher, on a personal exploration of other people's models to find my own model of the composing process. At a time of "back to basics," I am attempting to be basic about writing, to move towards a more complex understanding of the whole composing process in the belief that unless we teachers find a comprehensive theory of the process, the teaching of writing will be subject to potentially toxic localized tinkering and transplanting. As an additional safeguard against "feverish alliances," I intend always to be moving *towards* a model, or models, of the composing process.

Hypotheses and Definitions

I begin with the common-sense assumption that the writer's *composing behaviors* will vary according to the kinds of constraints and influences bearing upon the social act of writing (even writing for oneself is considered to be an act of communion). I hypothesize as well that the actual *sequences* of the composing behaviors, and time spent on each, will vary for any one writer according to these constraints and influences. This is not to discount the possibility that any one writer may have a distinguishable composing *style* across various writing tasks. Finally I hypothesize that across all writing acts there are identifiable common *stages,* recursive not linear, but essential in that no piece of writing could be completed without the writer passing through each of these stages. *"Stage"* is a difficult word in that it usually suggests "this-then-that." I define "stage" as one necessary phase of the composing activity which interacts dynamically with other phases.

In retrospect for any piece of writing, I suggest that it will be possible to identify certain common stages through which the writer has passed. The emphasis in terms of energy or time spent on various stages will vary according to a range of factors. The "composing process," then, means the *process* by which a writer *sequences* a set of *composing behaviors* in a certain *style* in order to make a piece of writing. It embraces all *stages* from the taking up of an intention to write through to the completion of the writing act.

The model towards which I am working will need to account for an infinite number of possible options and combinations of composing behaviors. It must also avoid the kind of reductiveness which certainly occurs the moment one removes a piece of writing from its "context of situation" and "context of culture" (Malinowski, 1923).

Constraints and Influences

As a first step, I have identified in Figure 1 the significant factors which may constrain and influence the composing process.

---

12 Factors Affecting the Composing Process

1. TASK   the nature of the activating demand, challenge, task
2. THEME   the significance to the writer of the meaning to be made (tenacity to communicate it)
3. FUNCTION   the function and purpose of the writing
4. FORM   the requirements of the chosen or imposed form (conventions; genre rules)
5. AUDIENCE   the nature of the audience (power relationships; familiarity)
6. SETTING   the "field" or context of the discourse (home; school; business; accepted protocol; "linguistic table manners")
7. CULTURE   contemporary "poetics" and "aesthetics" (what is considered to be pleasing by writer and reader; what is expected)
8. MATURITY   the maturity of the composer (cognitive; experiential; moral; linguistic)
9. KNOWLEDGE   the degree of familiarity of the writer with the subject (and affection for the subject)
10. ATTITUDES   the attitudes of the composer to self, to society, and to writing
11. MODELS   degree of exposure, past or present, to appropriate writing models
12. VEHICLE   the writing vehicle (dictation; handwriting, typing)

Figure 1

To explicate briefly by contrasting examples, a mature-age writer usually antipathetic to writing, who has to write a letter of condolence for reasons of advancement rather than from deeply felt grief, within the context of the business world, to a "high society" audience and who chooses to dictate his letter, will almost certainly exhibit a quite different set of composing behaviors from the educated adolescent who writes by hand a love letter within the context of a school social group to a person who is suspicious of "flowery" language.

Before the composing begins, there is a complex web of constraints which strongly determines what can and cannot be said. In Halliday's term (Halliday, 1973) there is a significant difference in "meaning potential" in the two situations.

Classifying a Piece of Writing

One could go on classifying the two pieces of writing above in infinitely more subtle gradations, proving that every piece of writing is unique. For teachers as for linguists this might be a fascinating but eventually unrewarding analysis in terms of its usefulness in yielding clues about possible action in the teaching of writing. Given the bewildering scope of things one might attend to, it is necessary to develop a means of classification based on a simple but fundamental set of discriminators.

Britton et al. (1975) and Moffett (1968) have developed closely related models for classification based on a two-dimensional analysis of function and audience. This has already proved useful to teachers as a means of "placing" writing that comes to them and as a map for charting likely growth in control and range in writing over time. I doubt whether such "placing" has led teachers to consider the effect of function and audience on composing strategies, but it has certainly helped them to be more aware of how to organize writing contexts to generate new kinds of writing.

While accepting the powerful effect of audience and function, the Victorian-South Australian group (Kress et al.) whose speculations about writing stimulated me to write this paper concluded, after examining samples of children's writing, that form or genre had been a major influence on the composing behavior of the writer, especially on semantic and lexico-syntactic options which had been taken up. Some writers seemed almost mesmerized into the governing conventions of the style, meanings, and wordings of the genre they had chosen, while others, seemingly more intent on meaning, were able to exploit the form without capitulating to cliché and conventional strips of language.

In discussing this important influencing factor, we found ourselves having to define "genre" much more broadly than is customary. When a writer chose to write a *story* about *detectives* investigating a *murder,* we used the term *genre* to cover the tradition of "that sort of writing." There are conventions and "poetics" (culture specific writing formulae) about *stories,* particular conventions and "poetics" about *detective stories,* and even more specific conventions and poetics about *murder-mystery-detective stories* (as distinct from *missing-jewels-mystery-detective stories*). Where there is a discernible shared set of audience assumptions ("aesthetics") about a certain kind of writing as in the murder-mystery-detective story, we chose to call this a *genre.* The influence on composing of a chosen "genre," with its attendant communal aesthetics or audience demands, seemed so strong to us that I have added this to audience and function as a major discriminator in "placing" a piece of writing. In terms of likely effect on the composing process, the significant feature seems not to be so much the *type* of genre but rather the *degree* to which the writer submits to the conventions and poetics embedded in the genre. It is possible from our experience to place a piece of writing on the continuum "bound by convention"—"not bound by convention," where "convention" refers to the written and unwritten rules of wording, syntax, style, content, and sequence adhering to a particular genre. Consideration of these three dimensions should be useful in helping teachers to speculate about what kind of composing behaviors might be necessary to produce a particular kind of writing.

There are, then, three significant tensions with which all writers have to contend:

What is my purpose?
Who is my audience?
What form shall I use and how conventional shall I be?

There is some danger in seeing "poetic" writing as necessarily more mature than "expressive" or "conventional" more than "nonconventional" or "public writing" more than "private." There are many pieces we know which would confound such a judgment. Nevertheless, tracking growth along the three dimensions will indicate present range and control and will help teachers to diagnose where the range and control might be extended.

Even so, manipulation by teachers of these three dimensions without a subtle apprehension of all the other constraints and influences inherent in the "context of situation" would be most damaging.

Stages in the Composing Process

After reading some major contributors to an understanding of the composing process, Emig (1971), Graves (1975), and Murray (1980), and after reflecting on my own experience as a writer and teacher of writing, I submit that there are three stages in the process—prewriting, writing and postwriting, to put it most simply and uncontroversially (Graves, 1975). Different terms may be used to describe each stage but there is little dissension about the kind of activities which belong to each stage.

In Figure 2, I have represented three views—Graves, Murray, Boomer—adding, as a starting point rather than a stage, the point of conception, ideation or challenge at which the writer takes up the intention to write. While there is to some extent linearity in the stages, it being logical that exploring will come before composing and composing before evaluating, the stages are also obviously recursive. Murray (1980) gives a good illustration of this in his depiction of drafting behavior as a cyclic repetition of rehearsal, drafting, and revising by which the writer's exploration of new ideas is gradually curtailed as clarification emerges (see Figure 3). It is also apparent that a writer during composition may through evaluation be led to reconceive the whole task. The stages are therefore fluid and interactive.

Although the identification of these stages seems so obvious as to be almost banal, it seems that this view of writing has been far from obvious to many teachers of writing. From the student writer's perspective, writing is still often a one-shot affair where prewriting and postwriting activities are

Stages in the Composing Process*
(from Graves, Murray, Boomer)

I		II	III	IV
Conception		Prewriting	Writing	Postwriting
				(GRAVES)
Incubation		Rehearsing	Drafting	Revising
Idea	Intention		(Discovery	(MURRAY)
"Ignition"			Final)	
		Exploring	Composing	Evaluating
Challenge				(BOOMER)

*N.B. Recursive, not linear

Figure 2

The Dynamics of Drafting or the Emergence of Meaning
(Murray)

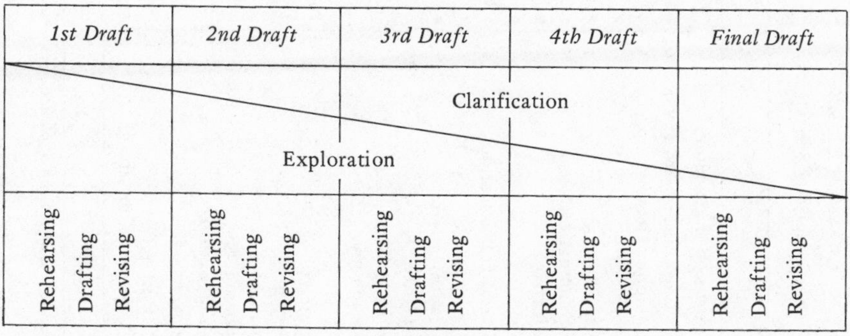

1st Draft	2nd Draft	3rd Draft	4th Draft	Final Draft
		Clarification		
	Exploration			
Rehearsing Drafting Revising	Rehearsing Drafting Revising	Rehearsing Drafting Revising	Rehearsing Drafting Revising	Rehearsing Drafting Revising

Figure 3

the province of the teacher. Even this crude level of analysis has profound implications for teaching.

Composing Behaviors

Thanks to the pioneering work of people such as Emig, Graves, Hayes, Flower, Nolan, Scardamalia and Bereiter, who have developed and are developing techniques for monitoring the "cognitive moves" (Bereiter, 1979) of composers, we are beginning to take our understanding of the writing process beyond the insights yielded by introspection and the anecdotes of famous writers (perhaps great writers being so close to their art can in the end only tell us lies). The techniques yielding new information depend largely on getting the writer to think aloud which enables tracking of the basic moves or strategic elements in the act of composition.

Bereiter acknowledges that we are still in "early days" with this work, but he believes that it is possible and useful to consider what a complete model

"Cognitive Moves"*
(Composing Behaviors)

Imagining	Exploring	Selecting**	Applying	Evaluating
• Finding significance	• Unformed writing	(Focus on the medium)	(Focus on the message)	• Reading back
• Discovering a theme	• Seeking information	Making choices with respect to:	• Shaping and uttering (together)	• Presenting
• "Conceiving"	• Reading models	• graphics (handwriting, typing)	• Composing	• Publishing
• Imagining	• Notetaking	• spelling	• Thinking and writing (alternating)	• Revising
-the audience	• Imitating models	• punctuation	• "Pen wielding"	• Seeking interim evaluation (self and others)
-the finished product	• Practicing	• lexicon	• Pacing	• Reformulating
• Indwelling in the theme	• Expressing in another medium (e.g. drawing)	• syntax	• Sequencing	• Proof reading
• "Lateral" thinking	• Testing different "frames"	• textual connections	• "Write-reading"	• "Read-writing"
• "Framing" (finding organizing principles e.g. scenario)	• Testing the "taboos" of the genre and social context	• purpose	• "Para" behavior	• Seeking final response
• Daydreaming	• Various avoidance behaviors (delaying, etc.)	• organization	-pen chewing	• Assessing the power and effectiveness of the writing
• Storytelling	• Planning, plotting	• clarity	-head rubbing	
• Reading and listening to others' stories	• Talking to explore and classify	• rhythm	-bodily contortion	
• Playing	• Organizing information	• euphony		
• "Brainstorming"		• style		
• Assessing the *potential* of the idea		• metaphor		
		• symbol		
		• analogy		
		• layout		
		• illustration		
		• genre		
		• scenario features		
		(**often automatized)		

*To be read as dynamically interacting behaviors

N.B. *Personal style and maturity of the composer plus other constraints will affect the sequence, time spent, flow and balance of behaviors.*

Figure 4

of the writing process would be like, "even if it can only be sketched roughly" (Bereiter, 1979). He sees a model having three aspects: an inventory of cognitive moves and how they are organized, a scheme showing levels of processing from the highly conscious and intentional to the unconscious and automatic, and a description of how processing capacity is deployed to these various functions to enable writing to go on (Bereiter, 1979).

My own work in analyzing the composing behaviors of a seven-year-old dictating a story to an interacting scribe (Boomer, 1979) has led me to construct an inventory of cognitive moves which I have modified through my reading of people like Nolan, Emig, Graves, Murray, Bereiter and Walshe. (See Figure 4.) At the risk of oversimplifying, I have found it useful to consider these moves under five broad categories of composing behavior: *imagining, exploring, selecting* and *applying* (these two being almost inseparable) and *evaluating.* While one would expect imagining and exploring behaviors to predominate at the prewriting stage, applying and selecting to occur during actual composition, and evaluating behavior to emerge in the postwriting stage, the history of any one composing act will show a complex interacting movement backwards and forwards across categories and behaviors.

The sequence, flow, and relative balance of behaviors will depend on the kind of constraints and influences already discussed, but they will also be subject to the personal *style* of the composer. Some writers seem to plunge straight into applying, imagining, and exploring as they write; others like to let the idea incubate over time; others engage in careful planning before the act. Some edit assiduously as they go along; others write while "hot" and practice the art of blotting later. Nolan (1979) and Boomer (1979) document interesting case studies which illustrate specific behaviors at work. Scardamalia (in press as quoted by Bereiter) makes the point that each cognitive move may go on at different levels of consciousness and deliberateness and that it is quite essential that the writer *not* be conscious of all the moves.

> Even a casual analysis makes it clear that the number of things that must be dealt with simultaneously in writing is stupendous: handwriting, spelling, punctuation, word choice, syntax, textual connections, purpose, organization, clarity, rhythm, euphony, the possible reactions of various readers, and so on. To pay conscious attention to all of these would overload the information processing capacity of the most towering intellects.
>
> (BEREITER, 1979)

Stages of Maturity in Writing

Bereiter (see Figure 5) sees maturity in writing as the development of control over cognitive moves subject to higher and higher levels of organizing principles. Thus, the beginning writer composes egocentrically and associatively, one word or idea inspiring the next in a kind of "data driven" composition. Then the young writer gains control over conventions and style ("performative writing") from which point there develops a growing capacity to affect the reader as desired ("communicative writing"). From here the writer becomes able to take a reader's critical, evaluative stance towards his or her own writing ("unified writing"). Finally, with control over all these levels, the writer can use written language as a vehicle to assist in the personal search for meaning ("epistemic writing"). Neat though this may be, I find it a peculiarly naive and mechanistic view of the writing process. The work of Britton and my own work convince me that children can and do use writing "epistemically" from the earliest stages and that, if physical constraints of pen wielding are removed, and if they have something of great personal significance to express, they will carry out "performative," "communicative" and "unified" writing strategies. My own view, then, is that maturity of writing involves a gradual increase in control and sophistication *simultaneously* in all of Bereiter's categories. Writing from the earliest stages involves all categories.

Stages of Maturity in Writing
Harrison I to V and Bereiter (a) to (e)

Writing to Communicate	I	Expressive stage (What do I sense, feel, experience in the world?)	(a) Associative writing ("data driven"; egocentric) (b) Performative writing (controlling convention; style) (c) Communicative writing (controlling effect on reader) (d) Unified writing (becoming reader over one's own shoulder)
Writing to Learn	II	Reflective stage (What effects do these experiences have on me? How do I respond?)	
	III	Identifying stage (How do I identify with the people and things relating to me?)	(e) Epistemic writing (personal search for meaning, language and thought together)
	IV	Organizing stage (What values and aims and concerns do I hold on behalf of my world?)	
	V	Integrating stage (What values emerge from all my relation-ships? On what do I claim to found my beliefs?	

Figure 5

Harrison (1979) provides an antidote to Bereiter's linguistically oriented scheme by looking at the writing process according to the psychologic of the writer as one who intends to make meaning. He suggests that the nature of the composing process and the composition will change as the writer's world view expands, and as personal morals and values emerge. Wilkinson (summarized in Bennett, 1979) has done some interesting work along similar lines. In correspondence with Harrison, Bereiter has suggested that Harrison's stages II to V are increasingly more sophisticated aspects of his "epistemic" writing. (See Figure 5.)

In examining many samples of children's writing, our Victorian-South Australian group seemed able to make clear distinctions between those pieces of writing where a powerful "conception" was at work and those where the writer was performing perfunctorily. We were also able to make broad judgments, not unlike Harrison's, about the writer's maturity and ability to evaluate experience. Discussion kept returning to the notion of "conception" or "personal significance" as the overriding influence on the composing process and the composition.

It is interesting to note that Bereiter (1979) seems to undermine his own case by citing Menig-Peterson and McCabe (1977) who observed "that while young children tend to produce incomplete and unfocussed narratives under ordinary task instructions, they frequently produce complete and well-integrated narratives when stimulated to tell about an event of strong emotional import."

Both Harrison and Bereiter, regardless of the "truth" of their representations, alert us to the need to develop a model of the composing process which takes account of variations in the process according to maturity and control of the medium.

Levels of Organizing Activity

We are now led to speculate about the cognitive processing that must go on to produce a piece of writing. Independently, Bereiter, Halliday and Kress et al. write similar "stories" about what might be happening.

In Figure 6, I have tampered with Bereiter's construct by adding "conception" as the ultimate level of ordering. Bereiter sees a high level "executive scheme" directing the whole writing operation in keeping with the kinds of purposes and constraints already discussed in this paper. At this level the writer's overriding consideration will be the function of the writing. Below this Bereiter sees "genre scheming."

> A genre scheme consists essentially of the knowledge available directing a certain kind of writing. . . . The beginner, who has never before written a letter of recommendation and who may not even have read one, will lack a specific scheme for this genre and will have to use some other available scheme . . . such as a general business letter or a scholarly writing scheme.
>
> (BEREITER, 1979)

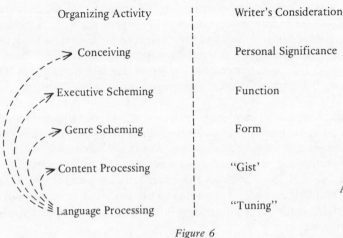

Figure 6

Writing: Levels of Ordering

(adapted from Bereiter)

At the next level the "content processor" draws semantic material from memory and organizes it according to instructions from the genre scheme. In Bereiter's terms the writer develops a "gist" which will make sense to the audience. The "gist" then goes through the "language processor" according to "tuning instructions" from the genre schemes (what can and cannot be said in this form).

Halliday (1973, p. 101), though not specifically referring to writing, offers a diagrammatic representation which makes for interesting comparison with Bereiter's. He begins with the assertion that input to semantics is "social and specific" whereas the output is "linguistic and general" (Halliday, 1973). Each social context and setting offers a range of alternatives for meaning making but the meaning potential is constrained by each specific situation. The grammatical options however are "general to the language as a whole" (p. 101). Halliday sees a movement from the *general* social categories to the *general* linguistic categories with specific categorizations occurring at the interface.

As I understand this representation, Halliday sees language users having to select from a general pool of uses of language in keeping with a specific situation in which they find themselves. Language uses available and situations together generate "meaning potential." The language users now operate the macro functions, "the most general categories of meaning potential, common to all users of language" (Halliday, 1973, p. 100), considering the expression of experience (ideational), the user's role and stance towards others (interpersonal) and the structuring of information (textual). These three categories offer new perspectives but have some similarities with Bereiter's levels of ordering. They can also be related to the three dimensions of our grid: function (ideational); audience (interpersonal); form (textual).

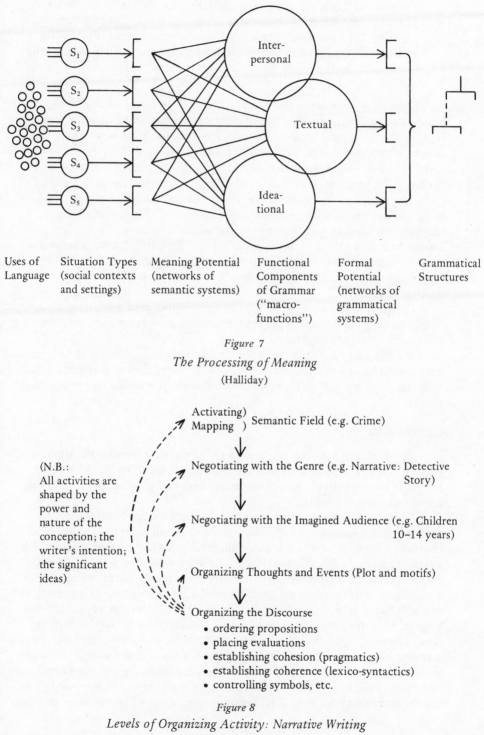

Figure 7

The Processing of Meaning

(Halliday)

Figure 8

Levels of Organizing Activity: Narrative Writing

(after Kress, Garner et al.)

The options in the semantic network determine the choice of linguistic forms by "pre-selection" of particular options within the functional components of the grammar. These grammatical options are realized in integrated structures formed by the mapping on to one another of configurations of elements derived from each of the macro functions.

(HALLIDAY, 1973 p. 101)

Kress et al. have developed a similar "story." In brief, we suggest that subject to the overriding influence of a personally significant theme or conception, the writer will begin by activating and mapping out what we have called a semantic field (cf. Bereiter's "executive scheming"). Thus, the theme may be "crime" which leads to activating of semantic networks related to "crime." The potential meanings are then pushed through the sifting grid of a particular genre. At this point, there is negotiation. The genre, through custom, brings with it embedded structures, meanings and wordings. These must be brought into tension with what the writer wants to say. Some genres are more constricting than others in this negotiation (c.f. Bereiter's "genre scheming").

Then the writer must take into account the imagined audience before organizing thoughts and events in a way which will be comprehensible (c.f. Bereiter's "gist").

The final step is to organize the discourse, which means ordering propositions, placing evaluations in the text, establishing cohesion and coherence and controlling symbols, etc.

It is not suggested that this is top down organizing activity. We see organizing beginning at any level and moving fluidly in any direction according to a vast range of possible influences and constraints. It is not as simple as it might appear.

Conclusion

One of the aims of this exercise was to complicate popular but simplistic conceptions of the composing process. That aim has, I think, been achieved. But having complicated, I now need to synthesize, if possible, in order to render my explorations useful.

Figure 9, which should, like all models, come stamped with "hazard" signs, represents my present synthesis. Within a broad context of culture and context of situation, a writer with a unique personal history and familiar with a certain range of language uses, intends to write either because of external demands, because a certain idea has incubated and taken hold, or in response to a combination of external and personal challenges. The intention is constrained and influenced by a range of factors (see Figure 1). From the tension between ideas and constraints, "meaning potential" (Halliday, 1973) is generated. A set of semantic networks is activated, which on the way to eventual graphic manifestation is subject to processing through at least three "sieves": purpose and function (ideational considerations); form or genre (textual considerations); and audience (interpersonal considerations). Throughout the composing process, the writer may revert to a deliberate consideration of any of these matters.

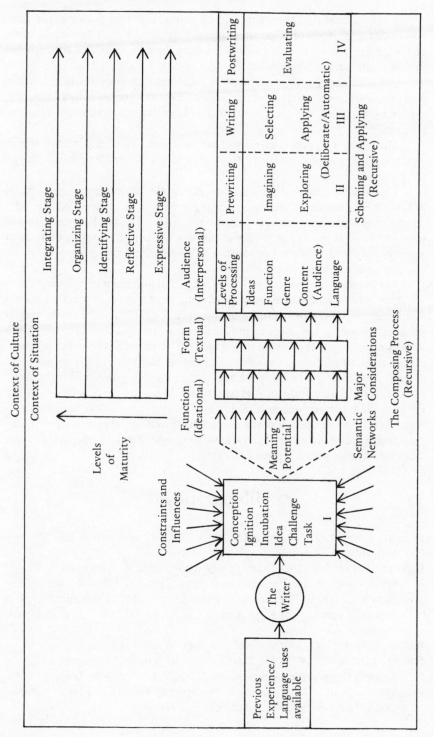

Figure 9

It is suggested that the writer will operate at different points of the process, on different levels of processing (ideas; function; genre; audience-content and language). This processing will range from the deliberate and conscious to the automatic and subconscious.

The composing will comprise three identifiable stages (prewriting, writing, postwriting), each characterized by "cognitive moves" or behaviors (imagining, exploring, selecting, applying, evaluating). These stages are recursive, fluid, and interactive.

The degree of deliberateness and the nature of composing behaviors will vary according to the constraints, the task, and the writer's level of maturity (cf. Harrison, Figure 5).

This model of the learner's journey during the composing process has implications for teachers of writing. Teaching writing involves establishing and maintaining conditions conducive to the act, diagnosing at what point, in what way, and at what level to intervene in the process, and the framing of appropriate responses to the finished product. The model offers a map of useful points of entry or observation to the teacher.

For instance, one writer may need help in deliberately considering the audience. Another may be linguistically competent but conceptually bankrupt. Some may be in need of exposure to appropriate genre models; others may be omitting imagining behaviors to the detriment of the quality of the message. Writers operating at the "expressive stage" may need access to other people's reflections on and evaluations of the ideas being addressed in the writing.

As a teacher, I have explored one of the complex games which children have to learn to play and which teachers have to teach—the process of composing in writing. I am convinced that linguists have much to offer teachers, if, with a sensitive apprehension of the teacher's problems, they can develop appropriate ways of giving access to what they know. Perhaps this exploration will suggest some possible points of entry.

Bibliography

Bennett, Bruce (1979) "Learning to Write," *English in Australia* No. 50, November.

Bereiter, Carl (1979) "Development in Writing" in L. W. Gregg and E. R. Steinberg *Cognitive Processes in Writing,* Erlbaum, Hillsdale, NJ.

Boomer, Garth (1979) "Becoming The Reader over One's Own Shoulder," paper delivered at the Fifth Annual Conference of the Australian Reading Association, Perth.

Britton, J. N. (1970) *Language and Learning,* Penguin, London.

Britton, J. N. et al. (1975) *The Development of Writing Abilities 11 to 18* Schools Council Research Studies, Macmillan Education, London.

Emig, Janet (1971) "The Composing Processes of Twelfth Graders," National Council of Teachers of English, Urbana, IL.

Flower, L. and Hayes, J. R. (1977) "Problem-Solving Strategies and the Writing Process," *College English,* No. 39.

Graves, Donald (1975) "The Child, the Writing Process and the Role of the Professional," *The Writing Process of Students,* No. 1.

Halliday, M. A. K. (1973) *Explorations in the Functions of Language,* Arnold, London.

Harrison, Bernard (1979) "The Learner as Writer: Stages of Growth," *Language for Learning,* Vol. 1, No. 2, Univ. of Exeter.

Malinowski, B. (1973) "The Problems of Meaning in Primitive Language," supplement to C. K. Ogden and I. A. Richards, *The Making of Meaning,* Routledge and Kegan Paul, London.

Moffett, James (1968) *Teaching the Universe of Discourse,* Houghton Mifflin, Boston.

Murray, Donald M. (1980) "How Writing Finds Its Own Meaning," in *Teaching Composition: Theory into Practice,* Timothy R. Donovan and Ben W. McClelland eds, National Council of Teachers of English, Urbana, IL.

Nolan, Frank (1979) "How Do Children Write? Let's Ask Them," *English in Australia,* No. 50, November

Rosen, Harold (1972) "Written Language and the Sense of Audience," *Educational Research,* U.K.

Walshe, R. D. (1979) "What's Basic To Teaching Writing," *English in Australia,* No. 48, June

Response

DOWN TO EARTH
(THE COMPOSING PROCESS—SO WHAT?)

GARTH BOOMER

(Written in response to a request from teachers to demystify the preceding article. The complaint was that I had lost my voice in the attempt to be academic.)

Right: Theory into practice. Let's take this ridiculously complex diagram on page 145 and turn it into a set of principles for all my teaching, but especially for the teaching of writing.

First of all, I need to begin with a view of how kids learn to write. That's not in the diagram, but what I do will be nonsense if I haven't got the learning theory right. Here's my "pocket" size guide:

- Kids learn to write by being in the company of people who are writing with pleasure or to some effect.
- Or rather they learn in such company if these people *expect* them to do it too and interact with them.
- But that's not enough in itself. The kids will need to be imagining what use or *pleasure* will accrue when they can do it.

- Then, if they have a chance to interact with the others and ask questions and *pretend** to do it, it will be almost impossible to stop them from doing it.
- Of course, they will do it better and faster if they are inundated with opportunities to watch others doing it and to listen to them talking about it.
- It will also speed things up if they can take their developing pieces to someone *they choose* to get some expert responses (i.e. It's good to check it out.)
- They will also learn by reading what others write back to them.

There's more to it than that, but that will do for the time being. I have fixed the classroom context problem.

Practical Implications:

- I will write a lot, talk about and show my writing and obviously take pleasure in it and use it to effect.
- I will expect them to become writers.
- I will do a range of things to get them imagining that the effort will be worthwhile.
- I will inundate them with demonstrations of the kind of writing I want them to learn (I will of course do it myself, too).
- I will challenge them to *pretend* doing it and to ask questions of me when they are stuck.
- I will give them advice and judgments when asked.
- I will write back to them.

Now to that diagram. Basically, I've already fixed that "context of situation" box, though for specific writing challenges, they will need to have a clear audience and purpose. The context of culture bit is not so easy. Writing has a bad name culturally for most people. (We set it for punishment in schools.) Most parents hated doing it and avoid it whenever possible, while insisting that their kids learn to do it. Clearly, there is also little resemblance between writing in school and what people do in living outside school.

Practical Implications:

- I need to explain my writing program clearly to the parents and invite them to change their views, if necessary, about the way writing is learned and why it is important.
- I need to make writing inside my room as varied and purposeful as writing outside.

---

* I use "pretend" deliberately to let you know that it is all right to play at doing the real thing. Playing at a version of "it" *is the first step* to doing "it."

Back to the diagram.

"Previous language uses available"

Every kid has a present repertoire of potential meaning and potentially realizable texts in speaking and in writing, even before the ability to write physically is achieved (i.e. by dictating "writing"). This will depend on what texts and ideas kids have been exposed to, what they've attended to, and what they've imagined doing or have done.

Oral text-making potential will exceed written text-making potential. In certain situations, then, contexts and challenges and previous experience will lead to the conception of a potential text. Until it can be imagined it cannot be realized. I cannot imagine a letter to the editor if I haven't been exposed to a letter to the editor. I will only imagine what I have experienced or versions of what I have experienced. In this sense, I cannot create new forms or uses of language. I can only deploy what I already have.

Practical Implications

- I need to have folders of kids' past work and records of writing forms and purposes they have encompassed so that I can assess their present written text-making potential.
- I need to introduce new forms and give practice in these new forms if I want such forms to be realized.

Back to the writer in the diagram. The writer must according to my diagram have some *ideas* he or she wants to convey (ideational stuff), to someone where the vibes or pressures are strong enough to encourage or force the act (interpersonal stuff), and then there must be an available language form in the repertoire that suits the situation (textual stuff). And the writer must be confident enough to take a punt that the ideas are realizable and communicable in writing. (A past history of having some success at this is pretty important!) Clearly, according to the "big" theorists (Britton, Graves et al.), and my own common sense, the writing exercise will be pretty abortive if the *intention* is not there.

Practical Implications

- I need to help students find the ideas that they want to write about and are worth conveying to someone else (or even exploring for self).
- I need to work on making available the possibility of *corresponding* recipients of the writing that is done.
- I need to exude a tough (but caring) attitude of "you can do it" (but it may be a painful struggle).
- I must enter into contracts with the writer about what he or she and I will do during and after the process.

Around that crucial box in the diagram (conception, ignition, etc.) are arrows of constraint and influence. These are the "yes buts . . ." which are real and perceived by both teacher and writer:

TEACHER: "I'd like to let them choose their own topics *but* this would be chaotic and some have no idea what to write about."

STUDENT: "I'd like to be a writer *but* I've had six years of being kicked in the bum and failing."

TEACHER: "I'd like to let them set their own writing texts *but* the school requires me to grade their work."

STUDENT: "I'd like to write at school *but* there are too many loudmouths fooling around. I need quiet."

etc.

Practical Implications

- I need to table *all* of the "yes buts," mine and theirs, and acknowledge the ones that can't be countered and change the ones that can (e.g. I need to face the fact of school assessment schemes and talk openly with the class about how to make the best of it).
- I need to state clearly the personal and political consequences of *not* learning to write with power as well as the consequences of learning to do it (which can be equally negative).
- I need to recognize that *I* am not responsible for some of the shitty things that cut across my teaching and stop feeling guilty about my "impurities" as an English teacher.

O.K. So we've finally decided to have a go despite the constraints because the imagined goal is potent and the intending brain intends. With a clear view of the purpose and ideas (function), having chosen a *form* for saying it and knowing the audience, the writer begins to push potential into a realized text (that is, begins to write down the ideas). If the ideas aren't clear, the writing will fall apart; if the purpose is not clear, the writing will wander; if the form chosen (e.g. business letter) has not been learned, there will be indiscretions (the writing equivalent of breaking wind in church); if the audience is not properly imagined as a responding reader, it won't make sense as intended; and if the wrong words, or style or tone or spelling get used, various unintended impressions will be made.

Practical Implications

- I need to know *for every child* where the strengths and weaknesses lie in the process of pushing intended meaning through the various filters.
- This will allow me to find profitable points of entry with students having trouble in getting started.

  Have you got your ideas clear?
  Are you clear what you want to achieve?
  What's the best way of saying it?
  Can you control that way of saying it?

How will your reader react to that?

Will your reader tolerate the language you're using and the cosmetic flaws?

Now the model takes us into organizing for the learning writer to pass through a process of exploring, drafting, reshaping, publishing and reflecting on the consequences.

Practical Implications

- I need to make sure that I have made arrangements for the writer to pass through all these stages with support.
- Nothing to it. Well, what about 30 kids in a class? What about time constraints and the need to get on with the course? What about the tension between each kid contracting a different piece of writing and the demands to have common outcomes in terms of writing "standards"?
- What price drafting, conferencing, using models for writing, writing aloud, reading aloud? What about scribing, using talk and drama for the clarification of ideas, self-evaluation, publishing, etc? They are fine *if* they respect the principles and the theory implicit in all that has been said so far.

The Principles or Tenets?

1. The responsibility for writing lies with the writer.
2. Intention is the key to writing achievement.
3. The teacher's writing theory must be made available to the writer.
4. The most potent form of teaching is showing how, when asked.
5. All deliberate learning requires intention, exploration, trial and error, testing (by self) and reflecting, powered by imagination.
6. Information should be given at the point of need.
7. A good teacher is a lazy teacher (caring teachers are a menace if they take over the problems).
8. Student adventurousness and confidence is directly proportional to teacher "readability" and explicitness.

I have many more, but these are enough to start the discussion. There is nothing more practical than a good theory.

XII

By 1982, the English teacher was undergoing metamorphosis. His career had taken him away from English into the wider field of curriculum development and in-service education. It was a logical progression because talking language inevitably leads one to consider learning, and learning is at the heart of all education.

Despite his fascination with the wider field, the first love lingered, but more significantly the brain kept worrying away at loose ends. He felt compelled to try to pull all that he had learned about English teaching in the past ten years into one all-encompassing map of the territory.

He became intrigued, if not obssessed, by the dream of establishing some "universal principles." At a time when so many teachers excuse themselves for remaining tied to outmoded habit on the grounds that "the experts can't agree," he felt that some things that we "know" could be asserted.

Until someone is prepared to make a stand and offer a manifesto based on scientific advances, English teachers may rightly claim that fashions come and fashions go. ("Wait where you are and eventually your style will come into vogue again.")

"The Literacy Machine" is the third draft of an attempt to pull together an inclusive theory for practice. The metaphor of the inference machine is amusedly speculative, but the contents are meant to be taken seriously.

The Literacy Machine
Towards a Universal Program for Literacy

Introduction

In computing science, the development of *inference machines* is fascinating. As I understand it, the inference machine is fed with the intelligence and knowledge of world authorities, translated into rules and relative weights, so that later various pieces of evidence may be presented to it. The machine offers inferences, leads, and recommendations to those seeking solutions. Attempts are made to build processing structures into the machine reflecting the complicated processing of the minds of the authorities who have been commissioned in the development of the computer program. Thus, in medicine, various symptoms of a particular illness can be fed into the inference machine and the machine will make a diagnosis, a prognosis, and recommendations for possible action. Should the doctor using the machine be mystified by the inference made, he or she can ask the computer what significant connections it made in reaching its "conclusions." The "minds" of leaders in specialist fields of medicine are thus potentially available, by proxy, to practitioners all over the world. And those minds can be subjected to interrogation, leaving the essential decisions to be made according to the judgment of the user, augmented by the cold scrutiny of the machine.

Of course, the power of the machine depends on the ability of the thinking minds which inform the program to articulate and codify what it is that they do when they think. The machine can only replicate what the informant can recognize. Thus, if the informer, let's say an eminent physician, has always worked on some hunch about the connection between read hair and lung cancer, and knows it, then this can be fed into the computer as a rule with some kind of weighting according to its relative strength compared with other indicators. The mind boggles at the awesome particularity that would be needed to embed into a computer what one currently knows and how one currently processes ideas on a certain topic or in a specific field.

I think it was T. S. Eliot who said that poets can only lie about their composing processes. Inference machines may therefore be little more than plausible liars if the doctors and scientists used to inform them are blind, or unconscious, with respect to significant operations of their own brains. On the other hand, I would feel privileged to have access even to Jerome Bruner's *version* of his own head, or James Britton's, or Yetta Goodman's, or Courtney Cazden's or indeed hundreds of others I could name. I would like to interrogate a machine instructed by such minds, because I'm sure that they would build in the subtlest of disconfirming and questioning strategies. They would, I believe, help me to follow up likely leads and to move more closely to the heart of the matter.

Knowing some of these people, and knowing particularly their modesty and humility in the face of what is still unknown, I find it hard to imagine them agreeing to become informants of an inference machine. It needs some degree of arrogance or foolhardiness even to commit one's present knowledge and frameworks to paper. To commit them to a computing machine, thus investing them with the infinitely more generative power, authority, and seeming correctness associated with the computer, one would need to be highly adventurous or at least slightly megalomaniacal. Still, I remain fascinated because I know that information understood is power, and I seek continually to become better informed. I would like to sit at the feet of the Bruner machine, playing and interrogating in endless patterns. Then I might, in my dreams, play with Skinner or Engelman just to experience an alien planet. Thus might I eventually follow or discard the mind prints of those who have gone before me into new territory. Just as processed food packages are required by law to detail their ingredients, so I would envisage legislation to require inference machines to detail their value systems, basic orientations, and brain hazard characteristics.

While I am conscious of the extreme complexities of the human sciences and recognize some of the likely limitations of inference machines, I am intrigued when I imagine the positive effects such technology might have on those of us who labor in the field of language development and literacy. People in our field are notoriously reluctant to preempt. We tend, in the name of negative capability, to hold our hunches close to the chest. We rarely expose our whole hand (or head). Those who do usually get done in by academic space invaders, appropriators, and demolition groups. It is hard to pin educators down because, in my experience, educators rarely pin themselves down.

I also suspect that behind the public information, the articles and books and talks at conferences, there lies a huge mass of know-how and subtlety which remains occluded. The innocent receiver might thus mistake what are really only trees for the wood. The complexity of a single tree might obscure the simple principles of the wood, or conversely the isolated examination of the tree might blinker the observing eye from the infinitely rich context in which the tree lives. In other words, our present public experiences of the mind at work are likely to be exposures to highly censored, even rigged, performances designed, wittingly or unwittingly, to protect the performer and to conceal more than they show. When it comes to mind we are continually "magicked." The sleight of mind is a special and pervasive brand of wizardry. Inference machines would begin to expose the deeper workings of mind.

The development of inference machines in the field of language development and literacy would, I believe, force all of us to be much more rigorous and deeply questioning about our theories and beliefs. Users of the machines, acting upon the inferences, would quickly reveal shortcomings or dangers inherent in the advice given. Gradually we would become more certain about where we still need to be very uncertain. The machines would at the same time help us to define the boundaries of what we know. They would also help us to confirm any universal principles and rules which apply across cultures.

> It was only with the advent of computers that people actually tried to create "thinking" machines, and witnessed bizarre variations on the theme of thought. . . . All of a sudden the idiosyncracies, the weaknesses and powers, the vagaries and vicissitudes of human thought were hinted at by the new-found ability to experiment with alien, yet hand-tailored forms of thought—or approximations of thought. As a result, we have acquired, in the last twenty years or so, a new kind of perspective on what thought is, and what it is not.
>
> (HOFSTADER, 1979, p. 337)

I prefer, therefore, to welcome this new technology rather than to dwell on the insidious kind of mental paralysis it might induce in the lazy and exaggeratedly genuflective amongst us.

> We make guilty of our disasters
>   the tele, the computer, and the chip,
> As if we were fools by technological predominance.
>
> (UPDATED SHAKESPEARE)

Of course, I am well aware that when we feed a computer "knowledge," we also feed it the value and ethics inseparable from that knowledge. I am also aware that owners control access so that such machines could simply be conscripted in the service of keeping knowledge and information from the oppressed.

Furthermore, the leads and inferences offered by the machine are still subject to interpretation and application within the value system of the users (which may be evil). Despite all these risks, idealistically I must support any advance which has the potential to assist the global sharing out of information and knowledge capital.

I therefore intend in this paper to adventure into some speculation about what I might feed into a "universal" inference machine for teachers of language development and literacy. While taking responsibility for the currency of my own knowledge, I need to acknowledge many influencing minds, not so that they can be dragged down with me when I go, but so that you can assess to what extent I have abused and distorted them—G. H. Mead, Jerome Bruner, James Britton, James Moffett, Susanne Langer, Douglas Hofstader, George

Kelly, Donald Graves, Dale Spender, Harold Rosen, Susan Cosgrove, Christine Davis, Robert Pirsig, John Fowles, Michael Halliday, Basil Bernstein, and many others. My speculation will lead me to consider principles, rules, and beliefs which might hold across cultures. As I proceed, I shall appear for the duration of the exercise to be assured, when in fact I am deeply aware of the profound questions I am begging.

> Can the mind be understood without understanding the lower levels on which it both depends and does not depend? Are there laws of thinking which are "sealed off" from the lower laws that govern the microscopic activity in the cells of the brain? Can mind be "skimmed" off of brain and transplanted into other systems? Or is it impossible to unravel thinking processes into neat and modular subsystems? . . . To understand the mind, must one go all the way down to the level of nerve cells?
>
> (HOFSTADER, 1979, p. 309)

Holism, reductionism, or both? Or is the premise of the question itself wrong?

Food for the Machine

> You lose explanatory power unless you take the higher level into account.
> (HOFSTADER, 1977, p. 321)

Eventually I want a teacher working with a particular learner (or learners) in a particular setting in a particular culture to be able to come to my inference machine for leads as to what might be done to improve the present language and literacy development of the learner. I must therefore begin to program my machine working from broad conceptions of influences on teaching into more narrowly focused pedagogical principles and then into specific principles related to language learning.

There will come a point where I can no longer assume that the inferences might hold across all imaginable cases. At this point more localized and operation-specific inference programs would need to be developed. For instance, my machine will eventually at some point lose predictive power with respect to language development in tribal aboriginal settings in Australia, or for adult literacy teaching in English for Vietnamese refugees or for the teacher of Year Six in Littlehampton Primary School. The machine can offer principles, general processes, and the outline of strategies. It cannot contribute greatly to the specifics of organization and delivery.

Since this is to be my machine, I must attempt to map my mind onto it. To begin, I must instruct my machine about "the cosmic egg" (p. 158; see Boomer, 1982), about the valencies of the containing and influencing forces surrounding the teacher of language development and literacy.

I picture the teacher in a state of continuing tension as his or her own constructs of the world alternately clash and coincide with the ruling constructs of the culture within which the teaching occurs. To complicate the map of the teacher within the circles of the institution, the textbooks, the examination structure, and societal values, it is necessary also to be aware

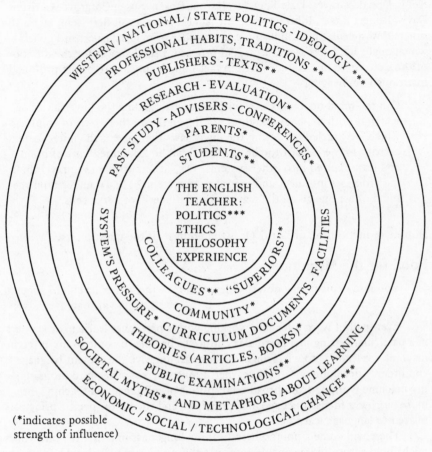

(*indicates possible
strength of influence)

The Cosmic Egg of English Teaching
(Garth Boomer, 1982)

that each child to be taught is also subject to containment from his or her own cosmic egg.

My machine must be alerted to seek further information about context and influences if clients do not supply significant contextual data. Asterisks indicate the kind of relative weighting that the machine will bring to bear in making inferences about where the problem may lie. Of quite remarkable significance are the political and ethical affiliations of the teacher.

I must also map onto my machine a picture of the curriculum composing and enactment process so that the machine can help to spot at which point of the process problems may be occurring. In my diagnosis I would assert that any stage of the process omitted puts the program at risk. The following outline represents my view of the process.

The Composing and Enacting Process

Stage 1: Planning a Unit of Work. Teacher planning. "Mapping the territory."

Stage 2: Negotiating with the children. Teacher-class negotiation and organizing. "Preparing for the journey."

Stage 3: Teaching and Learning. Student exploration, research, trying out and improvising, etc. Specific teaching.

Stage 4: Performing. Consolidating learning to show understanding through various "outcomes."

Stage 5: Evaluating. Teachers and students reflecting on the quality of the process and the outcomes.

This conception of the five stages (each of which is subject to continuing evaluation) needs to be linked with a taxonomy of seven necessary elements in curriculum. Failure to attend appropriately to any one element in one's planning and teaching is likely to lead to shortcomings in learning outcomes.

The Elements of Curriculum

Content— "Worlds to be explored"	*Problem or intention.* This is the content or territory which we want children to explore. We decide upon this on the basis of our knowledge of the children and our own intuitions about what would be worthwhile and suitable. The content may be a poem or story, the students' own stories or anecdotes, a theme, or a social studies topic, etc.
Justification of content	This is where we justify the content chosen and make hypotheses about what things may be learned. *Aim.* To decide what they already know and then to introduce new perspectives. *Key questions.* This is where we outline the key questions which we think will be addressed. They may not be specifically treated by the children but they will lie beneath all that is done. N.B. The quality of the question will affect the quality of learning. The key question offers the teacher a philosophical framework which will give purpose, direction, and shape to the learning activities. It will almost certainly imply a value stance.
Products	Here we list what the teacher would hope children will be able to *say* and *do* as a result of the work. *Can say.* Through sharing language and new experiences in the process students will accumulate a wider set of meanings in the "world" they are exploring and be able to articulate some of their new thoughts about the "world" in a finished product.

	Can do. Students can make some representation of their understanding in a performance, etc.
	Unforeseen outcomes. Add to the planned goals above things which were eventually achieved but not initially planned for.
Skills to be built up and *media* to be practiced.	To achieve the planned goals children will have to develop various skills and use various media such as enactment, mime, puppetry, talking, painting, and mask making.
	Unforeseen skills and media practiced. Children may take divergent paths and in the process practice applying other skills and media.
Learning activities (Process)	This column can only be completed after negotiation with the children. It may not be fully completed until after the work has been completed. However, whatever specific learning sequences and activities are decided on, *all stages of the learning process should be covered.*
	Teachers will come to the students with suggested approaches, but these will be modified and polished in discussion. The constraints on what can and cannot be done should be made quite clear to the children.
Aids and resources	Here we list the resources which will help. These will vary according to the topic. Some things that might be used are the students' experience, the teacher's experience, the experience of other people around the school, stories, poetry, films, pictures, and music, etc.
	Unforeseen resources. In retrospect, it will be possible to add resources which were not envisaged but proved to be useful.
Methods of evaluation	Here teachers and children list the kinds of evaluation they will use to see how well they have done. They will evaluate both the *process* and the products. Methods may include keeping a journal, performing to an audience, sharing criticisms, formal testing, making tapes, and comparing with others.

(EDUCATION DEPARTMENT OF SOUTH AUSTRALIA, 1981)

Thus, if a language development program does not take rigorous account of the need to provide a justifiably rich context or "territory" to be explored, then the program may be at risk, strong in process, but weak in conceptual demand. Likewise, should the teacher promote a mono-dimensional classroom in terms of learning media employed (e.g. language only) the comprehension of the learners may be less powerful than if multiple learning media had been used.

The machine at this point knows something about context, curriculum process, and curriculum construction. Now it must absorb some key principles and conditions for learning, some beliefs and assumptions about education and language learning, and some general strategies related to the principles and practice of good teaching as I see it.

First, some conditions or principles about human life and learning. (This is a package deal. No conditions may be omitted.)

Conditions for Learning

1. Human beings learn by being in the company of people who are doing "it" (where "it" represents what is to be learned).
2. Human beings learn by being in the company of people who take pleasure in it and/or use it to effect and *expect* young humans to learn it too (so that the young begin to imagine doing it).
3. Human beings learn by interacting with those who are doing it, asking questions of those who are doing it, and beginning to induce rules about how it is done.
4. Human beings learn by trying it, or aspects of it, under practice conditions where error can be used to indicate modification.
5. Human beings learn by seeking evaluations and advice from others (or from themselves).
6. Human beings learn by testing it out and reflecting on consequences.
7. Human beings learn by confirming and celebrating achievement.

These conditions need to be welded to a number of beliefs and assumptions.

About Learners

- Human beings are born scientists (i.e. they are theory builders).
- Human intention is necessary for human learning.
- Human training is distinct from human education.

About Society

- Ideally, human beings should share what they have and support each other in their struggles.
- Those in power should be subject to the wishes of the people as democratically expressed.
- To withhold information is to control the power of others to act.
- The ideal citizen will question and act on the basis of a coherent set of theories and principles.

About Teachers

- Teachers should be as explicit as possible about what they intend and how they intend to do it.
- Those in power should continually strive to empower others.
- The aim of teaching is to make students progressively more independent of teachers.
- Teachers teach what they are and what they can do.

About the Classroom Designed for Language Development

(Incorporating principles and beliefs about language learning)

The ideal classroom will be:

- *Active and interactive* (Language is learned in use through interaction.)
- *Collaborative* (We learn language in communities which ideally cohere and co-operate.)
- *Functional and Purposive* (Language is learned because it serves human purposes.)
- *Exploratory* (Language and thinking are dynamically interdependent; language serves thinking.)
- *Reflective* (Language learners are language theory builders, accumulating metalinguistic capabilities to explain what is happening.)
- *Multi-modal* (Reading, writing, speaking and listening interpenetrate and "feed" each other; they also relate to other modes of communication.)
- *Negotiated* (Meaning must be continually negotiated; the message interpreted is never exactly equivalent to the message sent; failure to negotiate will tend to increase alienation in the classroom.)
- *Contextually Supportive* (The richer the supporting and encouraging context, the more likely that language will be learned.)
- *Observed and Tracked* (Just as parents track and celebrate the unfolding language potential of young children, so teachers must observe, track, and support the unfolding capacities of their students.)
- *Experienced-based* (In moving toward the new, students need to activate what they already know from experience which relates to the current challenge.)
- *Conceptually Demanding* (Because language development goes hand in hand with cognitive development, language learning is enhanced by conceptually challenging the learners.)
- *Unbounded* (Language is learned powerfully outside "language arts" lessons and outside schools; good programs will seek to extend the boundaries of the classroom and to open it to community influences.)
- *Cumulative* (Language resources are personal resources which grow organically in interaction with others; language is a growing reservoir, not a set of building blocks.)
- *Text Conscious* (Language learning involves the capacity to pay close attention to texts [oral and written] and relate those texts to the context.)

About Teaching

The following general strategies will help the machine generate more specific strategies with respect to aspects of the language development program.

- *Imagining* (Getting learners to imagine what it will be like when they can do it.)
- *Demonstrating* (Arranging for demonstration of what is to be learned, ideally commissioned by the learner.)
- *Theory building* (Encouraging learners to induce patterns, rules, and principles and to act upon them to test them out.)

- *Transforming and Translating* (Requiring learners to transform or translate what they have expressed in one medium (e.g. painting) into another medium (e.g. writing) as a means of intensifying knowledge and diversifying skills.)
- *Analogizing* (Using analogies, metaphors, anecdotes, and illustrative examples to help learners make connections, and encouraging learners similarly to use these devices to consolidate understanding.)
- *Predicting* (Encouraging children to guess and hypothesize about possible outcomes, including prediction about the curriculum itself: "Where is the journey heading and what will we find?")
- *Telling and Withholding* (Judging when to give information directly and when to withhold to ensure maximum independent thinking from the learners.)
- *Questioning* (Basing teaching on the belief that learners learn most when they are asking questions, thereby keeping one's own questioning to genuine inquiries and providing problematic situations which will lead learners to questions.)
- *Testing* (Basing teaching on the belief that learners will learn most if they set their tests according to criteria they have identified, or at least if they are involved in the setting of tests.)
- *Negotiating* (Basing teaching on the belief that learners will learn more if they know in detail what the teacher intends, have helped in the construction of the curriculum, and have been able to contribute some of their own preferences.)
- *Collaborating* (Acting on the knowledge that learners together can usually achieve more than an individual and that in the act of working together the less able learn [from the more able].)
- *Teaching* (Allowing as many opportunities as possible for learners to teach others who do not know, as a means of stretching and consolidating their own understanding.)
- *Reflecting* (Ensuring that learners collectively and individually have the opportunity to value the quality and effectiveness of what has been done and learned—including the processes used to get there as well as the product.)
- *Formulating* (Allowing learners to use media—e.g. talk—exploratively and expressively to shape and investigate new ideas, concepts, and theories.)

At this point, I would try to put into the machine all I know about various general approaches to the teaching of language development (e.g. language experience, direct instruction, thematic teaching, skills-based approaches, etc.) including information about strengths and weaknesses. I would also take specific segments of Language Arts and English courses (e.g. spelling, conventions, reading, writing, speaking, listening) and supply listings of specific strategies (gleaned from my own practice, listening to described practice, and reading books on practice) which relate to these segments and are consistent with all the principles and beliefs I espouse. In addition, I would need to supply the machine with a workable set of "maps" (some grammars) on language development. (If I could gain permission I would "ride" on the work of Moffett, Britton and Halliday in this regard.) Add to this a range of general knowledge about sexism, cross-cultural concerns, self-concept, powerless groups, institutions, and practical aspects of organization and management.

Imagine, now, that I have painstakingly embedded, weighted, and wired up all the significant connections between the data and instructed the machine how to generate inferences and leads from information provided by users. We are about to test a hypothetical attempt to build an inference machine on language development which might be universally useful.

Case Study 1

A teacher feeds in the following initial information appropriately coded:

Age: 41
Female
Middle class
University trained
Teaching in a working class area (Australia)
Year 6 class (11 year olds)
Political orientation: liberal / democrat
Basic educational orientation: humanist, progressive, child-centered
Basic Language Arts orientation: language experience approach, activity
    methods, crossing subject boundaries, anti-exercise and drill work.
Present problem: Poor performance in spelling achievement. Dissatisfaction
    with spelling program.

(The machine asks for further specific information.)

Symptoms:
- Little improvement over 6 months
- Carelessness
- Spelling as it sounds
- Previous history of poor spelling (taught under sequenced word book scheme)
- Low self-concepts (students)
- Parental displeasure
- Complaints from colleagues

Method(s) being used:
    No sequenced spelling program.
    All spelling taught through writing which students do followed by editing.
Contextual information
    25 in class
    School requires testing in spelling by grade.
    Conservative school philosophy.

She requests: "Please indicate possible leads for investigation."
This is the reply:

Spelling, language experience approach, working class students, conservative school structure, "liberal" teachers.

Possible causes:

1. insufficient exposure to words, thinking about words, experimenting with words, inducing rules and patterns
2. lack of student confidence in having a go
3. lack of teacher demonstration and illustration
4. teacher inexplicitness about what is expected
5. habituation of poor strategies learned previously
6. lack of intention to spell correctly for a specific purpose
7. tasks not "owned" by learners
8. inadequate student spelling, evaluation, and reflection procedures
9. inadequate one-to-one tutoring
10. inadequate general reading
11. lack of cohesion, co-operation, and mutual support in the class

Choose one for investigation or indicate need for further leads.

Teacher chooses number 1 and asks how this inference was made.

Reply:

Principle 3:   We learn by building theories about what we are exposed to.
"Language experience":   strong on exposure, but often weak on theorizing and structured investigation.
Activity is necessary but not sufficient.
Do you wish to know more?

Teacher responds "Yes," asks the computer to print out some recommended reading, and also seeks guidance on possible specific strategies.

Reply:

Spelling program: Theory Building (Principle 3)
Strategy I
Spend time each week with learners looking at unusual words. Students guess spelling. Guesses compared. Teacher leads discussion about which may be correct. Correct spelling noted. Similar words discussed.
Strategy II
Learners collect random words for group investigation and discussion with teacher. Notes written on each word. Word knowledge books compiled.

Teacher asks machine to indicate "toxic side effects."

Reply:

Possible toxic side effects—theory building, spelling, specific strategies, working class learners, "liberal" teacher.

- learners not interested: boredom, disenchantment
- teacher may not believe in method: hypocrisy, perfunctoriness
- spelling given exaggerated attention: atrophy of composition skills

- words out of context: alienation from meaning
- guessing considered wrong by school and parents: conflict of values
- teacher overly technical: student mystification, and rejection

The teacher, satisfied with this investigation, has the machine return to the initial leads and asks how inference number 11 was made (lack of cohesion, co-operation, and mutual support in class).

Reply:

Principle 2:   We learn by interacting with others who are also doing what we are learning.

Belief: Language is learned best in a co-operating, mutually supportive community. Language experience/low self concept/working class/liberal teacher/conservative school.

- may be discipline problems
- children may reject middle class regime/values
- low self-concept learners may put each other down
- liberal philosophy may emphasize private enterprise rather than social sharing and support
- individual programs may isolate and dilute student experience
- students may be confused by ideological contradictions in school

Do you wish to know more?

Teacher replies "Yes" and seeks elaboration of the final point, "Students may be confused by ideological contradictions in school."

Reply:

Ideological Contradictions in School
Mismatch between teacher beliefs, beliefs of authorities, beliefs of system, beliefs of students. Some likely effects:

- teacher tension
- imposition of sanctions visible and invisible
- different student responses: rejection
                              confusion
                              disruptive behavior
- energies spent on maintenance of stance rather than on learning

Possible solutions

- capitulate to authorities
- compromise with authorities
- negotiate with authorities
- negotiate with students
- convert students
- question and modify own ideology

Note: There will always be ideological contradictions in schools.

The teacher proceeds in this way until she is satisfied that she has enough information to support her problem solving. She prepares a modified spelling program, feeds this information to the machine and asks for inferences about potential strengths and weaknesses of the program. She then goes ahead to try out her plan with a few more modifications.

Case Study 2

Teacher information:

Age: 25
Male
Middle class (working class background)
University trained
Special training in Aboriginal education (Australia)
Teaching in Aboriginal reservation school
Class of 8, 9, 10 year olds
Political orientation: socialist
Basic educational orientation: humanist, belief in structured and sequenced program; strong motivator
Basic Language Arts orientation: E.S.L. approach based on controlled vocabulary. Basic structures first. Continued practice through simulation games. Audio visual approach.
Present problem: Lack of significant progress in reading and writing. Dissatisfied with reading and writing program.
Symptoms:
  • Little interest
  • Inattention
  • Lack of grasp of basic structures
  • Reading without understanding
  • Few signs of independent reading and writing
  • Use of oral patterns in writing

Methods being used:
  • Regular exercise with word knowledge text (sequenced exercises, drills)
  • Use of pictures and sound tapes to stimulate writing (talk before writing)
  • Use of basal readers designed for Aboriginal children (culturally relevant)
  • Reading stories to children
  • One-to-one tutoring of each child
  • Attempt to involve mothers in school as co-learners
  • Careful correction of all work

Contextual information:
  • 10 in class
  • 1 other teacher in school
  • 250 km from nearest town
  • no parents read and write

- mixture of Aboriginal language as first language and pidgin English as first language
- all homes use pidgin English regularly
- parents support the teaching of English

(The machine asks for further information: "Features of oral program?")

Oral program:

Regular practice of sequenced phrases, patterns, structures

Use of language games

Attempt to overcome shyness through puppet work

(The machine asks for still further information about the learners.)

The Learners:

Very shy and passive

Inattentive

Irregular attendance

Interested in art and craft only

Tend to guess rather than think

Uncomfortable in school

Do not enjoy reading and writing

Teacher requests: "Please indicate possible leads for investigation."

Reply:

Reading and writing, structured approach, Aboriginal students, Aboriginal language/pidgin English, low interest, student discomfort, committed teacher.

Possible causes:

List 1:

1. insufficient time spent *imagining* the pleasurable effects of reading and writing (lack of student *intention*)
2. insufficient use of reading and writing for a purpose
3. lack of teacher demonstration and illustration
4. mismatch between learning style of learners and structured, "Westernized" teaching approach
5. teacher reliance on texts rather than common sense
6. possible mismatch between ideology in texts and teacher ideology
7. possible negative approach to error and interim grammars

Do you wish to see List 2 at this stage?

(Teacher replies "Yes.")

List 2:

8. lack of texts created locally, relating to the life of the community
9. lack of literacy behavior in homes
10. "strangeness" of meanings in prepared texts
11. reliance on motivational techniques, reinforcing passivity
12. lack of publication

13. lack of celebration and sharing
14. failure to make links with skills in art and craft
15. teaching reading and writing as special instructional periods separate from other activities

Choose one for investigation or indicate need for further leads.

The teacher studies the list for a long time and eventually asks for reasoning behind number 1: "Insufficient time spent *imagining* the pleasurable effects of reading and writing (lack of student intention)."

Reply:

Principles 1 and 2

1. We learn by being part of a community which is doing it.
2. We learn by seeing others in the community doing it with pleasure and effect.

Structured sequenced approach, exercises, games, prepared texts, lack of parent demonstration.
Strong on: instruction
           drill
Weak on: relevance to learners from a different culture
           rich demonstrations
           engaging purposes
           cultural reasons and expectations
Sequenced instruction may decrease student engagement and sense of responsibility.
Without a sense of the benefits of doing it, learners will tend to be passive.
Do you wish to know more?

Teacher responds "Yes" and asks the machine to suggest possible strategies.

Reply:

Increasing the power of imagining the pleasure and effect of reading and writing.

Strategies

1. Teacher continually demonstrates his/her own reading and writing with pleasure and effect.
2. Classroom/school becomes an intensified reading and writing community (signs, books, newspapers, publications . . .).
3. Parental education leads to involvement of parents in the program, as learners and encouragers.
4. Teacher chooses and reads relevant, engaging, pleasurable stories regularly.
5. Visitors are invited in to talk about reading and writing and how it works for them.
6. Children dictate stories and articles which are scribed, typed, read to the class, taken home, and displayed.

7. Those children who are enjoying reading and writing are encouraged to tell others about it.
8. The classroom involves lots of talking about reading and writing, who does it and how it works.

The teacher asks for a display of any warnings.

Reply:

Caution: *reading and writing, awakening, imagining.*

Beware:

- overkill
- teaching to copy the teacher's form rather than to emulate the process
- parental misunderstanding leading to confused advice to learners
- artificiality in finding *purposes* and *audiences* (leading to inauthenticity)
- teacher may not get pleasure (therefore teaching hypocrisy)
- moving too quickly from old regime to new

At this stage the teacher, having taken notes, seeks the reasoning behind lead 14, "Failure to make links with skills in art and craft."

Reply:

Observation Literacy involves making marks to represent meaning. It has its roots in drawing.
Belief Literacy programs should feature the preferred learning modes of the learners (cultural and individual) as bridges to new modes.
Assumption Art and craft are culturally significant modes for these learners.
Inference Beginning with drawing and illustrations and moving to accompanying text is likely to prove effective in preserving learner engagement.

The teacher proceeds to seek strategies related to lead 13, "Lack of celebration and sharing."

Reply:

Celebration and sharing:

Strategies:

1. Turn the written pieces into plays and hold a performance of work done
2. Display illustrated work and invite other children in
3. Make an illustrated book, with photographs of authors, for taking home *or* keeping in the school library
4. Read work done aloud to the whole class in a relaxed session
5. Record the writing on tape
6. Use video to make a film of a class story

Note: Celebration and reflection on work done is crucial to human learning.

The teacher is by this time hooked on the machine and proceeds to "read" it in fine detail, following up each lead, seeking connections, noting reading lists, and feeding in new possibilities to seek responses. Eventually, he begins to reconstrue aspects of his own teaching. In particular, he decides to abandon the sequenced readers, to use a "book flood" approach (lots of good stories even if culturally different) in conjunction with a "make our own readers" drive.

* * *

The object of this exercise has been to examine what a practical theory of education in language development might look like and how it might inform and shape teaching. Whether or not you reject the notion of an inference machine as unachievable or misguided, I would like you to remain speculative and open to the question of developing an all-embracing practical theory for teachers (in a new discipline called educology where teachers are the applied scientists in their own classrooms).

I have certainly confirmed one of my own predictions. The act of imagining how I would instruct an inference machine has forced me to unearth (or rather to begin to unearth) the enormously complex chains of knowledge—embedded-in knowledge—that I bring to bear on any specific instant of teaching. The exercise reinforces my belief that it is worth trying to pull together what we know about teaching and learning in order to discover any universals and in order to combat the rampant fragmentation of education which has allowed itself to be differentially colonized by other disciplines (psychology, philosophy, sociology, linguistics, science, etc.). I would be pleased if some of the principles and assumptions I have espoused in this paper stand the test of applicability across cultures and across time. On the other hand, as each is disconfirmed I shall celebrate new knowledge.

* * *

Bibliography

Boomer, Garth (1982), "The English Teacher, Research and Change (1966–1980)" in R. D. Eagleson, ed. *English in the Eighties.* Australian Association for the Teaching of English.

Education Department of South Australia, R–12 Drama Curriculum Committee (1981), *Images of Life.* Education Department of South Australia, Adelaide.

Hofstader, Douglas (1979), *Gödel, Escher, Bach: An Eternal Golden Braid.* Penguin, London.

Response

BEYOND THE MACHINE

JONATHAN COOK

I guess I could call myself an "educologist." I try to be an applied scientist, a practical-theorist, operating as a practitioner in my classroom, yet also always conceptualizing in and about it. I'm an English teacher. My "discipline" is literature and language development; my field is learning and teaching. I like to ask myself—and anyone else who'll listen—the why, what, how, when, for whom, and how well questions, and I thirst to become more consciously knowledgeable in my field, as well as in my discipline. After all, the relationship between the two is all-important.

My theory for the learning and teaching of language development and literature is pretty much the same as Garth Boomer's, and I delight in it. I welcome the chance to explain why I do. The theory does several things for me which I couldn't do when I started teaching in the mid-60s. It enables me to *explain* what I'm doing and why I'm doing it; it *generates* ideas and issues and in turn helps me *resolve* them; and it enables me to become increasingly *rigorous* and scientific in my classroom—without losing the freedoms beloved of literature teachers, or my own personal style, and without forcing me into unblinking, learning-inhibiting, lock-step prescription and mindless recipes. The theory *empowers* me as a rational, informed *decision-maker* in my classroom, as I tackle the complex curriculum task of helping my students grow in understanding and in learning power: which is what literacy and language development are really to do with. And there's one more thing: the theory generates theorizing just as it generates informed practice, and the emerging theory is essentially generated *from* the practice.

Having said that, I'd now like to respond to this machine that "knows" Garth Boomer's "mind-scapes"; and, because the machine's program is so complex and all-embracing and so deeply process-oriented, I'll ask it to reveal the essence of its theory (x-ray the theory, and uncover the bones and structure). Finally, I'll admit my present set of practitioner-problems to the machine. While it considers them (because I don't think it can fully resolve them), I'll be in my educological field, trying to work them out for myself, and with the help of my fellow educologists! Who knows—in five years time, we may have a whole new program to feed into the machine. And that, of course, is precisely what Garth Boomer wants. It's how the theory lives and grows.

Machine, you're strong stuff! You remind me that it's not just microtechnology that has advanced so much in the last twenty years; it's also the *human* understandings which inform you. Machine, we couldn't have made you in 1964; in 1984 we probably can. But then again we couldn't have programmed you in 1964 with the remarkable developments in the science of learning and teaching we've made since then. So you've come a long way, and so have we. (I just thought I'd remind you, in 1984, that you still need us, as well as vice-versa!)

My question:	Before I can ask you specific questions about my specific problem and context, I need to know what *your* context is. What is "it" that I'll be selecting from for me? What are you?
The machine's answer:	(In effect, the title of the program) A universal set of principles and rules;
for:	teachers of language development and literacy:
who are:	both liberated and constrained by sets and networks of containing and influencing forces;
as they go through:	a curriculum and composing process;
which incorporates:	the elements of curriculum;
applies:	principles and conditions for learning;
embraces:	beliefs and assumptions about education and language learning and teaching;
and is illustrated in:	general strategies related to principles and practices of good teaching;
the combination of all of which is:	an all-embracing practical theory for teachers as applied scientists in their own classrooms.

I accept this, so now I pose a

PROBLEM FOR THE MACHINE

1. *Information*

   a. My context is that of a secondary school classroom English teacher. But my reality is not that of a lesson, or even a unit of work. It is a semester or year-long *course*. The same 30 children in the same classroom for perhaps 100 periods occurring daily over a semester, or even 7500 minutes in daily periods over a year.

   b. My "cosmic egg" operates; I know it; and I acknowledge all the areas of the practical theory you embody. Yet, in my classroom, it all comes down, day after day, to decisions about the curriculum elements: There's a set of them, and in every lesson they must interrelate. I call them *curriculum intertextualities*. They generate and react together and have a cause and effect interrelationship:
   - the stage of learning (or phase in the learning process)
   - the learning and teaching purposes
   - the activities
   - the content
   - the thinking processes
   - the language processes and skills
   - the classroom structures and organization patterns (individuals, small groups, whole class).

   Each impacts on all the others. Change a decision about one (for example, small groups instead of whole class; full draft and edit writing instead of once-off pieces; write to learn instead of write to be tested; kids' talk instead of teacher talk; read, talk, write, talk, write instead of listen then write), and the incremental growth in language development changes; different mixes of elements produce different outcomes.

c. I've got to *sequence* all this, day by day. Every lesson has antecedents and consequences. Something must *unify* the course and its separate lessons and units. Something must guarantee that the course grows and develops. It mustn't be an arbitrary collection; it must purposefully and defensibly *go* somewhere. And the growth and direction must be process and method conscious, not just content or syllabus determined.

d. I'm told that you can offer principles, general processes, and the outline of strategies, but that you cannot contribute greatly to the specifics of organization and delivery. Some teachers say that we all teach differently, in individual ways. This sits uneasily with me. Teaching *style* may be idiosyncratic, but surely teaching methodology and process is—or needs to be—more consistent. I'm only aware of about two or three broad categories of teaching method. Your program embodies one of them. Now, when I think that at present 1000 teachers might be coming up with 1000 different mixes of classroom curriculum elements, all in the teaching of language development and literacy, I become very uneasy indeed. They can't be all equally good. This is more than a matter of specifics or organization and delivery. This is the teaching and learning program itself—the enactment of the whole deal. I really feel the need to be more scientific and rigorous about it. *Not* lock-step rules and immutable patterns, please; but surely there is something more consistent, valid, and reliable to help practitioners make their daily teaching and learning decisions than the ad hocery of "I do it my way."

2. *My Questions*
   Therefore, I seek from you any contribution you can make towards:

   a. A practical theory of explicit *curriculum intertextualities*—to help me make my decisions about each curriculum element and the interrelationships between all of them, in each lesson, unit, and course that I teach.

   b. A practical theory of *sequence and consequence* for a language development and literacy course—to help me decide why I should use *this* set of curriculum decisions *now,* and *where from* and *where to.*

   c. A practical theory of *structural principles* upon which a curriculum or course in language development, literacy, and literature may be educologically developed and unified.

As far as I am aware, the inference machine cannot yet be programmed with rigorously developed answers to my problems. As Garth Boomer suggests, theorists must contribute to the resolution of practitioners' problems, and so must practitioners as applied scientists. And as I remarked earlier, I'll be out there giving it a go in that capacity.

XIII

The English teacher enters computerland, not as a Luddite but with due caution.

The computing center within the Education Department of South Australia is holding a summer school on Computers in Education (1982). They require a range of speakers to give participants different perspectives on the topic.

With nine months warning, the English teacher accepts the invitation to "have a go" and begins some intensive reading and thinking in the field. For instance, he gets to understand about half of Douglas K. Hofstader's book *Gödel, Escher, Bach: An Eternal Golden Braid,* where mathematics, music, and art are woven together with artificial intelligence and computing, helped by Lewis Carroll and Zen Buddhism. This reminds him of Pirsig's classic *Zen and the Art of Motorcycle Maintenance,* which among many other things is about people and machines. He had read it in the late seventies and later made connections between it and James Moffett's insights into meditation as a key element in writing. (*Coming on Center,* Boynton/Cook, 1981).

In addition to his reading, the English teacher, somewhat like the Ancient Mariner, begins to stop one in three subject consultants (whether in music, mathematics, or English) forcing the conversation around to the topic of computing. He also attends a "hands on" computer awareness course and experiences that first fine rapture of fingers on keyboards.

Then, as he writes his speech, he tries to connect all his new thinking with what he already knows. What emerges is a view of computing seen through the filters of a learning theory which began to take shape over ten years ago when he studied the amazing real intelligence of his own son. (See Chapter I.)

Zen and the
Art of Computing

It's all tied up with how we view and use machines. Machines have been blamed. Yet it is in our power to use machines for good or evil. Our machines will serve our values. The computer is an extension, an amplification of the mind and as such is an instrument for bringing into effect the potential of personkind. It is an analog of aspects of the human brain, but it has no mind. (It is a *selective mirror* of human thought processes.) Aspects of mind can be mapped onto computers. Thus, computers allow us, within limits, to look inside our own and other people's heads. Furthermore, they allow us to stand on the shoulders of other people's intelligence. They increase our scope, our vision, and our field of influence.

As an English teacher I wish to draw some parallels between writing and computers.

- Writing allows us to externalize our thought.
- Writing allows us to manipulate and detect inadequacies in our externalized thoughts.
- Through acting reflexively upon our writing we can reformulate and thereby rearrange, retheorize our internal thought processes. (In other words we can interact with our own writing.)
- Through writing we gain access to the externalized minds of others so that we can *converse* with their thoughts and ideas.
- Through writing we can order and sift chaotic thought.
- Writing allows us to record and therefore to retrieve information and thinking.
- Writing is capable of creating an illusion or a replica of anything which humans have ever done or are likely to do, so long as that experience is *available to the consciousness* of the writer. "Whereof we do not know; thereof we cannot write."

- On the other hand, writing is often a kind of dredge on the unconscious. Or, to change the metaphor, a probing searchlight into the darker corners of our head so that sometimes through writing we discover what we think and feel for the first time.

All these things, I suggest writing has in common with the art of computing.

Let's go further.

- Writing is a machine in the sense that it is a rule-governed system for conveying meanings encoded in orthographic symbols. It is an extension of the oral language capacities of humans, which is in turn an extension of their brains.
- Writing generates power for the user. It allows the user to act upon the world and on other people to get things done, to persuade and to control (through law, etc.).
- Writing is used as a weapon of subjugation and oppression as well as for liberating, empowering, and informing.
- Writing can convey indiscriminately whatever meanings and values drive the pen or the typewriter.
- Writing as a form can be used sloppily or precisely, with care for its rules or without.
- "Programming" a piece of writing can be done both before the writing and also progressively during the writing. (We can wind back writing, replay it, edit it, and even reconstrue it.)

I suggest that all the abuses which writing has suffered and caused will be suffered and caused by computers. Human beings will do with this machine what they have done with machines in the past.

The people who made the first automobiles obviously loved them. They "loved" their machines. Every nut, every metal pin, every working part was in effect a part of their souls and minds. They indwelt in that which they had made. So it is, generally, with anything we have invented or cultivated as our own. Witness the affection and affiliation of home gardeners for their vegetables and flowers. Witness the satisfaction and oneness with the creation of someone who has made a piece of furniture for the first time.

The rot sets in with reproduction, when the machines and creations are replicated and given to the world and are taken up by people who own them but have not made them their own, if you see the difference. What was an almost organic extension of the creator in a paradise of creation becomes a mere tool in the hands of potential Cains. What is more, the tools need to be maintained. And so, a race of maintainers is spawned, machanics generally as alienated from the machine as the owners except they have learned to follow the cold instructions of manuals prepared by the manufacturers (*not* usually by the *maker*). It is a rare mechanic who is more than a wrench twiddler. It is a rare mechanic who cares and lovingly indwells in the machine.

Between the mass-producing manufacturers and the wrench-twiddling mechanics and the alienated owners, what is beautiful is botched. Those who have botched the greatest machine of all, the earth itself amd life upon it, often seek out the indwellers when they become conscious of their botching. Perhaps the most potent indwellers on earth are the Zen masters (and mistresses!?) who seek to dissolve eventually all distinctions between self and other than self. They seek to read the world which includes themselves.

Robert Pirsig in a brilliant book which I have plagiarized in my title writes of *Zen and the Art of Motorcycle Maintenance*. In lovingly caring for his own motor bike he comes to question the whole of Western society with its separation of material things and spiritual things. Having just brilliantly discovered a sheared pin in his machine, by dint of thinking himself inside the bike, he reflects on the whole business of mechanics and manuals.

> While at work I was thinking about this same lack of care in the digital computer manuals I was editing. Writing and editing technical manuals is what I do for a living the other eleven months of the year and I knew they were full of errors, ambiguities, omissions and information so completely screwed up you had to read them six times to make any sense out of them. But what struck me for the first time was the agreement of those manuals with the spectator attitude I had seen in the shop. These were spectator manuals. It was built into the format of them. Implicit in every line is the idea that "Here is the machine, isolated in time and in space from everything else in the universe. It has no relationship to you, you have no relationship to it, other than to turn certain switches, maintain voltage levels, check for error conditions . . ." and so on. That's it. The mechanics in their attitude toward the machine were really taking no different attitude from the manual's towards the machine, or from the attitude I had when I brought it in there. We were all spectators. And it occurred to me there *is* no manual that deals with the *real* business of motorcycle maintenance, the most important aspect of all. Caring about what you are doing is considered either unimportant or taken for granted.
>
> On this trip I think we should notice it, explore it, a little, to see if in that strange separation of what man is from what man does we may have some clues as to what the hell has gone wrong in this twentieth century. I don't want to hurry it. That iself is a poisonous twentieth-century attitude. When you want to hurry something, that means you no longer care about it and want to get on to other things. I just want to get at it slowly, but carefully and thoroughly, with the same attitude I remember was present just before I found that sheared pin. It was the attitude that found it, nothing else.
>
> (PIRSIG, 1974)

I want to take up the ideas explicit and implicit in Pirsig's book and make some observations about the challenge facing educators when it comes to our handling of this latest brilliant machine in our schools and in the homes of our students. In particular I want to allude to the dangers of mere spectatorship and disengaged usership. The computer is not a machine isolated in time and space from everything else in the universe. It does have a relationship with all of us historically and in terms of how it is already interpenetrating in our daily acts of living.

Spectators, at least most of them, are "magicked." They gasp at wonders and feats of genius and are awed. They live vicariously through seeing the power of others, but when they leave their spectatorship, they are left with their relatively impoverished selves. They distinguish between the ordinary and the extraordinary and in so doing construe themselves as lacking power. Spectators not only become bodily flabby, their minds also atrophy.

Computers are the new magic of civilization. In one sense they will soon be common. In another sense they will be *unknown* and as inaccessible as writing once was, as television still is, by and large, and as silicon chipperys are coming to be. To the extent that most human beings remain spectators or alienated users (i.e. not indwelling and comprehending), to that extent will be humankind's capitulation to the few who possess the machines and the knowledge that feeds them. We will thus be possessed rather than possessing, owned rather than owning, acted upon rather than acting.

It is not mere chance that far more time and money in language learning in schools is spent on the *receptive* mode as opposed to the *productive* mode, on reading as opposed to writing. It is not mere chance that computers in homes and schools are in general making their advance as receptacles rather than as tools for acting on the world. Software programs abound. Programs invented by users are relatively rare. Thus we are programmed rather than programming; powered rather than empowered.

The computer revolution is impacting on schools which still in many ways have not caught up with the Gutenberg revolution. We still spectate on writing rather than write. How much more likely is it, then, that we will be taken by force or seduced by the computing machine? How likely is it, when writing is, I fear, taught largely by wrench twiddlers and armchair critics, that the new-wave art of computing will be taught in anything but a perfunctory disengaged manner, by mathematics teachers, as opposed to mathematicians? It will not, I suspect, even be taught as a science, let alone as an art. How many science teachers indwell in their science? How many history teachers indwell in history? How many teachers live in and through what they present?

You must by now have detected a certain pessimism about the future of computing in our schools. My rising despair is not about computers but about the nature of schools. They are, viewed objectively, machines which program children and reach solutions in binary terms of pass and fail, yes and no, advance and retire. They serve society well in this regard, reproducing existing structures and relationships. But they serve the evolution of the species poorly, if, as I contend, each citizen must be developed to use *nous,* if we are to survive into the 21st century. Before one can deal with computer education constructively, one must deal with the "machine," the institution, within which computing will be taught. The art of educating must come of age before the art of computing has a chance.

Schools, like computers, serve the values of those people who program them. In the book, *Negotiating the Curriculum* (Ashton Scholastic, ed. G.

Boomer, 1982), it is argued that students must be brought over to the teacher side of the student/teacher fence, to begin observing the art of schooling from the point of view of the programmers and furthermore to *begin programming* themselves. Teachers should deliberately reveal the secrets of making and shaping a curriculum and invite the students to become coplanners with them. In this way, students might come to indwell in their own schooling, to see the curriculum as an arbitrary construction, and to realize that alternative constructions are always possible. They would learn new perspectives on truth, defending themselves against publicly avowed Truths with the power of their own personal constructions and scepticisms. Paradoxically, by *indwelling* in a machine one is healthily alienated from it, in the sense of knowing its limitations. *By becoming it,* we control it. We lose our reverence and our fear.

In a school where children are not "magicked" out of reverence and fear, where the mechanisms of the schooling machine are owned and applied by students and teachers together, the advent of the computer will amplify the emancipation of each student and teacher and extend the capacity of everyone in the school to act upon the world. Conversely, in a school where the secrets of the schooling machine remain secret, the secrets of the computer will remain largely secret and the student clients will go out into the world programmed merely to receive and destined to be done in.

Computers, like writing, should not be considered separately from the purposes and values being served. I need therefore to look closely at the avowed and enacted values and purposes of schools. A good school, in my view, is one which has these features at least:

- It will believe that gaining knowledge means coming to know *personally*; it involves coming to understand information personally so that one can act as a result of that understanding.
- It will demonstrate by its teaching that one comes to understand through manipulating ideas using different media and tools in a variety of contexts for purposes where consequences can be assessed.
- It will demonstrate that individual power to act requires the learner to *produce* (to *make* and *do*) in addition to *consume* (to *receive* and *spectate*).
- It will believe in going deep into (indwelling in) the subject matter, the machines and the procedures which are part of the curriculum (as opposed to constant practice and exercise at a relatively superficial level).
- It will believe that education is a continuing process whereby learners come to penetrate further and further the various forms and contents of public discourse while at the same time nurturing their own private "knowing."
- It will believe, and demonstrate, that reflection is crucial to knowing.

Now, clearly, computers can be used to serve and enrich such a school and its students. They can, likewise, serve a school which believes that knowledge is objective fact which can be transmitted, that recitation rather than action will pass as knowledge, that most learners are incapable of understanding and that schools are places of basic training rather than of creative thinking and speculation.

Having stated some of my beliefs about the ideal conditions of schooling, I am in a position to consider what computers might offer. As with language, of which computers are a special sub-set, one can conceive of these aspects of computing in schools:

1. learning computing
2. learning through computing
3. learning about computing

I should make clear that I use "computing" in the broadest sense to include the whole range of operations now undertaken by computing machines—word processing, music making, graphic processing, inferencing and diagnosing capacities, etc.

Pursuing parallels with language learning I would make the following assumptions:

1. One learns to compute by computing for a purpose in a context where the consequences of one's actions are available for evaluation.
2. One learns to compute by acting and interacting with others who are computing, especially with more mature and sophisticated computing people.
3. One learns to compute by progressively inventing for oneself a more and more sophisticated "grammar" of computing (i.e. by progressively theorizing and retheorizing what one does).
4. Computing can be used tentatively and exploratively to try out ideas and notions during the process of formulating new products, operations or concepts (i.e. it joins art, video, language [oral and written], diagrams, model making, enactment, etc., as a medium with a *mathetic* or heuristic function).
5. One learns about computers by being able to observe the functions of computers and by having the opportunity to reflect and to develop a meta-commentary on what happens.

These assumptions would be a part of any school policy on computing if I had my way. The school program would then reflect the policy.

There are some immediate implications for teachers. All of us have to become what we would profess to teach with regard to computers, since it is obvious that, like language itself, computing will need to be used across the curriculum as it becomes established in society as a common medium. If we do not ourselves learn computing, we will teach alienation from the medium and powerlessness with respect to it. Let's not panic (myself firmly included). Stories are coming in from the schools about wide-scale post-figurative learning by teachers. (Margaret Mead spoke of three kinds of society—pre-figurative, co-figurative and post-figurative. In a pre-figurative society, the elders hand wisdom down to the young. In the co-figurative society, young and old pioneer together in the new learning. In the post-figurative society, the young teach the elders about the new technologies—e.g. New Guinea where the young educate their parents about transistor radios.)

At least in our schools we are, most of us, likely to find ourselves in a co-figurative learning culture which I find exciting to contemplate. The new language with its new operations will spread much as a second language might be learned. The more people around us practicing the language for real purposes, the more quickly will we acquire it. And it seems that the young, not so rigidly cemented into their constructs, may pick up the language more quickly than some of us. So be it. I shall not become paranoid about my relatively rusty head. My task, knowing what I know about knowing, will be to ensure that the *processes* and *purposes* being used by the young to learn the language are driven by emancipatory values and that the work they do is done with CARE (indwelling, reflection, and oneness with the machine). My task will also be to instigate continual *rebellion* against the language when it is in danger of becoming clichéd, moribund, or propagandist. Just as I have in the past urged the young to be critical of what they hear and read, so must I urge them to activate their crap detectors with respect to the language of computing.

Let me expand. To simplify, there are two kinds of novel, one which allows the reader to *escape* from reality and one which explores and illuminates reality through the fictive mode. One leaves us either slightly drugged against the world or at least unchanged, the other helps us to make new constructions on our own world and therefore enables us more subtly to act upon it. So it is likely to be with computer programs. Simulations or protocols with little more transforming power than "space invaders" are no doubt already on the educational market. It is our task as educators to eschew such child-minding palliatives and to seek out truly challenging and transforming programs. Some programs, because of their immediacy (the cheap thrill, the cheap effect), may appeal to teachers tyrannized by a generation who want it Now. We must, I believe, use such drugs sparingly in favor of programs which leave the user reflecting or require the user to interact and to bring meaning to the task.

I keep returning to the themes of power and control, to the key questions:

- Does the learner control what is going on?
- Is the interaction helping the learner to establish *new powers*?

Ideally, I wish the learner to practice using the machine, the medium as an *art*, lovingly, constructively, humbly, and sceptically (the world today is always at war with the intractable word). I imagine that the process of getting a poem to say what you want is very similar to the process of getting a computer to generate in response to your instructions (at once an exhilarating and fulfilling experience). You cannot cheat in poetry writing; nor can you cheat, I think, faced with an implacable machine. You must either come to terms or admit present inadequacy. When a poem or a computer program works, there will be sympathetic vibrations between creator and machine.

But, I am probably dreaming too fast. The productive mode is always difficult in schools. Economically it means providing enough machines for students to use. Pedagogically it means having teachers who themselves know how to produce. Politically, it means handing over the means of production to the workers (a prelude to revolution?). For these reasons, and others, I doubt that we will see a great deal of *production* through computing in schools for a decade or so. The home will outstrip the school in this regard. (Especially the privileged homes where mother and father know about power.)

If I am right, then the least we can do is to make sure that learning with the assistance of computers is carried out by learners who are active, critical, and *in control.* So long as what we receive and use is under continued critical scrutiny, students will not become mesmerized by the values embedded in the programs.

In a fascinating education evaluation called Understanding Computer Assisted Learning conducted in the U.K. in 1977, Stephen Kemmis et al. identify four paradigms of C.A.L.

1. *The Instructional Paradigm* which presents content and motivates students through fast feedback where at best, the computer is seen as a patient tutor; at worst a page turner.
2. *The Revelatory Paradigm* which simulates information handling and gradually reveals information according to appropriate structures and sequences; where at best the computer is seen as creating a rich learning environment and at worst is a glib amplifier.
3. *The Conjectural Paradigm* where the computer is a manipulable space or field or "scratch pad" or language for creating or articulating models, programs, plans, or conceptual structures; where at best the computer is seen as a tool or education medium and at worst an expendable toy.
4. *The Emancipatory Paradigm* where the learner is construed as a laborer who can be helped by having access to a computer as a labor-saving device and where the computer is deliberately *commissioned* to operate in any of the other three modes in order to emancipate the learner from the constraints and blocks of time and materials, or bring about increased efficiency for the learner.

Clearly, we would all like to see the "at best" aspects of the first three paradigms operating in schools. And clearly, from what I have already said, I support Kemmis et al. in their dream of the emancipatory paradigm devoted to power and control for the learner.

Ideally, in some future classroom I can conceive of each child having his or her own portable computer which is maintained, handled, and used as attentively as one cares for oneself because it is an extension of oneself. By playing with their computer from the earliest age, and by using it in multiple contexts (increasingly with less and less adult guidance), it will be as if they have "grown" it. It will, indeed, be their friendly computer. In an interacting community of computer users, the children will progressively learn more subtle language and employ their machines in ever more subtle services of their minds.

As an English teacher, I will use the word processor as an integral part of my teaching of composition. Each child will be required to learn how to operate a word processor. Through the word processor I will teach sentence structure, text construction, discourse analysis, and transformation of text to suit different purposes and audiences. I will use the graphics tablet to map out movements in drama, to graph plot intensity in novels, and to provide visual starting points for writing.

In seeking out appropriate software, I will, by and large, bypass instructional and revelatory programs, but I will introduce the best conjectural and inference programs I can find. I can see very useful interactions between learners and programs designed to explore meanings in particular texts. (I imagine a program similar to some of the diagnostic programs now used in medicine.)

On the productive side, I will help children towards more and more precise formulation of what they require in the English language and then help them to translate this into programmable computer language.

These are the embryonic, half-baked thoughts of a layman in computerland. I intend to learn quickly and to help my teaching colleagues to learn because, as you may have inferred, I see the new computer era as a battle for civilization itself.

History teaches that those in power will use the better technology for better domination. The owners of the machines will have access to all the stored up and projected power of humankind. If we, the potentially dominated and oppressed, do not penetrate, demystify, and dwell in this new form of public discourse, we will find ourselves powerless as it penetrates and absorbs our private consciousness.

We need access to great computer programs as we need access to great books, but as bonafide computers and writers in our own right. To enter into the new conversations of computing, we must become conversant with, and confidently articulate in, the medium. Let's hope that we do better with computers than we have done with writing.

* * *

Bibliography

Boomer, Garth (1982), *Negotiating the Curriculum,* Ashton Scholastic, Sydney.
Kemmis, Stephen with Atkin, Roderick and Wright, Eleanor (1977), *How Do Students Learn?* Working papers on computer assisted learning. UNCAL Evaluation Studies. OCC Publication No. 5. CARE, Norwich, U.K.
Pirsig, Robert (1974), *Zen and the Art of Motorcycle Maintenance,* Bodley Head, Great Britain.

Response

ZEN AND THE ART OF COMPUTING: A RESPONSE

CLAIRE A. WOODS

"It's all tied up with how we view and use machines." So Garth Boomer begins the paper "Zen and the Art of Computing," originally presented to a group of teachers at the tenth annual Summer School conducted by the Angle Park Computing Centre in South Australia.

He prompts, provokes, and prods his audience with a dancing barrage of words and a flurry of ideas which operate rather like the shock tactics of the Zen master, designed to jolt the lecture hall audience with insights into computing, curriculum learning, teaching, and technology. In short, he challenges us to view machines in education critically.

His underlying concern for valuing the learner's power in the midst of systems constraints, of the competing energies of new and old resources and in relation to the potential of any new technology, is clear. The "layman in computerland" as GB calls himself, urges his listeners to "enter into the new conversations of computing" with their focus on the learner and *not* on the machine.

This is a paper written for the listener and not the reader. The ideas are those of the orator and deserve to take wing. Captured on paper for the reader, some statements settle uneasily and demand closer consideration.

"It's all tied up with how we view and use machines."

I reread GB's paper. I review a word processing program for a computer. I read through stories written by primary school children at their computer terminals. I draft this with a pen and on a micro-computer. I, like GB, write and talk with other teachers about children, language, and writing. I am, like GB, fitting computers into my teaching repertoire. I write. I lament the lack of time for writing. I curse my typewriter and my miserable typing skills. I have graduated from pen to simple manual typewriter to electric typewriter to word processor. I now choose my weapon or tool whenever my thoughts seek an audience. I control the choice, the machine, the medium.

I choose. The writing process is still my own. I can "indwell" on that. The micro-computer amplifies the writing process for me and it makes the mechanics of it easier.

I watch young children learn to move between pencil, pen, and computer to write and solve problems. I see the computer extend their writing processes.

GB points his listeners to some parallels between the writing process and variously computers and the art of computing. There is a need for caution about such neat comparisons. Writing is a means, a symbol system for communicating and thinking. Computers are tools for manipulating that symbol system. Computers and writing are of two different orders.

Computers may well do the things GB claims for them; for example, computers allow us to record and retrieve information. However, a simple substitution of the words *computer* or *the art of computing* for the word *writing*, as he suggests, is less than helpful or accurate. It denies the distinction between mode, process, *and* the tool. Yet at the same time he hints at the dynamic interplay between them. Thus, we might note the similar function writing and computers might serve for the individual.

We need to recognize, however, that the computer is a tool, a machine, and that we use language via the tool to do the things GB ascribes to the writing process. Unless teachers have a sense of the writing process and indeed of the individual child's relationship to his or her own learning, thinking, and meaning-making processes, then the tool will remain merely a tool, a machine, an object which can control the learner and keep learner and learning at an impersonal distance.

When the teacher adds another tool to her teaching repertoire, she must adjust her methods to take advantage of the potential offered by that new cultural resource. Taking on board a new tool or resource whether it be book, film, video, graphics, tablet, or micro-computer, ought to force us as teachers to reconsider anew our philosophies of learning and of educational practice and our understanding of what thinking and learning is. It may force us to remake our learning theories.

GB notes how readily we can take on board a new machine and just as easily how, because we do not "make them our own," the rot sets in. To prevent this happening we don't need to indwell in the micro-computer, but we do need to understand how it can extend thinking and learning. We need to understand anew that learning is a linguistic and cultural process: a process in which individuals interact with and act upon an outside world using symbol systems (language and gesture) and tools. Between the cultural context and the learner there is an interplay that is instrumental to cognitive, social, and personal growth. It is a *dialectical* process in which whatever tools are available to the individual have a potentially significant effect. We know well how young children take hold of anything new in their surroundings and attempt to manipulate it and turn it into an object for doing something, acting in the world. Enter the teacher!

The teacher is a culture-broker: a trader in tools, resources, and environments for learning. So, her role is vital when a new machine enters and begins to remake the social and cultural contexts for learning.

GB is acutely aware of this. He urges teachers away from "mere spectatorship and disengaged usership." And it is easy to be a spectator when confronted with the "new machine." Yet my experiences working in a school where teachers and children are using computers for writing as part of their Language Arts program is that it is also possible to be a participant, or owner of a learning process. Indeed, it is easy to be a sharer in a learning partnership, where teachers and children are both engaged in creating new and complementary environments for learning writing and reading in which computers have a role.

GB writes "Where the mechanisms of the schooling machine are owned and applied by students and teachers together, the advent of the computer will amplify the emancipation of each student . . ." I see that happening. I see the writing process extended for children when word processing/editing is integrated into their Language Arts programs. I see children writing both with pens and computers. I see them gaining confidence in themselves as writers. I see them revising their ideas, detecting errors, sharing their stories with others. They accept the computer as another tool, and the computer room as another writing environment: one complementary to their classroom.

GB points to parallels between language learning and learning computing. Of course he is right in this. But he is right only when schools see the computer as a tool for language and thinking and not as an administrator of pattern.

Donald Graves has suggested "Let children show us how to teach them to write." One could rewrite that to include the word computing. Some of the children I observe know more about computing than I or their teachers do. The pre-figurative society is to a certain extent with us if we can take the risk and become teacher-learners. I sit near children as they write at the computer and what matters is not the machine but the writing and thinking processes of Lisa, Ben, Simon, or Talia.

They own their writing. They own their stories. Many feel a new pride in their work. It looks good. They can revise it easily. They can share with others. Their hands are on the keys. They and not their teacher make changes. The choice to delete or save is theirs. They write a story on the computer and continue it in their classroom and vice versa.

Children have no difficulty in adding a new tool to their learning and living repertoire. When they work to write a program or use the word processor, they construct with their language. They think. They play. They solve problems. The children direct their learning and they teach themselves.

We have no word in English for the notion of a close dialectical relationship between teaching-learning, or learning-teaching. This is what happens when children can "own" the tools and processes and skills with which to extend their understanding of the world in which they live. It is what happens when children and adults are able to create opportunities for independent and collaborative learning.

GB, in citing the four paradigms working "at best" suggested by Kemmis et al. looks ahead to such ownership. It is possible when teachers are prepared to rethink their teaching and learning to the degree necessary to view the computers as a potentially dynamic tool and *not* a panacea. It is possible when they add computers to their repertoire in such a way that they emancipate and don't chain teaching or learning. It is indeed all tied up with how we view and use machines.

GB is right. We do need to "enter into the new conversations of computing" by being conversant with the medium. More important, however, we have to reopen our conversations about learning and teaching.

XIV

While chronologically this chapter pre-dates Chapters XII and XIII, it is the most appropriate as a close to the story-so-far about the growth of a teacher. It represents a kind of mid-career swansong for the English teacher who has changed into a generalist in-service educator.

The International Reading Association Convention in Chicago in 1982 featured a strand on "literacy worldwide." The brief of the Australian English teacher, kindly invited to take part, was to report on the "state of the art" in Australia.

Now this may not seem surprising, but it is. Because of their isolation and their historical starting points as a colony of the Motherland (and no doubt for other reasons, too) Australians tend to be awkwardly unsure of their own voices on the international scene. The cultural cringe to England lingers, symbolized in our literature courses by the predominance of English as opposed to Australian literature.

Australian English teachers' conferences with one or two exceptions have featured, almost as if it were mandatory, the visiting guru from either the U.S.A. or England. Invitations in return are very rare indeed. So, here was a glorious chance to blow the Australian trumpet. Here was a chance to celebrate the considerable achievement of Australia Felix, the lucky country. Perhaps the prospects of a closer international network of actors and sharers might be enhanced if our overseas colleagues listened to our voice and admitted that we exist.

The Wisdom of the Antipodes

What's Working for Literacy in Australia

The Australian Context

Australia is a continent the size of the forty-eight contiguous states of the U.S.A. It is populated by 15,000,000 people representing a very wide spectrum of cultures and living predominantly in six state capital cities dotted around the extensive coastline. It comprises six states and two territories, each state and territory with its own government under a federal government super-structure. Education is funded partly federally and partly by the states. State education systems are centralized, and schools within each system work to centrally prepared curriculum guidelines with varying degrees of freedom to adapt, modify, or reject such guidelines. Alongside the state system, there is a Catholic Education system, partly centralized, and a private system where there is loose affiliation between some schools but basic independence from outside prescription or guidelines.

The dominant culture is white European with a strong Anglo center. The parliamentary system is British in origin. There is a very slowly growing multi-cultural perspective on life and society and a possibly slower realization that our small aboriginal population should be given back some of its land and all of its rights.

Australians, by and large, enjoy a very high standard of living, but there are substantial pockets of poverty and disadvantage. Measured literacy compares favorably with similar measures in other Western countries.

The state education system of South Australia in which I work has a teaching force of about 17,000 serving some 620 primary (or elementary) schools (grades 1 to 7) and 150 secondary or high schools (grades 8 to 12). These schools, until recently in our history, have followed central prescribed courses of instruction. Now they are required to take account of, but not necessarily to use, central guidelines. Schools have parent councils, but the power of such councils is rarely used to influence basic curriculum offerings or staffing.

Many of the myths, legends, and songs of Australia glorify the underdog, the outsider, the battler, and the bushranger. We like to celebrate our egalitarianism, but in truth we have subtle class structures based on wealth, and we are owned, more than we usually care to admit, by huge multi-national organizations. I leave it to you to compare Australia with your own country.

Literacy

Before talking about what is not working and what is working for literacy in the Australian context, it is necessary to say what I mean by "literacy."

There is an infinite range of situations and contexts which make, and will make, demands on people's ability to shape and comprehend meanings couched in the written word. To be able to make and comprehend meaning in any one context is to be literate *in that context.* Literacy in one context does not ensure literacy in another. It is more accurate to think of a multiplicity of "literacies" than to speak of a unitary achievement called "literacy."

"Literacy" is often used to denote basic functioning where rudimentary decoding and encoding are mastered. This is sometimes termed "functional literacy." I believe this to be a potentially confining concept. I prefer to talk about *active* literacy in whatever context is being considered. By this I mean the ability to inject one's own thoughts and intentions into messages received and sent; the ability to transform and to *act* upon aspects of the world via the written word.

To function in this way, learners must go much deeper than the coding and encoding of written symbols. Beneath the surface iceberg of this ability is the ability to revise, to arrange, and to deploy personal experiences and thoughts as well as the ability to imagine other people doing the same thing.

Literacy is a fundamental game of our culture which children begin to learn the moment that they are exposed to marks and signs which stand for something else.

What Things Are Not Working for Literacy in Australia?

At the risk of appearing glib I will comment briefly on five things that are not working for literacy:

- formulaic texts and kits
- the media
- experts with solutions
- habits
- national testing

Formulaic Exercise Texts and Kits

To my dismay, Australian schools are massively stocked with publishers' remedies, catechisms, and incantations for literacy. These tend to be based on the notion that teachers will not achieve literacy without the aid of "literacy food" for children, the equivalent of pre-packaged T.V. dinners with preservatives added. These materials, many of them concocted in the U.S.A. and exported, contain exercise work on parts of language, de-contextualized comprehension rituals, language games, and sequenced protocols which purport to increase literacy skills. Some are less toxic than others but, in the main, these materials come between children and authentic (real world) reading and writing. They encourage teachers to consider themselves deficient in knowledge and skills; and they invade schools and their children with cultures and meanings from *elsewhere.*

Sometimes, in some circumstances, short term gains appear to be made, especially if the test instrument is based on the materials used, but there is plenty of evidence from research and plain observation to confirm that there are long term negative side effects of such a diet.

Australian children first need to read what is around them in their own culture (local and national) and to write about what concerns them and the people with whom they live. The alienation effect of imported language texts and kits is incalculable but patent to the observer in the glazed eyes of the children who use them. One such text title in Australia has been scored out by children in thousands of classrooms across the nation: "Let's Make English Live" has become "Let's Make English Die."

The Media

Television and newspapers rarely report good news about literacy. In 1975 the results of a national literacy survey were variously quoted and misused in the media to feed what I call "the illiteracy scare." Rather than reporting that nine out of ten ten-year-olds *could* write simple correct sentences, newspapers blazoned the negative:

"One in ten Australian ten-year-olds unable to write a simple sentence"

In 1980 when the survey was repeated showing marked advances on quite a few scores, the argument was advanced that since improvements had been effected during a period when educational funds were being cut back, there is obviously no relation between funding and literacy. A comfortable solution for the politicians.

The effect of the negative press coverage on literacy is to lower teacher morale, increase uninformed community pressure for "the good old methods," and create a panic climate in which some of the desperate measures already described are prescribed more out of fear than out of belief.

Teachers are battling against "big stick" strategies which are on the increase the more unemployment rises: "big sticks" to beat teachers into line; "big sticks" to diminish and deny teachers' brain power. You would recognize the slogans:

- "Unemployment results from inability to write job applications"
- "Language exercises and corrected homework—that's what we need"

- "Forget the frills and get back to the 3 R's"
- "Let's have phonics and direct instruction"

The effect, where schools are not strong, is ironically to drive teachers and children away from their own common sense. It is even more ironic because there are strong indicators that more young Australians in the last decade have learned in common-sense programs to *give voice* in writing to what they believe and to make choices in reading which give them access to the kind of information that increases personal powers.

Experts with Solutions

We need knowledge and information. We need to have access to research and to inspiration. How and when information is delivered to teachers is a matter of delicacy. Australia is slowly learning not to pour good money down the drain on hit and run visiting gurus and consultants. Advisers are gradually learning that to work long term alongside teachers on the job is better than dispensing "smart pills."

Research and my own observations as a consultant indicate that teachers rarely take up gratuitous advice and act concertedly upon it over time. It is tempting for consultants to give solutions and schemes because teachers often seem to demand answers. But the Australian experience is that teachers so treated tend to become addicted, forever looking for the next guru and the next "fix." This paper explores in some detail an alternative.

Habits

While there is a good deal of exciting teacher experiment and growth in Australia, there is also a huge repressed mountain of established teacher practice contained and shaped by the structures and values of the institution of education. (Some of this is sound teaching; some of it has been shown by research to be harmful.) Most change agents tend to be ineffective in transplanting new ideas into our institutions through which the soothing and settling piped music of custom wafts. For those who believe that the function of schools is to fit most children to be relatively acquiescent citizens, the phenomenon of habit and inertia in education is not surprising.

My own research has led me to conclude that teachers are not to blame for their failure to take up new ideas based on sound theory. Our teachers and our children are literally framed by the established ideology and structures. In order to promote effective teaching of literacy we are at war, not against resistant teachers, but against the very substance and structure of Western society.

The difficulty in fighting habits, of course, is to know which are the bad habits.

National Testing

One could write a book on the current growing hysteria about accountability, standards, minimum competence, and "core" curriculum.

National testing and other forms of standardized testing are political instruments with little educational justification. They do not help teachers diagnose problems and they do not point the way to a more effective pedagogy. They simply measure, in a crude way, something that they call literacy but which bears little relation to the "active literacy in context" to which I have referred.

While they give no help about *how* to teach, they have a profound effect on *what* is taught. As is the evaluation so is the curriculum. Thus, as testing of this kind increases in Australia—a likely prognosis—teachers, spurred on by the publishing industry, will tend to teach for the tests. What is good will be sacrificed for what appears to be necessary.

What Is Working for Literacy in Australia?

I believe that there are some distinct advantages in having centralized education systems. Australian teachers are now supported by state and national official writing which, in my view, represent some enlightenment and wisdom. I call this the Australian orthodoxy and I believe it is working for literacy.

The Australian Orthodoxy

In 1980, I was part of a national Language Development Project team which had the task of consolidating world-wide wisdom about literacy and putting it in readable form for a national curriculum development center pamphlet on language and literacy* (for teachers and the wider community). It was a difficult but pleasurable task; difficult because eventually it had to be censored and endorsed by each Australian state education system; pleasurable because at last, after ten years of fighting for a clearly articulated positive national statement on literacy, I was actually engaged in the historic act of writing it.

Our own voices were altered in the consultation process but most of the ideas survived. For instance, here is my original contribution:

> Learning to become literate is very much linked with learning to be confident in your own ability to make sense of others and for others. Children who are fearful, lacking in self-respect or ashamed of their own language for some reason, will tend not to use language, especially in the presence of those who have the power to judge them. It is crucial to the development of literacy that homes and schools be loving and accepting institutions sensitive to and respectful of the language which each child possesses.

This became, in the pamphlet:

---

* Language Development Project, *Language and Literacy* leaflet, Curriculum Development Centre, Canberra, 1980.

Schools should be a place where parents, teachers and children support each other, care about each other, trust each other and want to communicate with each other.

If there is a strong tendency towards negative comment and the exacting of penalties for errors in language, or for the use of non-standard language in informal talk, children are likely to become cautious and stilted in their language performance. This will impede their language development.

On the subject of texts and kits the pamphlet contains the following advice:

Schools should:

- teach children the patterns and rules of the English language as they use and meet them in their own reading and writing tasks.

Where an excessive amount of time is spent on grammar in isolation, fragmented language exercises and drills, as opposed to "on the job" help with writing tasks, the children may be failing to learn their craft even though they get their exercises right.

- allow children plenty of time for private reading of material, especially books which they have chosen for themselves.

Where there is more use of artificially constructed language laboratories, kits and workcards than the reading of real books and materials, long term progress in reading is likely to be adversely affected.

The following excerpt perhaps best summarizes the message, the spirit, and intention of the pamphlet.

. . . the school should be a rich language workshop where children are actively engaged in talking about how it works and in evaluating the quality of what they have done so that they can do it better next time.

It may come as a surprise to you that such a pamphlet could be endorsed and promulgated in every state of Australia as *relatively uncontroversial.* There have been no media attacks on the document. 100,000 copies have been distributed and it is still heavily in demand by teachers and parents. The profession has stated where it stands and it can support what it says with research and sound theory.

In each of the official state curriculum guides for English and Language Arts, similar orthodoxies are echoed. Our national platform has coherence and internal consistency. It is something solid and refreshing for teachers to test themselves against. It is also an invitation to constructive debate. It has gone a long way to clearing the air and it is a powerful defense weapon for teachers under sttack and pressure to do other things. It is also a healthy spur to some schools to consider change.

There is no necessary connection, of course, between what is nationally espoused and what happens in schools. What we have done nationally is to produce an ideal set of generalizations. Teachers, however, have to contend with children and literacy in a context which is in many ways obstructive to change. They need practical theories and plans which will help them to move towards the ideals once they have agreed on those ideals.

Towards a Theory and Practice of Teacher Development

If teachers cannot develop practical working plans, the national orthodoxy will remain a pleasant dream. It is in this field of teacher action that I believe things are beginning to work for literacy in Australia. This brings me to the central assertion of this paper. To be succinct: *teacher power is working for literacy in Australia.* Conversely, *teacher powerlessness is working against literacy.*

I now need to make my meaning rich with information and example.

Participants in the two major Australian projects which I shall describe briefly have come to understand that theories of literacy and language development rest on certain views about life, learning, and society. The theory implicit in the national pamphlet represents a certain *frame of mind* which must be taken into account in the quest for literacy. People with a basically different frame of mind will either reject or abuse the principles which the pamphlet endorses.

In the course of two major projects we have learned two simple things:

1. New practices in the teaching of literacy in schools are doomed to failure if they are applied by teachers who are not changing their frame of mind along with the practice.
2. Projects aimed at changing teachers' minds are similarly doomed if they use methods inconsistent with the learning principles which they espouse.

Our contribution to literacy, then, is not new tests, not new materials, not new ways of teaching teachers how to use new schemes, but how to work with teachers to develop their power. Much that I have said in looking at the negative aspects of literacy in Australia can be traced back to a pervasive lack of faith by society and educational administrators in teachers. Similarly, when one looks at classrooms where active literacy is not being achieved I believe that much of it can be traced back to a lack of teacher faith in children:

What we say about learners of literacy we can also say about teachers learning to "read" and to act more effectively in their classrooms.

We have come to feel in our bones from experiment, failure, partial success, and hard-won experience that teachers learn just as children learn:

- Teachers learn by showing, sharing with each other and by trying things out.
- Teacher learning requires access to demonstration of what is to be learned.
- Those teachers with low self-esteem and a history of powerlessness will learn and grow only as they begin to assert and believe in their own worth.
- Teacher development is best achieved where the subject matter relates to the culture and concerns of the teacher.
- Teachers learn more from consequences than prescriptions.

Two National Projects

Let me illustrate this with two examples.

The Language and Learning Project

In 1975 the national Schools Commission funded a *Language Across the Curriculum Project* in South Australia. Two project officers worked in four secondary schools for two years to support individual teacher inquiry into problematic aspects of language development and learning. There was a quite explicit language development and learning theory underpinning the project (very similar to those outlined above), but in the belief that explicit statements of this theory would preempt teacher findings, this was withheld.

Volunteer teachers set up small action-research investigations into such problems as the impermeability of science textbooks (an experiment with student rewriters of the adult text), the effects of different kinds of assessment on language performance, and the effectiveness of peer-to-peer teaching in mathematics. Inquiries were documented and made available to other teachers in the four schools and in the wider system.

The hunch was that teachers would build for themselves explanatory theories, that other teachers on the staff would be drawn into the discussion and speculation, and that eventually each school would begin to articulate a "language across the curriculum policy."

Those of us working on the project had designs on the schools in which we worked. We were inspired by a naive view that wisdom similar to ours would ripple out from the inquiring teachers and that our designs would be achieved by means of induction within the school.

This did not happen for various reasons but mainly because we had not made ourselves vulnerable by being explicit and we had not taken sufficient account of the power of custom to neutralize individuals in an institution. We had not built in supports for our inquiring teachers. But the obvious growth by the participating teachers in articulateness about their own practice convinced us that certain of our basic principles were sound.

- Teachers learn by inquiry into their own practice.
- Teachers who take risks in critically assessing themselves will grow in independence and ability to act to overcome problems in their own teaching.
- Teachers doing this kind of work need outside and inside support.

In 1977, this project was taken up by the Education Department of South Australia as the Language and Learning Unit. The model was modified. The unit began to work only in schools where the principal and certain senior staff were willing to work with a *group* of teachers on a project when intentions were negotiated and agreed upon.

The theories, values, and beliefs were made much more explicit, not as dogma but as ideas to be tested in practice. Once again the experiments were documented. A teacher network was established so that findings could be shared. Social occasions and conferences were arranged to help bind and support the work. Our newsletters and occasional papers began to fill with teacher writing as the power of writing to liberate the writer and to engage colleagues became more obvious to us.

During the same period three other states of Australia had established similar units working on a similar philosophy of teacher development and a similar view of language learning. We began to share across state boundaries.

In 1978 the work was recognized by the National Curriculum Development Centre, which set up a National Working Party on the Role of Language in Learning, comprising all but one state of Australia. The strength of this working party was its Australia-wide network of inquiring teachers and schools. The price of entrance to any language and learning conference was the commitment to undertake an experiment and to write about it. Publications now document this work.

By 1978, we became convinced that a crucial aspect of teacher growth was the building of a personal theory of learning which could then be tested by teachers in their practice in schools. Our conferences worked unremittingly to this end with considerable success. We accumulated evidence that a personally owned learning theory liberates and empowers the teacher. *An effective way to language development is to begin with the teacher's learning theory.*

More and more we were learning, as teacher developers, that we should come clean about our own beliefs and intentions so that we could be judged as teachers *according to our own criteria.* We had advanced from our earlier romanticism to the point where we acknowledged and took account of different levels of power, where we recognized political and institutional constraints, and where we realized that ideally all contracts between "change agent" and teacher (or teacher and child) should be *negotiated.* We were less coy about initiating, challenging, and informing, knowing that we were putting our own theories on the line. We became convinced that above all else you teach what you are and what you do. *You* are the most powerful demonstration of your own theories.

Funding for the national working party ceased in 1980, and the units in all but one Australian state have now been disbanded by the education systems. The work continues under other names and in other projects.

The National Language Development Project

The second project, the National Language Development Project, took hold as the first project was phasing out. This is an interesting example of a potentially "top down" curriculum intervention project which, by adopting principles of teachers' learning similar to the Language and Learning project, set out to *negotiate* with systems and teachers, thereby incorporating many of the strengths of a "bottom up" endeavor. While the politics and history of the project are fascinating, I intend to concentrate on the effects of the project in my own state, South Australia.

Suffice it to say that the project *negotiated* tasks with each state, offered a sound theoretical framework for states to consider, and provided limited central support for the state developments. The aim was to produce national teacher development and curriculum materials for grades 5 to 8 of schooling.

South Australia opted to work on writing development with a focus on the documentation of "good practice." The theory was that without highly authentic demonstrations of how sound language theories could be put to work in schools, teachers would not be likely to imagine ways in and likely benefits.

The Language Development Project task force of advisers established in South Australia knew that teachers needed access to the explosion of information on language, much of it iconoclastic in effect, but we also knew that they would not dynamically engage with that information without concrete demonstration of the practice which was implicit in the information.

By use of the equivalent of grapevines and underground networks, we identified thirty teachers across fifteen schools who were considered, by fairly loose criteria, to be "good" teachers of Language Arts or English. The requirement was not that these teachers could theorize but that they taught well. The teachers, in negotiation with their principals, were then invited to join the project knowing that they would be asked to document aspects of their own practice for other teachers. With varying degrees of enthusiasm or suspicion most agreed to be in it supported by a co-ordinator and a group of advisers and consultants.

At a five-day residential conference, the teachers and the task force hammered out a set of goals, strategies, and understandings, not without tension, and then individuals set about documenting, as a base-line, one aspect of their present teaching that they considered to be of possible interest to other teachers. Even though these were in effect hand-picked "stars," there was a high degree of humility, self-doubt and, in some cases, fear amongst the teachers. Most were absolute novices in the business of writing about education in their own classrooms and a good many entered into quite extreme manifestations of avoidance behavior. They faced the truth of Donald Graves' assertion that authentic writing is an advanced form of strip tease.

Writing for one's local peers is challenging enough without the added awe of addressing the nation in a pioneering language development project. But project leaders insisted that the task be completed even if the writing never reached an audience. Support was available for those who wanted to talk through their writing difficulties. With no precedents and no models, finding a voice and a format was problematic. Yet they all made it, after many drafts and heartburns, and their work has been subsequently published in draft in three volumes, *WRITE ON, I, II* and *III.* * Teacher response to these materials

---

*Despite the range of background, age, and teaching experience of the writers it is interesting to note the conclusions about them of a cognitive psychologist, Dr. J. Biggs, who was commissioned to examine the L.D.P. materials to assess the match between espoused L.D.P. theory and teacher writing: "The *WRITE ON* series thus conveys a strong impression of theoretical unanimity and an innovative array of classroom practice that give practical expression to the common theoretical stance." "Assumptions about learning contained in the L.D.P." J. Biggs, Unpublished paper, Curriculum Development Centre, 1981.

across the nation has been quite overwhelming.

The South Australian project teachers realized that they were not only *literate* with respect to this language task but that through print, they had become valued public property. A mild form of panic followed. The writing and reflection on their own practice, as predicted by the teacher development principles upon which we were working, had led them to develop some articulate theories about their own practice. But it also exposed unsettling contradictions and absurdities. Their practice was not nearly good enough. The teachers almost unanimously asked for input, access to information, research data, and the writing of experts. With such information at their command they planned for the next stage in which each individual undertook an experiment into some aspect of writing. Reflection on their own practice plus new information led them to seek improvement.

They decided in 1981 to become self-supporting groups commissioning input. They had recognized the loneliness and precariousness of individual work. In groups in 1981 and 1982 they have gone from strength to strength producing very powerful and effective materials which will allow other teachers to repeat the process which has made them strong.*

The Language Development Project model had more change than the Language and Learning Model because it was, for a while at least, blessed by the Federal Government, because it worked at *all levels* to make room for change (classroom, community, state education system, national system), because it aimed at *production* of tools which could be taken up by other teachers, and because it offered specific *demonstrations* of practice to its clients. It also gathered and gave access to the best of what is currently known. But both projects *at the core* rested on the major assumptions that teachers must come to feel their own *power to act* according to their own hard-won theories. In order for this to happen, change agents and participating power figures (hierarchically speaking) must demonstrate their own fidelity to this tenet. They have to demonstrate what they espouse in their own actions. They also have to be able to negotiate. In such a model there is no room for patronizing "help" or "facilitation." All participants have to be bona fide coworkers and learners, each vulnerable in his or her own sphere. Each participant has to be willing to make a stand and be open to scrutiny. Conflict, contradiction, and resolution are essential elements. Struggling teachers, strengthened by such a process, will teach children to struggle productively. This is what novices in the quest for increasing literacy must learn above all else. Thus, *some* of us are becoming wiser.

---

* Kevin Piper, the national evaluator of the project, writes of this feature of the project:

   ... there is also a growing sense in which, through the process, the ownership of the Project is becoming vested in the actors. This growing sense of "ownership" among project participants in turn has produced a growing sense of commitment and involvement. The open-ended, exploratory element likewise contributes an air of uncertainty, and sometimes an impression of inaction; but it is also contributing towards the building of a solid foundation of understanding on which practice can be based and on which theory can be modified. ("Evaluating a National Curriculum Project" in *English in Australia,* no. 58, December 1981.)

In assessing the quality of a literacy program, look to the demonstrations, the enactments of the teachers in living and teaching. There can be no easy grafting of new methods and ideas onto teachers. People who accept grafts are likely to be powerless functionaries who will teach powerless functioning (not to mention grafting).

Towards the end of 1980, the Minister of Education announced that the national Curriculum Development Centre (and with it the Language Development Project) would be disbanded by June 1982. As Kevin Piper* the national evaluator of the Language Development Project says:

> The irony is that the L.D.P. may well have succeeded in pioneering a model of national curriculum development genuinely suited to the peculiarly difficult Australian context at a time when the concept of national curriculum development itself is being abandoned.

Other Australian Work

In speaking of only three Australian initiatives, I do not wish you to leave with the impression that this is all. If I had time I would expand on the "hands on" work of people like Brian Cambourne in tertiary institutions, on Stephen Harris' and Michael Christies' pioneering work in the Aboriginal schools in the Northern Territory, the growing collaboration in teacher support between national associations (Australian Association for the Teaching of English, Australian Reading Association, Primary English Teaching Association, Australian Applied Linguistics Association) and on many other "action research" type projects now gathering strength across the nation. They all have in common the belief that in any act of learning the *locus of control* must be with the learner if we are to promote growing independence and personal power. This applies both to children learning to read and write *and* to their teachers.

But I do not wish to depict Australia as the great south land of promise and insight. As indicated earlier in this paper, we share struggles similar to yours and we despair as often as we struggle. In closing, however, I wish to rise above despair. I prefer to be constructive, and slightly comic. In summary I offer for your consideration a synthesis of some developing ideas which may eventually warrant the status of universals in the quest for literacy.

Some Features of a Universal Program for Literacy: A Modest Proposal

Some Basic Views About Learning and Literacy

- The human being is a born scientist, actively processing the world and inducing "rules."
- Humans learn interactively and collaboratively by showing, sharing, and trying things out.

---

*Piper, K. "Evaluating a National Curriculum Project" in *English in Australia*, no. 58, December, 1981.

- Human learning requires access to accomplished demonstrations of what is to be learned.
- Literacy is learned in use when it has *purpose* for the learner (when there is intention to learn).
- The aim of literacy is to produce increasing independence and ability to act on the part of the learner.
- Those with low self-esteem and a history of powerlessness will achieve active literacy only as they begin to assert and believe in their own worth.
- Literacy is best achieved where the meaning being made relates to the culture and concerns of the learner.
- Skills and information offered at the point of need are more effective than skills and information taught separately from the act.
- Human beings learn best when they *own* the problem.
- Human beings learn more from consequences than prescriptions.

At the base of all these views, I suggest that there is a formula:

group/personal power + intention/purpose + information (access to demonstration ➤ learning ➤ more group/personal power.

Such a view of learners and learning values sharing, working together, acting, and transforming. It is for dynamism, change, and reconstruction. It is non-determinist and non-behaviorist in its orientation.

Features of a Literacy Program in Schools

If: group/personal power + intention/purpose + information/access to demonstration ➤ learning

then teaching for literacy will need to have at least the following features:

- genuine belief by the teacher in the power of the learner's head
- engagement with meanings arising out of and related to the cultural, socio/political reality of the learners (cf. Freire's work)
- emphasis on *production* and *use*
- demonstration, thinking aloud, and on-the-spot information delivered by the teacher *when commissioned* by the learner (either implicitly or explicitly)
- where possible, rich exposure to and immersion in a community of readers and writers who share and talk about their craft (the classroom itself will be a supportive community of apprentice readers and writers)
- access to inspiring examples of mature reading and writing (and ideally to those who produced it) to help learners imagine what it is that they might eventually seek to be and do and why this might be pleasurable
- encouragement of the learners (by example) to induce rules and patterns (to build their own emerging theories) about what they read and write
- pervasive valuing of, if not insistence upon, tenacity, question asking, risk taking, and imagination
- access to explicit demonstration of *consequences* following as closely as possible after the literacy act

Features of Projects and Teacher Development Programs

Because teachers teach what they are and what they can do, a "universal" teacher development program would aim to ensure that teachers learn to:

- negotiate with and defend themselves against those in authority over them
- read and write for a variety of pruposes and theorize about their own comprehending and composing processes, and about the complexities of each act within its context
- articulate their own developing theory of learning, and of language learning in particular
- give access to what they presently think about reading and writing (and anything else for that matter)
- analyze constraints and taboos that operate and where necessary make compromises but not capitulations
- reflect upon their own performance and invite others to do the same
- ask questions, seek advice, or find demonstrations in areas of personal puzzlement, dissonance, or anxiety
- say "I don't know" when this is so
- contradict and provide frank appraisals with respect
- evaluate information, research data, and opinion in the light of their own principles
- try things out systematically to see if they work
- apply Kelly's first law of psychology: "When in doubt, ask the clients"

The "Fronts" on Which Workers for Literacy Must Fight

Because any of these plans for children, teachers, and change agents can be aborted by ruling ideologies and structures, any literacy program must also try to address the following influences and constraints in order to make room for the main actors to operate:

- local and national assessment/evaluation instruments and diagnostic tools must be challenged to value those things which are consistent with desired theory and practice
- local and national education councils, funding agencies, and political leaders must be provided with evidence (and voter pressure) that sound educational theory works in practice
- parents and the wider community must be informed, shown, and convinced that the program works
- publishers of materials which run counter to the knowledge, processes, and values of the program must come under pressure from teachers, education systems, and parents
- official local, state, and national education curriculum policy statements, guidelines, and instruction manuals should endorse and legitimate the tenets of the program

- school boards and principals must come to value the program and appreciate the need for some school structures, habits, and rules which impede the program to be altered
- teachers' unions and associations should be helped to understand and to endorse the program and, if necessary, to be convinced to take action to secure it
- media mythologies need to be effectively challenged and corrected
- teacher educators should provide undergraduate and graduate courses in keeping with the program
- children, if necessary, must be helped to unlearn expectations of schooling and teacher requirements, methods, and rules incompatible with the tenets of the program

Conclusion

Finally, if you ask me, it is all about power and the struggle by individuals and groups to win some space and control. But consideration of constraints can so easily lead to despair. It is much more constructive to look at how much we have won (and why) by struggling over the past twenty years.

As some of my colleagues noted in a recent position paper on writing:

> Despite constraints, teachers still largely rule in their own classrooms, and where one rules one can make changes.

Change requires courage. In Australia, we are backing teachers to make a difference.